PAUL 'BEAR' BRYANT

What Made Him A Winner

Paul 'Bear' Bryant:
What Made Him a Winner

For Vision Press
Editors: C. Joanne Sloan
          W. David Sloan
Production and Design: W. David Sloan
                       Cheryl S. Wray

Vision Press
P.O. Box 1106
Northport, Alabama 35476

Reed, V. (Virgil) Delbert
Paul 'Bear' Bryant: What Made Him a Winner

ISBN: 1-885219-01-6

Printed in the United States of America

ACKNOWLEDGMENTS

Paul W. Bryant Jr.
Mary Harmon Tyson Moman
Paul W. Bryant Museum, University of Alabama
Jack Engelhart Photography
Barry Fikes Photography
Calvin Hannah Photography
Wayne H. McDaniel, University of Alabama
Kirk McNair, *Bama Magazine*
Texas A&M University Office of Sports Information
Columbus (Miss.) *Commercial Dispatch*
Tuscaloosa News
University of Alabama Office of Sports Information
University of Kentucky Office of Sports Information
University of Maryland Office of Sports Information
University of Oklahoma Office of Sports Information
University of Tennessee Office of Sports Information
West Alabama Gazette

About the author

Delbert Reed is an award-winning journalist who came to know Coach Bear Bryant well during a 17-year newspaper career (1960-1977) as a sports writer, sports editor, city editor and managing editor with the *Tuscaloosa News*, *Nashville Banner* and *Columbus* (Miss.) *Commercial Dispatch*. He maintained that relationship until Coach Bryant's death as a close associate of Paul W. Bryant Jr. and covered several Alabama games for the *Tuscaloosa News* during Coach Bryant's final season as University of Alabama coach (1982).

Reed's work has been published in state, regional and national publications in addition to newspapers. His sideline observation of Coach Bryant during the 1970 Alabama-Southern Cal game in Birmingham was selected as Alabama's sports story of the year, and he was chosen Mississippi's sports columnist of the year in 1976. He also won awards nationally in 1988 for writing and research on journalism history and has won several additional writing awards.

Reed holds B.S. and M.A. degrees from the University of Alabama.

PAUL 'BEAR' BRYANT

What Made Him A Winner

Analyses, Comments, and Memories
By Those Who Knew Him Best

By
Delbert Reed

VISION PRESS
Northport, Alabama

Dedication

• To those fans, including my own father, who never met legendary football coach Paul "Bear" Bryant, yet who admired and respected him for the winning spirit and positive attitude he inspired and taught wherever he coached.

These fans are proof that Coach Bryant exemplified excellence not only on the football field, but in life, and that his influence reached all corners of the states in which he coached and beyond over a span of five decades. His accomplishments swelled the hearts of all those who knew what it was to work hard and long to make ends meet, play hard just to have a chance to win, or fight against long odds just to stay alive.

• To those hundreds of thousands of anonymous fans who never saw him along the sideline in person, yet who were inspired by Coach Bryant almost as much as those who played for him or those of us fortunate enough to have known him in some small way.

These fans never once shared a moment of glory in his presence, a handshake or a meal with him, yet they still believed in the standards of excellence he set for himself and his teams and all else that he stood for. They are the truly loyal fans of Paul "Bear" Bryant.

• To those quietly appreciative working-class fans who hung his picture or a football schedule on the walls of their gas stations and country stores and barbecue joints and coffee shops and chalked up the scores after each autumn Saturday game and talked about "Ol' Bear" with their co-workers and customers and children home from the college they never had the chance to attend.

Somehow, even they felt close to and a part of the greatness that was Coach Bryant.

• To those fans who never experienced the intensity of one of his fiery practice sessions in the rugged building days at Kentucky, Texas A&M or Alabama and to those who never marveled at his serenity on an otherwise chaotic sideline when it was third and long, his team behind late against Tennessee in Knoxville or driving for that last-second victory over Georgia Tech at hostile Grant Field or clinging to a narrow lead over LSU in Baton Rouge.

They may not have been there, but somehow they knew him and shared the confidence he inspired in his teams.

• To those fans who never held a pair of Alabama-Auburn tickets or made it to the Sugar Bowl for a national championship game.

They had to be satisfied listening to the games on the radio and catching one on television now and then. Still, they felt a part of it all, even from a distance, and they too believed in his miracles.

I hope those fans, old and new, who missed the many moods of Coach Bryant in person can enjoy these collected bits and pieces of the brilliant and complex Bryant character who played equally well the role of country bumpkin or Wall Street genius and get to know him in some small way—perhaps even feel like they, too, met him once when he stopped in at the local diner for a cup of coffee or some country store for a pack of Chesterfields on a recruiting trip or on the way to make a speech somewhere.

—Delbert Reed

CONTENTS

"I don't know what he had, but he had a lot of it."

—Bobby Marks

1

More Than the Records Show

"As long as someone has to be the winningest coach, heck, it might as well be me."
—Paul "Bear" Bryant

IT WAS NOT ONLY WHAT HE DID, BUT HOW HE DID IT

How do we explain the man and legend known as Paul William "Bear" Bryant?

How do we understand his dogged determination not only to be the best, but to be the best ever?

How do we place into perspective his brilliant record as a college football coach and an even more impressive mark as a leader of men?

How did one man, in just 38 seasons, compile such an astounding list of records and honors, including more wins (323) than any NCAA Division I coach in history; national coach of the year three times; six national championships; 15 conference championships; 29 bowl appearances; national coach of the decade twice; Southeastern Conference coach of the century; 24 consecutive bowl games as head coach at Alabama; Southeastern Conference coach of the year ten times, and an astounding average of 9.3 wins per season during his brilliant 25-year career at Alabama?

The list, with appropriate accompanying honors, stretches on and on and on. It boggles the mind, looking at it all at once now. But, at the time Bryant was piling up the records, his winning came to be expected, even taken for granted. The wins were news, but rarely surprising news. That was just how things were supposed to be. After all, he was Coach Bryant, and none who knew him was ever surprised by a Bryant victory—only by a Bryant defeat.

It is difficult to imagine anyone ever again weathering the pressures of college football coaching long enough to accomplish even half what Bryant did. It is even more difficult to imagine anyone devoting the time and energy to football that he did. A young coach starting out today with an eye on Bryant's won-lost record alone (323-85-17) would have to survive as a head coach for 32 seasons and average 10 wins a year just to get close.

The many other Bryant records are equally amazing; yet, the records tell only a small part of the near-epic Paul "Bear" Bryant story.

It was not only what Bryant accomplished as a

Page 2: During a head coaching career that spanned almost 40 years—most of them spent at Alabama—Coach Paul "Bear" Bryant epitomized college football.

Bryant was happiest on the football field.

football coach that set him apart; it was as much the way in which he went about doing it.

So how did he do it? What was his secret? What was so unusual about him?

How did he adjust and endure through all the years of changing times and schools and conferences and players and formations and rules and assistant coaches and opponents and still win big from start to finish, 1945-1982, in the major leagues of college football?

What was different about Bryant as man and coach that made him the unsurpassed winner that he was so driven to be and became? What special character trait or event forced or inspired him to such greatness that he became perhaps the single most recognizable sports figure of his time and a hero to millions who never met him and perhaps many millions more who never even saw him up close?

How did he motivate those who played for him

to give far more than they ever thought they had to win for him? What did he have that inspired even opponents to strive harder, to spend themselves physically and emotionally, giving their best trying for that rare, near-sacred, season-saving victory against "The Bear," especially during his last dozen seasons?

Just what was it that made Paul "Bear" Bryant a winner?

More than a dozen years after his sudden and shocking death on January 26, 1983, less than a month after his final game, Bryant continues to be remembered and analyzed almost daily by his former associates; yet his formula for success remains difficult to describe and impossible to duplicate.

Was there some rare, mysterious trait or charm or ingredient that made Bryant better at what he did than anyone else?

Was it simply luck? He often acknowledged his extraordinary luck.

Perhaps timing? He often said timing was everything.

Was it the hard life of his humble Arkansas roots? He certainly learned to work and endure difficulty there.

The questions are easy, the answers elusive.

Bryant was often asked these same questions during his coaching career. He always modestly claimed not to know the answers. Perhaps he didn't for certain. He also said slyly that he wouldn't tell even if he did know. He modestly explained his unusual self motivation simply as a fear of having to return to the hard life of the Depression-era farm of his boyhood in Arkansas, "driving those mules and chopping cotton for 50 cents a day."

But Bryant's inspiration was not born out of fear of labor or long hours; he was noted for his long work days, even in his gloried later years. There had to be something far more which stirred his heart and soul.

He Was Different Things To Different People

Those who knew him best—former players, assistant coaches, staff and associates who spent years close to him on and off the football field—remember Bryant as a unique man in many ways, inwardly and outwardly. They knew and remember him as intelligent, organized, disciplined, determined, always solidly focused on his goals, demanding, poised, confident, always in total control, hard as hickory and even a bit mean if the sit-

Coach Bryant with familiar pose at goalpost as he watches pre-game activities.

Bryant continues to be remembered and analyzed almost daily by his former associates; yet his formula for success remains difficult to describe and impossible to duplicate.

On Sept. 12, 1981, Bryant studies with intensity the game day ahead for him and his Alabama team.

uation demanded it. And he was predictably unpredictable—always.

But he also could be compassionate, humble, courteous and brilliant. His personality was magnetic and complex. He was part evangelist, part barroom brawler, part thief, part dictator, part gambler, part teacher, part philosopher, part psychologist, part humorist, part showman, part mad scientist, part salesman, part carnival huckster, part spiritual healer, part obsessed madman and part leader. He had the mood, manner, attitude and demeanor for any situation. He was whatever and whoever the situation demanded, and he played all his roles perfectly. But then a coach—and especially a great leader—must obviously be all these things.

Bryant had an uncanny awareness of all that was happening within his program and with his players and coaches. He could read faces and moods, and some say even minds. He was direct and often plain-spoken. His stare could sting your skin; his words could cut to the bone. He was imposing in size at nearly 6-4, but he lived and coached at closer to 7-4. He was big in heart, too, genuinely caring about his players and their success outside and after football. And he had power— all the power in the world—it seemed. He never let anyone wonder who was in charge of what fell within his domain. It was always crystal clear: He was.

His style was an unflinching, unwavering, my-way-or-hit-the-highway style, both on and off the field, from start to finish. To him, everything was black or white. You were either with him 100 percent or against him. He didn't compromise, back down, apologize or admit mistakes. And he never thought of being anything less than the best—not even once. He didn't plan for winning seasons or conference championships; his goal was the national championship.

He looked people in the eye when he spoke to them and asked the same in return. You might have wondered what he said now and then, but never what he meant. He was a motivator and teacher who prepared his players not only for football, but for life, though they might not have known it at the time. He was tough, mentally and physically, but he had a soft heart and a keen sense of humor.

He was deceptive in a poker-playing sense. He never tipped his hand until all bets were down. And he never bluffed. At least no one ever caught him at it. If he asked a question—and he didn't ask many—chances were better than even that he already knew the answer; he was just seeing if anyone else did. He could lull you to sleep with his folksy, plowhand pretense of country bumpkin ignorance, but he was a long time and a long way from that Arkansas bottom land, and it was all just part of his act.

He worked himself and his players and coaches hard and long, promising always not to be outworked. He got more out of his players than they ever believed possible, not only because he asked more of them, but because he could convince them, motivate them, sell them—whether by fear, hate, love, pride or whatever—on his ideas and goals. He

*His style was an unwavering
my-way-only style.
To him, everything was black or
white. You were either with him 100%
or against him.*

Coach Bryant gets a close-up view of the pre-game warmup prior to a Crimson Tide game.

could make them believe in him, the goals he set, and more importantly, in themselves. He encouraged dreaming, challenging his players to be the best, just as he was. As a result, his teams found a way, almost always, to win.

He had an unusual and special presence about him. It was more than an air, more like an atmosphere. Some call it charisma. He would probably call it class. "I can't define class, but I can recognize it a mile away," he often said. Whatever it was, he had it. And as all agree, he had a lot of it.

Bryant blended unusual intelligence, a unique personality that was both tough and compassionate and a stubborn desire to win with discipline and hard work to make football history. Upon reflection, most of his secrets for success seem not to have been secrets at all, but simple, common-sense methods mixed with his own special gift for knowing, or finding out, how to get the most out of people. Mostly, he succeeded simply by leading, something he did with a natural ease. And he did it with discipline, sacrifice and hard work.

Blessing Or Curse, He Had Something Extra

But there always seemed to be something more, something he could never overcome, which drove him throughout his life to achieve success beyond even the dreams of ordinary men. Bryant seems to have been blessed—or cursed—with a double portion of that inner force which causes man to rise before dawn and work into the darkness each day, striving for greatness or immortality or even lesser things. Perhaps it was simply survival instinct. Perhaps it was part of his character by birth, honed by the difficult, Depression-era times in which he grew up and the people and events which touched and shaped him. Perhaps it was a single word or event, or several. Whatever the source, it never left him, even when times were good. It was his strength, and perhaps in another sense, his weakness.

Bryant hinted at what might well have been his

strongest inspiration several times when he recalled the ridicule he experienced as a barefoot farm boy from Moro Bottom selling vegetables from a mule-drawn wagon in Fordyce. Schoolmates from Fordyce "would come along and make fun of me and those old mules. I still remember the ones that did it," he said 40 years later in a *Sports Illustrated* interview. He set out then to show those "city slickers" who had laughed at him that he was as good as anyone, maybe even better. Perhaps it was this determination to prove himself, to be accepted by his childhood peers, that really ignited the fire inside Bryant and triggered his rise to fame.

One of the many ways he proved himself early was by fighting, and being bigger than most boys his age and tough from farm work, he frequently won, gaining acceptance and a degree of respect through intimidation, a tactic he carried into his coaching career. He also drew attention to himself by being something of a daredevil and showoff, pulling such stunts as wrestling the bear that led to his nickname and throwing a cat into a church service. Most were typical boyhood pranks, and most drew the standard punishment in addition to earning him rank with the other boys. "I must have craved attention, and maybe this has something to do with shaping a man," he said in the 1966 *Sports Illustrated* interview.

At age 13, Bryant was introduced to football, and his life from that moment on took a new direction. His physical size, toughness and an aggressive nature made him a natural at the game, and he was an instant success. He eventually earned All-State honors and played on two state championship teams at Fordyce High School. He had found a new way to gain attention, and the life-long journey that carried him to 31 bowl games, seven national championships (six as a head coach and one as a player) and a dozen other records had begun.

Bryant was indeed lucky, starting with his time and place in history. His formative years in football (and other sports in high school) came during an era when sports was king in America. There was Knute Rockne and his fabled Four Horsemen at Notre Dame; Babe Ruth and Lou Gehrig with the Yankees; Red Grange and Bronko Nagurski in college and professional football; Jack Dempsey and Joe Louis in boxing; Jesse

People noticed Bryant for one reason or another. He often saw to that himself, but he wasn't a hard man to spot in a crowd or on a football field. He was tall and handsome, and he was drawn to the spotlight or thrust into it for more than 50 years through the game of football. Bryant standing before the goalpost before a game became a well-known scene with fans.

Owens in the Olympics; Babe Didrikson in women's sports; Bobby Jones in golf and Alabama's cross-country train rides to the Rose Bowl under Wallace Wade and Frank Thomas.

The time was known as a golden era in sports, and it was glamorized by the best writers of the day. The tough times of the gangster-dominated twenties and the Depression and Dust Bowl thirties left little else to write or cheer about, and those who excelled in sport seemed destined for certain fame and fortune. Bryant was one of those. He claimed every opportunity, and made headlines for himself and his teams for more than 50 years as player and coach.

His year-by-year coaching exploits have been well documented, from the abrupt start at Maryland to Kentucky, Texas A&M and the quarter-century finale at Alabama. At each school, he turned losing programs into winners, and he did it quickly and soundly. He was sometimes considered controversial, as truly great leaders often are because they are frequently misunderstood and sometimes feared, but he was always considered a winner.

He Was "All That His Nickname Implies"

Although Bryant earned much of his coaching fame at Alabama, he was anything but a late bloomer. Whatever the magical mixture of his character, it was visible early and continued throughout his life. People noticed him for one reason or another. He often saw to that himself, but he wasn't a hard man to spot in a crowd or on a football field. He was tall and handsome, and he was drawn to the spotlight or thrust into it for more than 50 years through the game of football. He was, as a 1930 Fordyce newspaper picture caption noted, "all that his nickname implies." He had a certain flair about him, a certain style. He was more than a bit of a showman, and created a stir, if not a controversy, wherever he went.

His fierce desire to win drove him to use every trick and loophole in the book, and even to bend the rules from time to time, especially in his early years before he knew just how good he really was, or believed in himself and his magic as much as his followers did. There were times, without doubt, when his teams won because the opponents believed in Bryant, too, in spite of themselves.

He kept assistant coaches and conference officials busy checking the rulebook, and rulesmakers busy tying up the loopholes as he employed such

Bryant as a young Alabama assistant coach

tricks and genius as quick kicks; forward fumbles on fourth down near the goal line; the tackle-eligible pass; a signal-calling specialist who never ran a play; tearaway jerseys; signing football players to basketball, baseball or academic scholarships; slapping fumbles or blocked kicks toward the goal line; the whoopee pass, etc., and who knows what else. Some of it didn't amount to much, but it contributed to the confusion of the enemy, and Bryant loved it. It was all legal at the time, of course, but not many people knew about the loopholes and even fewer took advantage of every opportunity as Bryant did. He used every edge in recruiting, too. Once, at Texas A&M, over-zealous supporters—whether with or without his knowledge—cost his Texas A&M team two years probation for recruiting violations, teaching him a bitter lesson he vowed never to repeat.

Bryant literally turned the Southeastern Conference on its ear when he arrived as head coach at Alabama in December 1957, bringing with him a brand of hard-nosed, kill-or-get-killed play that rival coach Ralph Jordan of Auburn later described as "helmet-busting, hell-for-leather, gang-tackling football." The new style of play shocked some, but it thrilled and inspired Alabama followers, and Bryant's first Alabama team won more games (five) than the school had won the three previous seasons combined.

The high-spirited play of Bryant's Alabama teams, coupled with the unfortunate injury of an opposing player, soon prompted a magazine article accusing him of teaching brutal, dirty football. Shortly after, another article accused him of "rigging" a game. The articles caused him his greatest anger. He wanted blood, then jail, for the offenders, but sued instead and eventually collected more than $300,000 in a libel suit settlement over the articles. He never forgave those responsible, however.

Bryant acknowledged the frequent controversies in his career without apology in his autobiography, saying, "If you stick your head above the crowd, you're going to have people trying to knock it off. We've done it wherever I've been, gotten it up there pretty high, and they've tried, and I've been darn active defending myself." One thing for sure: he

didn't run, and he didn't hide. The spotlight might have been a little hot at times, but he never dodged it.

For Only a Moment, He Was Human After All

Bryant experienced what to him was a disastrous slump in the late sixties, going 6-5 and 6-5-1 in 1969 and 1970. He appeared to have suddenly been left behind in a rapidly changing time. Some "faint-hearted" fans even began to grumble and mumble about Bryant, then pushing 60, being too old, and how it was maybe time for him to retire, run for governor or accept one of the professional coaching jobs he was frequently offered.

But there was more to the two lean years than first meets the eye in the recordbook. First of all, the game of football, especially defensive sets and strategies, had changed suddenly, and Bryant's famous small, quick players could no longer handle the bigger players.

Secondly, some players, reflecting a changing mood and time, worried more about the length of their hair than they did the next game, and even openly stated that they wanted to be treated the same as other students. It was a trying time in America, and Bryant's team and the University of Alabama campus did not escape the nationwide student unrest, Vietnam War protests and trauma of near rebellion as leaders such as Martin Luther King and Bobby Kennedy were assassinated Even Alabama governor George Wallace was shot as he campaigned for President in 1972. Some of this anti-establishment attitude eventually permeated even Bryant's football team.

Thirdly, the loss of potentially promising black players from the state due to Alabama's non-recruitment of blacks added to the weakness of the teams, at least in theory. Alabama lost to some of those outside teams such as Nebraska, Missouri, Southern Cal, Penn State and Colorado before starting to recruit blacks in 1970.

And Bryant himself, perhaps for the first time in his career, was distracted by outside factors, including two important personal losses. Former Alabama quarterback Pat Trammell, the leader of the 1961 national championship team and Bryant's confessed favorite person ever, died of cancer in early 1969. Carney Laslie, a teammate of Bryant's at Alabama in the early thirties and an assistant coach with him at Maryland, Kentucky, Texas A&M and Alabama, died a year later. These losses, and others within the next few years, were heartbreaking to Bryant, whether he let it show to more than a few close friends or not; and for once, for a time, football didn't seem as all-important to him as it had for so long.

At the same time, other SEC teams had gradually caught up with Alabama after being forced to play Bryant's kill-or-get-killed brand of football in self defense. Tennessee had been playing tough, aggressive football for years, but Bryant attracted the most attention with it at Alabama due to the reputation he earned at Texas A&M.

Then, finally, as implausible as it may sound, it is possible and even likely that Bryant and the Alabama staff had grown complacent, spoiled by the startling success of the previous nine seasons during which Alabama had posted a record of 84 wins, 11 losses and four ties while winning four Southeastern Conference championships and three national titles. During that time, Alabama had

(Left) Most eyes and cameras focused on Coach Bryant before the game.

Bryant on telephone to President Ronald Reagan after getting his 314th win

such notable quarterbacks as Trammell, Joe Namath, Steve Sloan, Ken Stabler and Scott Hunter, and had slowly evolved into a team driven more by offense than the ball-control, defense-minded teams of Bryant's past. Not surprisingly, with abundant offensive talent at hand, Bryant had stepped slightly away from his personal style of play, and when the quarterback talent ran thin, Alabama didn't win as often as before.

The likely answer to the "why" of the dismal 1969 and 1970 seasons is a combination of all these factors, and probably as many more unnoted. The spoiled Alabama fans at the time didn't look for answers, however, and Bryant was on the hotseat

Coach Bryant surveys the crowd before one of his last games.

once again. Speaking as an Alabama alumnus, Bryant expressed his own dissatisfaction with the two sub-par seasons. And speaking as athletic director, he promised a quick change in direction or a change in head coaches. Speaking as the coach, he said he wasn't about to quit.

A lesser man would have retired to the cozy position of athletic director and enjoyed the 199 wins and wealth Bryant had already accumulated in his first 26 seasons of glory. He did consider going into professional football briefly, turning down at least one attractive offer, but he never considered quitting coaching. "Losing doesn't make me want to quit," he said through clinched teeth shortly after the end of the 1970 season. "It makes me want to fight that much harder."

He pushed aside the distractions, regrouped his forces, told the "faint-hearted" fans and a few others where to go, installed a new offense which emphasized ball control, and proceeded to stun college football in his last dozen seasons by winning 124 games, three more national championships and nine Southeastern Conference titles. Remarkably,

his Alabama teams lost only seven conference games during his last 12 seasons, and three of those came during his final season.

Former Pupils Carry On As His Impact Continues

Bryant's approach to the game of football was almost evangelical, and he won many disciples for his cause. Because of that, no one has had a greater lasting impact on college football, and perhaps football in general, than he. In 38 years as head coach at Maryland, Kentucky, Texas A&M and Alabama, he inspired, encouraged and assisted nearly 50 former players and/or assistant coaches in following him into head coaching at the college or professional level. That number will surely rise in coming years as his former pupils continue to follow his lead. Countless others have become college or professional assistants and high school coaches. He coached thousands of players in his career, and his former pupils are coaching thousands more, who in turn will coach thousands more. The chain is unending; therefore, his influence will be felt for all time in football. This accomplishment alone places him at the top of any list of college football coaches and is perhaps his greatest tribute among so many he has earned.

But Bryant did more than win football games and turn out more football coaches in his likeness. His contributions to the universities, communities and states in which he coached were also great, though far less noted. His winning programs brought pride and recognition and money to improve facilities wherever he went. At Alabama, he turned ragged, run-down facilities and programs into one of the nation's best. The wins on the field brought in bowl and television money, and the money built not only athletic facilities, but class-rooms and science labs and funded pay raises for the faculty and scholarships for students. He personally donated hundreds of thousands of dollars of his own money for scholarships to non-athletes. Because of the Southeastern Conference formula for sharing bowl revenue, Bryant and Alabama helped pump millions of dollars into every other school in the conference. He also brought national recognition to the conference by playing such national powers as Notre Dame, Penn State, Nebraska, and Southern Cal and winning much of the time. In addition, he made other teams and coaches in the conference better, too, because they worked harder to try to meet the standards he set.

Most Alabamians still see Bryant as one of the state's greatest heroes, as surely he was. Those who knew him before in Texas and Kentucky and even Maryland have voiced the same sentiments. For those of us who know him primarily for what he did at Alabama, he is "ours." He made us all better with his constant sermons year after year about class, sacrifice, character, discipline, perseverance, pride in winning and holding your head high win or lose. Through his weekly television shows, he reached an audience far beyond his football team. And he made us all not only feel better, but better, period. We admired and respected him not only for the games he won but for the hope he gave to all of us still struggling to get ourselves and our children away from the mining and mill towns and cotton fields and make something of our lives. He believed; he made his players believe; and he made the rest of us believe, too.

All of a sudden, it seems now, Alabama, which had not won a single football game in 1956, was beating Nebraska and Oklahoma and Penn State and Southern Cal and Ohio State, and was doing it

Bryant's heyday lasted all of his life. He lived in a time and a world that seems now to have belonged only to him.

with scrawny little boys from big towns and little towns and country crossroads throughout Alabama, some of whom maybe couldn't even have played anywhere else or for any other coach.

We held our heads up again because "Alabama" came to mean Alabama football, not racial problems in Selma or Birmingham. He helped us as a state and as a people to overcome the shame and ridicule we had to endure because of our time and place in history. As sports had done for the nation in the thirties, Alabama football gave Alabamians something to cheer about in the turbulent sixties and seventies.

Just as Bryant had overcome the ridicule of his classmates in Fordyce through football, he helped Alabama and the South to overcome national ridicule, whether he intended to or not. He had done the same in Kentucky 15 years before, to an extent, and was named Kentucky's Outstanding Citizen of 1950 for "having helped give Kentucky nationwide publicity by uplifting UK's football team from mediocrity to a place near the top in national standings and for his contributions toward building character among young men of the Common-

Bryant's teams won with no strutting or bragging—just class.

wealth." What he did in eight seasons at Kentucky he did a thousand times over in 25 years at Alabama.

But Bryant brushed aside praise for his larger contributions, just as he often did for winning football games, saying, "I don't try to save the world, I just take it one football player at a time." His focus may have seemed narrow, but his vision was broad.

Midway through his coaching career, in the midst of his first three national championships at Alabama, Bryant went home to Arkansas for induction into the Arkansas Hall of Fame. He went home a proud hero, walking down the streets of Fordyce with his head held high, as he had many times before. He had proven himself to all the world, but this time, in 1964, he finally forgave those who had made fun of him so long ago. Before, he had gone back to "big-dog it." This time, he was humbled.

After all, the home folks had gone beyond the mere acceptance he had once coveted; they had brought him home to pay him tribute, and he was touched by it. Perhaps he realized, too, that they might have been partly responsible for the spark that propelled him to fame. Perhaps he was being generous, as he often could be. He certainly had not forgotten, but he had finally forgiven.

By the end of his career, even Bryant himself seemed to recognize that Paul "Bear" Bryant was truly something special, that others recognized all that he stood for, and that he was perhaps something more than just a football coach, whether he had set out to be or not. He had become, in a way, a legend even to himself. He had done all he had set out to do and more. He had all the records and honors. But he had a few regrets, too, for time not spent with the family that loved and admired him probably far more than he knew or understood.

Briefly now and then Bryant would enjoy something other than football—a round of golf, a fishing or hunting outing, a rare trip to Las Vegas or a baseball game. But he could never get his mind off that next game for long, even in the off-season. It was something of a curse, but football had gotten him out of the Arkansas cottonfields, and he had given his life to it in return. He never once grumbled about the deal.

Maybe He Wasn't Perfect, But He Came Darn Close

Bryant was a brilliant, often gruff and tough, groaning, grumbling, mumbling character who became a folk hero to those who follow football. He was a man of compassion to those who knew him off the football field. He placed team goals above individual goals and honors. He taught all-out effort, one play at a time every play, for victory on the football field, and all-out effort, one day at a time every day, for a winning life. His teachings went far beyond the simple matter of winning football games as he became a standard of excellence for all who admire and honor achievement.

His followers and pupils all agree that Bryant was indeed a special person, that he had a knack for "reading" people, choosing people and motivating people and that he wanted to be known and remembered as a winner. He never once claimed to be

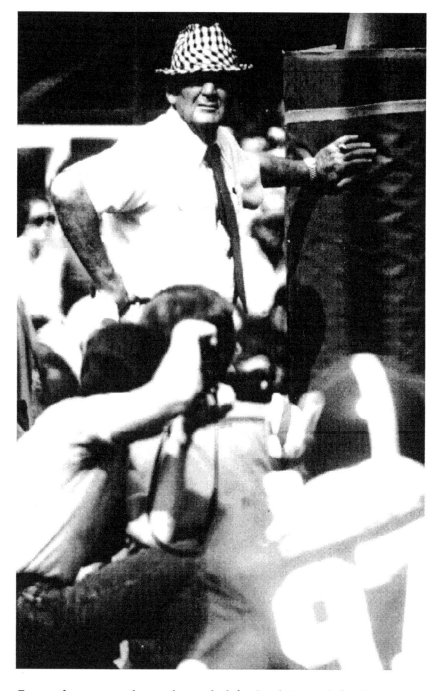

Fans and cameramen knew where to look for Coach Bryant before the game: at his usual spot in the end zone.

and meant what he said, then some; and you knew what he meant even if you didn't catch every word he spoke. He had a way of getting his message across. It was not only what he said, but how he said it and when he said it that gave it the special meaning that only Bryant could give it.

He didn't fret over the losses, although he hated losing more than most. He simply went to work preparing for the next game, figuring a way to keep from losing the same way twice. Now and then he got mad; most often he got even. He was very much human, but he worked hard at keeping anyone from knowing it.

Fans wrote songs and poems about him and sent tons of fan mail to him. In return, he sent out scores of thousands of autographed pictures, letters and momentos.

Bryant was news, and he and his teams made news. Mainly because of him, sports sections in newspapers in Alabama grew from two pages to five or six daily and from four or five to 10 or 12 on Sunday. He was on the cover of national news and sports magazines regularly, and nearly every word he spoke made the daily sports pages and newscasts, if not headlines. He made things happen.

He had a plan for every situation. He left no detail unattended, no possible situation overlooked. He even had a plan for a particular, very favored former player and assistant to succeed him as head coach at Alabama upon his retirement, a plan that did not materialize until almost a decade later following a chain of strange and unexpected or perhaps divinely orchestrated events.

Was Coach Bryant everything the admiring chroniclers then and now say he was? Is he still all we thought he was now that more than a decade has passed since his death? The answer is yes, and far, far more. Have we magnified him in his absence to a size greater than he truly was? On the contrary; only now, from a distance, can we see him clearly for what he was. The more we analyze the man and his record the more we come to appreciate all that he was and did and the unique way he went about it.

perfect or even a genius at the game of football. But as a motivator and leader, and as a winner in the game of football, he was as close as anyone has ever come.

Bryant was a unique and excellent communicator. Even though he mumbled lazily at times (and that was often just part of his act), he gave full, clear meaning to every word he spoke through eye contact and demeanor. He was never vague or guilty of hollow rhetoric. He said what he meant

He was first and foremost a teacher and disciplinarian. He was a philosopher, motivator and humorist. He was a leader, a worker and a thinker. He was more than we knew or even imagined then, and maybe more than we will ever really know.

Most of us thought of him only as a great football coach. We were wrong, of course, and that was partly his fault. He never claimed to be anything more, and often modestly claimed to be far less than a "great" coach. But he was, and he was so good at being what we thought was just a coach we never asked or looked for more from him. He gave us wins, and he gave us memories. But he gave his players and close associates—those who paid his asking price—far, far more. His statue is etched in all our minds and in some hearts, leaning nonchalantly against the goalpost watching pre-game practice in Legion Field; squinting intently from his tower on the practice field; standing serenely amid a chaotic sideline; or walking proudly off the field after another victory.

His life story reads more like some corny, fiction-filled movie script than reality. A handsome, dashing and daring hero from a simple, rural background makes it to the big time by walking a tightrope between mischief and trouble to achieve greatness.

Bryant and Jackie Sherrill celebrate after Alabama clinched the 1964 national championship.

But it was reality. He achieved perhaps more than anyone except him ever dreamed he would. He was a gifted, determined person who demanded more, gave more and won more than anyone during his time.

Another coach may one day eclipse his won-lost record, or his bowl record, or his record for conference or national championships. But it is not likely that another will inspire followers as Bryant did and impact football as Bryant did. And surely none will ever match the wisdom and wit and charisma that set him apart as a man.

Bryant's heyday lasted all his life, from the bear-wrestling incident of 1926 until his death in 1983. He lived in a time and a world that seems now to have belonged only to him. There were few low points, and those were short-lived. He sought and found, or attracted to himself, those like himself—those coaches and players with pride and dedication, unafraid of discipline and work, willing to pay the price, and to whom winning meant a little more than most. His teams and others around him, therefore, remarkably reflected Bryant and his personality. They were marked with unequalled discipline, determination, preparation, toughness, confidence and poise, just as he was.

And they won with no strutting, no taunting and no bragging—just class.

By the time Coach Bryant neared retirement, he had achieved more in football than most people had ever dreamed possible.

2

He Wrote His Own Script in Life

"If wanting to win is a fault, as some of my critics seem to insist, then I plead guilty. I like to win. I know no other way. It's in my blood."
—Paul "Bear" Bryant

BRYANT CAME TO SYMBOLIZE COLLEGE FOOTBALL

The pure, simple, unaltered facts of Paul William "Bear" Bryant's life stand alone as the stuff of which heroes and legends are born. There is no need for the addition of a single fictional twist or turn on a scriptwriter's part.

Bryant, at times seemingly driven by some demon genius, rose from near-poverty, Depression-era farm roots to become one of America's greatest sports heroes as college football's all-time winner over a 38-year career as a head coach. Along the way he became the symbol of the game itself as he surpassed record after record, setting standards of excellence which inspired not only his own teams but all others as well, including people outside the game of football.

At the time of his retirement as University of Alabama coach following the 1982 season, Bryant's list of records included national coach of the year three times; 18 bowl wins; six national championships; 29 bowl appearances as a head coach and 31 overall; 24 consecutive bowl appearances at Alabama; 15 conference championships; most wins for a Division I coach with 323, and consecutive home field wins with 57 at Bryant-Denny Stadium from October 26, 1963, until November 13, 1982.

He had been chosen conference coach of the year 11 times (10 times in the Southeastern Conference and once in the Southwest Conference), had been inducted into the Arkansas Hall of Fame and the Alabama Sports Hall of Fame, had been selected to the *Sports Illustrated* Silver Anniversary All-America team, and had been chosen Kentucky's Citizen of the Year and Alabama's College Administrator of the Year. He was honored shortly after his death with the presentation of the Presidential Medal of Freedom to his family, and was inducted into the National Football Foundation College Football Hall of Fame in 1986, in addition to earning many other honors.

And what may well be his highest honor is the fact that scores of his former pupils have followed

Page 18: Bryant (on step) and Alabama teammates depart for the January 1, 1935, Rose Bowl.

him into coaching. Nearly 50 former players and/or assistants have become head coaches at the college or professional level, indicating their deep admiration for him as well as their belief in his cause and style as they follow in his footsteps.

Coach Bryant did not set his many records with fancy formations and super talents, and he did not change the game of football. He did, however, dramatically change the way the game was played, and often the players themselves. He took special pride in turning what many considered ordinary players into winners with a few basic lessons based on discipline, pride, work, confidence and perseverance.

Although Coach Bryant is best remembered as Alabama's head coach for 25 years, he started his career at Maryland in 1945, then coached at Kentucky and Texas A&M before returning to his alma mater in December 1957. At each school, he turned losing programs into winners, and at each stop his reputation grew as much for his personality and charisma as it did for his winning teams.

A sometimes gruff, plain-speaking man with a style and demeanor like no other, Bryant was often controversial in his demanding practice methods as he taught hard-nosed, gang-tackling football through strict discipline and tough, boot-camp-like physical conditioning. His tactics brought results, however, as he averaged 8.5 wins per season over his 38-year career and 9.3 wins per year during his 25 years at Alabama.

Alabama was the winningest team in college football during the quarter century Bryant served as coach of the Crimson Tide, and his teams of the seventies were the first in NCAA history to win 100 games in a decade. Bryant seemed to improve with age, too, winning 124 games during his last dozen seasons (1971-82) to average 10.3 wins per year while claiming three national championships and eight conference titles and winning seven of his last eight bowl games.

Through the years, mainly due to his teams' many television appearances, the tall and ruggedly handsome Bryant became known to football and sports fans throughout the world for his winning teams; his ambling walk; his deep, gravelly voice; and the familiar houndstooth hats he wore on the sidelines. And he became what most call a legend.

Born September 11, 1913, in rural southern Arkansas, a few miles from Fordyce in an area known as Moro Bottom, Bryant was the second-youngest child in a struggling farm family of 12 children. His parents were Wilson Monroe Bryant and Ida Kilgore Bryant. His father was a semi-invalid due to high blood pressure.

Bryant often endured the ridicule of his class-

Bryant during his playing days in the early 1930s. He played on Alabama's 1934 national championship Rose Bowl team.

mates as a youth because of his deprived circumstances, mostly because he wore overalls and drove a mule team and wagon to school and to town on Saturdays to help his mother peddle vegetables, an endeavor which provided the family with most of its income. As a result of his classmates poking fun at him, Bryant developed a tough hide and quick temper early in life and became known by his early teen years as something of a ruffian, eager for a scrap or any mischief which might attract favorable attention or earn him the much-sought respect of his peers. He found that pulling such pranks as putting a turtle in an excitable girl's desk or tossing a cat through the church window at revival services attracted considerable attention. Some of it was unfavorable, of course, but it made him a hero with his less daring classmates, and he enjoyed such admiration then and throughout his life. The attention somehow helped to offset the shame and ridicule the awkward, overgrown Bryant felt when he heard the giggles of his more socially prominent classmates in his early years, and he developed a lasting fondness for the spotlight as a result.

Despite his later fame and success, memories of those giggles stuck with Bryant throughout his life; and in his autobiography, *Bear*, published a full half a century later in 1974, he said he still remembered the names of those "city slickers" who had laughed at him. Much of his inspiration and angry determination to succeed in life resulted from those early years as he set out then to prove that he was as good as anyone.

By age 12, Bryant was a gangly, labor-hardened lad of six feet tall who would accept any dare to win the admiration of his friends.

Bryant (lower left) shown with family members in the 1940s.

Bryant and Mary at the University of Alabama, 1934

It was by accepting one of those dares that he earned the nickname of "Bear," which came to symbolize to a large degree his personality and demeanor from that day forward.

Several cronies goaded Bryant into wrestling a carnival bear at the Lyric Theater in Fordyce in the summer of 1926 with the promise of a dollar a minute as long as the match lasted. The money and the prospect of catching the eye of a certain young girl in the audience were too good a deal Bryant to pass up, even without the dare.

The contest between boy and beast at first appeared to be a one-sided affair destined to fill his pockets with cash, as Bryant quickly threw the bear and pinned it in a choking headlock, grinning proudly at his pals and counting the anticipated cash as the animal's handler urged him to give the bear a sporting chance and provide the audience with a little more action.

Later, Bryant said he would have held the bear "until it died" except for a couple of technicalities. One, the bear's muzzle suddenly came off and Bryant was staring into a nasty set of unsmiling teeth. Two, Bryant wiped blood from a stinging ear and suddenly envisioned himself being eaten alive. He leaped from the stage, skinning his shins on the theater's front-row seats and forgetting about the money he had earned until too late. The man with the bear quickly skipped town, leaving Bryant with only a nickname. As he did with most opportunities, however, Bryant made the nickname one to remember.

Bryant turned 13 in the fall of 1926, and his size and natural aggressiveness made him an attractive prospect for the Fordyce Redbugs football team. He was invited to practice by coach Bob Cowan as an eighth grader, and after he crushed another player in his first try at kick coverage, Bryant knew he had found his niche in life. Bryant had cleats put on his only pair of shoes and played in his first game a week later.

Bryant devoted his life to football, for the most part, from that first game on until his untimely death on Wednesday, January 26,

Two football coaching greats—Bryant and Wallace Wade. Wade's winning legacy at Alabama was a strong motivation for Bryant to come to the school to play football.

1983, less than a month following his final game as head coach at the University of Alabama. His success at the game provided him with the attention, approval and respect he seemed to seek all his life. Bryant participated in sports other than football during his school years at Fordyce, and he continued to pick fights, hop freight trains for brief excursions out of town and engage in other borderline mischief. He had the size and taste for the contact of football, however, and he earned All-State honors as a tackle as the Redbugs won back-to-back state football championships in 1929 and 1930. He and several others on the team attracted the attention of college scouts from Alabama and Arkansas.

Alabama had won three national championships and four Southern Conference (later changed to Southeastern) titles and played in three Rose Bowls in eight seasons under Coach Wallace Wade (1923-30) and was by far the most popular and publicized team in the South. That, and the fact that several members of the Alabama teams of the era were from Arkansas, had already attracted Bryant as a fan. Wade had resigned following the 1930 season and had been replaced by Frank Thomas, a former Notre Dame quarterback under Knute Rockne. Bryant had once been a close follower of Notre Dame and Rockne, and the Thomas connection with Notre Dame and Rockne made Alabama even more attractive to him. He wasn't difficult to recruit.

Newlyweds Bryant and Mary Harmon at the 1934 Rose Bowl

Page 24: Bryant as Alabama assistant coach, 1939. This page: Bryant in Navy uniform during World War II

When Alabama assistant coach Hank Crisp rode through Fordyce in the late summer of 1931 with Bryant teammate Joe Dildy already on board and offered Bryant a ride back to Tuscaloosa with them, he was ready, even though he had to ride the rumble seat of a coupe all the way.

Bryant got off to a slow start at the University of Alabama. He first discovered that he had to attend Tuscaloosa High School for a semester to make up high school credits before he could enter college. He did practice with the Alabama team, however, and he quickly caught Thomas' eye as a hitter. He also found the discipline and demands of college life a bit binding, and was on the verge of leaving Alabama—of quitting something for the first time in his life—when he heard from Collins Kilgore, a cousin in Fordyce, who sent Bryant a telegram saying "Go ahead and quit just like everybody predicted you would." It reminded him of his classmates laughing at him in his overalls with those mules.

"I wasn't about to quit after that," Bryant said in telling the story many times through the years.

Bryant soon became what he later referred to as Alabama's "other end" opposite All-America Don Hutson, another Arkansas product and close friend of Bryant's. Bryant lettered three seasons (1933-34-35) as Alabama won two conference championships and a national championship in 1934 by beating Stanford, 29-13, in the Rose Bowl to cap a 10-0 season. Bryant had an outstanding game in the Rose Bowl, which featured the sensational pass-catch combination of All-America halfback Dixie Howell and Hutson.

The 1934 team also featured Arkansas natives Dildy; Tilden "Happy" Campbell, who later became baseball coach at Alabama, and All-Southeastern Conference guard Charles Marr.

Bryant was greatly influenced by Thomas, of course, and at some time early in his college career decided he wanted to go into coaching after college. Young Boozer, a teammate, roommate one year at Alabama and life-long friend, said Bryant knew he wanted to coach from the start, and never changed

Bryant and Mary Harmon after his return from duty in North Africa

his mind. "From the first day I met him as a teammate at Alabama, Paul always knew what he wanted to do. He wanted to coach," Boozer said.

Bryant earned his greatest fame as a player in his senior season (1935) when he played against Tennessee with a fractured fibula in his right leg. He had suffered the injury a week earlier and was on crutches the day before the game. The doctor took the cast off his leg and told him he could dress for the game even if he couldn't play, and Bryant actually had no thoughts of playing.

Thomas had a special dislike for Tennessee, which Bryant inherited, and after making his pre-game talk aimed at firing up the team, allowed Coach Crisp to address the squad. "I don't know about the rest of you," Crisp said during the brief but often-repeated talk, "but I know one thing: old 34 will be after them." The stunned Bryant was wearing number 34, and Thomas played him in the game. The performance turned out to be perhaps Bryant's best ever. He caught a pass early which led to a touchdown, and later caught one which he lateraled to All-America halfback Riley Smith, who carried it in for another score as Alabama upset Tennessee, 25-0.

When Bryant made headlines for playing with a broken leg, Atlanta *Constitution* sports editor Ralph McGill traveled to Tuscaloosa the next week and demanded proof of the broken leg. After seeing the X-ray, McGill wrote "As far as this season is concerned, Paul Bryant is in first place in the courage league. There was no bear story about Bear Bryant. He played football with a crack through one of his leg bones. Bryant showed true courage and determination by realizing the vital role that he played for the Crimson Tide. Putting aside all thoughts of pain, he went on to play one of the best games of his career."

Bryant earned second-team All-Southeastern Conference honors for play in his senior season as Alabama went 6-2-1. He also served as president of the A Club that year.

While still in college at Alabama, Bryant married Mary Harmon Black of Birmingham.

Bryant began his coaching career in the spring of 1936 when he landed a job as an assistant at Union College in Jackson, Tennessee, during spring practice. By mid-summer, however, he was back at Alabama as an assistant, where he remained throughout the 1939 season. The Crimson Tide went 29-5-3 during those four seasons, winning the SEC championship in 1937 and returning to the Rose Bowl where it lost, 13-0, to California for its only loss in a 9-1 campaign. Bryant, pushed by Mrs. Bryant, completed work on his B. S. degree during his tenure as an Alabama assistant, an accomplishment of which he was quite proud in later years.

Bryant left Alabama after the 1939 season and spent the next two years as the top assistant to Red Sanders at Vanderbilt. By then, Bryant's coaching talents were gaining widespread recognition, and when Sanders missed a game because of illness, he

After combat duty in North Africa during World War I, Bryant coached a base football team in North Carolina.

Bryant's first coaching job after WWII was at Maryland.

At Kentucky, Bryant was always in the background behind Adolf Rupp and basketball.

Bryant, Mrs. Bryant and Paul Jr., circa 1950

chose Bryant to handle the team in a 7-7 tie with Kentucky.

World War II Changed His Plans

Bryant had dared to dream of one day returning to his home state as head coach at the University of Arkansas, and that dream appeared to have come true following the 1941 season when he wrangled an interview for the job and seemed to have it nailed down at the tender age of 28. As he drove from Arkansas back to Nashville on Sunday, December 7, however, he heard the news of the Japanese bombing of Pearl Harbor, and his plans changed suddenly and drastically. If there was going to be a fight, he wanted to be in it. By the next day he was on his way to Washington to join the Navy, where he spent the next four years.

Bryant spent more than a year in North Africa, but his closest brush with physical harm during World War II came on the trip over when the ship he was on was rammed by another ship in the same convoy and lost more than 200 men. Following his duty in North Africa, Bryant was assigned to North Carolina Pre-Flight Training at Chapel Hill, where he coached football until the war ended in the summer of 1945. Within days of the end of the war, he had his first head coaching job lined up at the University of Maryland, and he carried 17 members of the North Carolina Pre-Flight team and most of the coaches and managers with him, arriving just five days before the first game.

Maryland had won only one game in 1944, and Bryant's hand-picked team matched that in a 60-6 victory over tiny Guilford in the opening game. The team finished the season with a 6-2-1 record highlighted by three closing wins. Elated Maryland President H. C. "Curly" Byrd, who had served as head coach at the school for 23 years, threw a banquet for the team and announced that Bryant had a lifetime contract as head coach. Perhaps the youngest head coach in the country at 32, Bryant was on top of the world.

Within a month, however, Bryant had angrily resigned. On his return from a Christmas visit to Alabama, Bryant found that in his absence Byrd had fired one of his assistant coaches and reinstated a player that Bryant had kicked off the team. His personality would stand for no meddling in his program, even by the school president. He felt he had no choice but to leave, and he did.

Bryant shuffled through the job offers which had

Coach Bryant enjoys Christmas in Kentucky with Paul Jr., Mrs. Bryant and daughter, Mae Martin, December 1950.

accumulated during his visit to Alabama and accepted the job as head football coach at Kentucky, even before going to see Byrd, who unsuccessfully attempted to change his mind.

His abrupt resignation and the circumstances which caused it touched off a strike by thousands of Maryland students urging him to stay, and it took two separate appeals by Bryant himself to finally convince them to return to classes. The story of the Maryland uprising made headlines, and at first Bryant feared it would get him off on the wrong foot at Kentucky. The publicity worked in his favor, however, and he was greeted by an even larger crowd on his arrival in Lexington.

Bryant spent eight seasons at Kentucky, winning the school its first (and only to date) conference football championship in 1950 with an 11-1 record. He remains the school's winningest coach in history even today with a 60-23-5 record, more than four decades following his departure. He carried the Wildcats to four bowl games, winning three, including breaking a 31-game Oklahoma win streak in

the 1950 Sugar Bowl. He was chosen the state's citizen of the year for 1950 as well as SEC Coach of the Year.

Five Kentucky players earned All-America honors during Bryant's tenure. Tackle Bob Gain, quarterback Vito "Babe" Parilli and end Steve Meilinger earned the honor twice each and guard Ray Correll was selected once. Meilinger was chosen all-conference three times (1951-52-53), and five other Wildcat players made All-SEC during the Bryant era. Parilli (1949-51) and George Blanda (1946-48) became the first of many Bryant-coached quarterbacks to go on to outstanding professional football careers.

Many of Bryant's Kentucky players were returning servicemen attending college on the GI Bill, as was the case at Maryland, and his practice sessions were demanding, even for returning war veterans. An indication of Bryant's rough and rugged coaching style came during the 1950 season when the Wildcats played North Dakota in the next-to-last game of the regular season. Kentucky, unbeaten at

Left: Mrs. Bryant and children

Bottom: Mrs. Bryant at Kentucky football stadium, 1951

9-0 for the season, led 70-0 at halftime. Bryant turned the game over to the scrubs in the second half and sent the first two teams to the practice field for additional work to prepare for the upcoming Tennessee game. Unconfirmed rumors had fans leaving the game to watch the more interesting practice scrimmage. Kentucky lost to Tennessee, 7-0, for its only loss of the season.

Bryant made a big first impression at Kentucky, to say the least, as his 1946 team went 7-3. It was the first Wildcat team since 1912 to win seven games, and Bryant was promptly rewarded with a pay raise and long-term contract. The press guide for the 1947 season spoke of him in glowing terms, calling him a tireless worker, patient teacher and "in a class by himself" as a recruiter.

"Paul Bryant is home folks, destined to become one of the greatest coaches of football," the item, written by long-time Birmingham sports writer Zipp Newman, prophetically concluded.

Kentucky was a basketball school and state, however, and Lexington wasn't big enough for two legends. Bryant could not escape the shadow of legendary Wildcat basketball coach Adolph Rupp, who produced conference champions year in and year out as the nation's winningest basketball coach of his time. Rupp was to basketball then what Bryant later became to football: the undisputed king of the hill.

Bryant grew unhappier by the year playing second fiddle to Rupp, and finally made up his mind to leave. He had plenty of offers through the years, but had a long-term contract which the school president was determined to enforce. Bryant finally had to ask the governor to help him gain his release from the contract in February 1954. At that time he had only one job offer on the table—Texas A&M. It wasn't exactly what he had in mind, but he was determined to move on to a school that placed football first; so he took the job.

Bryant and daughter, Mae Martin, circa 1951

Bryant at Texas A&M

His Reputation Soars at Texas A&M

College Station, Texas, did not offer the social life of Lexington, and the Bryant family, including Bryant himself, was shocked at the change in scenery when they arrived at the all-male military school. It took a while for the Bryants to adjust to the situation, but the Aggies immediately became Bryant fans, and with good reason. Several thousand uniformed cadets met Bryant on his arrival in College Station, and as he walked to the microphone to address them for the first time he took off his coat and tie, threw them to the ground and stomped on them. Then he rolled up his sleeves and told them he was ready to go to work. "Those Aggies went crazy," he wrote in *Bear.* But that was only the start.

Bryant's reputation soared, for better or worse, as coach of the Aggies. He made headlines and stunned the college

Top: Bryant with Paul Jr. and Mae Martin, circa 1955. Bottom: Coach and Mrs. Bryant check sports pages, circa 1960.

football world in the late summer of 1954 when he trimmed the returning Aggie squad of 115 or so players to 27 during a rigorous pre-season training camp held off campus in Junction. The team left College Station in three buses and returned in one. Most of the other players disappeared from the camp during the night, unable to meet the challenge of his demanding, helmet-busting practice sessions in the desert heat. The few who stuck it out managed only a 1-9 record during the 1954 season as Bryant suffered his only losing season in 38 years as a head coach. Members of that team always ranked among his favorites, however, because of the determination they showed in not quitting.

Bryant was asked about the incident many times through the years, and said he did the only thing he knew how to do at the time, but that he wouldn't do it again "because I know more now than I knew then—more about resting players, letting them drink water, more about other ways to lead them....I believe if I had been one of those players, I'd have quit, too," he said in *Bear*.

To add salt to the wounds of the 1-9 season of 1954, Texas A&M was found guilty of recruiting violations the following spring and placed on a two-year probation by the Southwest Conference. The Aggies refused to give up, however. They had more bodies in 1955 than the year before, and they were pushed by Bryant's angry, "we'll show 'em" determination to win. And they won seven games, losing only the first and last games of the season to UCLA and Texas, respectively, for a record of 7-2-1 as they served notice to Southwest Conference foes that the Aggies were returning to league contention, probation or no probation.

One of the most legendary

Left, top: Bryant and son Paul Jr. at Mae Martin's school graduation, early 1950s

Bottom: Coach and Mrs. Bryant vacationing, 1961

games of Bryant's career and Texas A&M history came during that 1955 season when the Aggies overcame a 12-0 deficit with less than four minutes to play to defeat Rice, 20-12. The game helped to establish a tradition for fourth-quarter comebacks by Bryant teams which continued throughout his career.

Texas A&M streaked through the 1956 season unbeaten at 9-0-1, won the SWC title and finished the season ranked fifth nationally. Only a 14-14 tie with Houston kept the Aggies from a perfect season. The probation, however, kept them out of the Cotton Bowl. Gene Stallings, Alabama's head coach since 1990, was a member of the Aggie teams of 1954-55-56, earning All-Southwest Conference honors at end in 1955 and serving as a captain in 1956. Dee Powell, also a member of the 1954-56 teams, also later coached at Alabama.

John David Crow, a rugged 60-minute player for the Aggies of 1955-57, was the star of the 1957 squad and became Bryant's only Heisman Trophy winner. Crow gained just over 500 yards rushing as a halfback, but was also outstanding as a pass receiver, punt returner and defensive back. Bryant, noted for rare high praise of individual players, endorsed Crow for the Heisman by saying he had led the league in "running over people." Bryant added that if Crow didn't win the Heisman "they ought to stop giving it." Crow won it. Following a professional career, Crow later coached for Bryant at Alabama. Bobby Marks, an All-SWC end, and Bobby Drake Keith, both members of the 1957 squad, also later coached at Alabama.

The 1957 A&M team was perhaps Bryant's best in his four seasons at the school, but finished the season with an 8-3 record. The Aggies won eight straight games to start the season and were ranked No. 1 nationally with two games to play before disaster struck. Word leaked out that Bryant would leave A&M to become the Alabama coach after the season ended. The disappointed Aggies lost their remaining three games after that, falling 7-6 to Rice and 9-7 to Texas in regular season play and 3-0 to Tennessee in the Gator Bowl. Bryant was furious with Alabama insiders who had failed to keep his impending return to Tuscaloosa quiet, saying they cost him a national championship. What might have been a glorious return to Alabama had suddenly turned bittersweet.

Texas A&M had an impressive 24-5-2 record

Top: Bryant with long-time Alabama radio broadcast team of Maury Farrell (L) and John Forney (R). Bottom: Bryant with Alabama Senator John Sparkman

Page 34: Coach and Mrs. Bryant at home at Texas A&M, circa 1955

during Bryant's final three seasons as Aggie coach. He had more than turned the program around and produced 11 all-conference players, four All-Americas and a Heisman Trophy winner in the process. Not surprisingly, Aggie supporters who had helped meet Bryant's demands for a lucrative, long-term contract when he arrived in College Station were openly displeased with his sudden departure. As with his two previous jobs, he practically had to crash through roadblocks to get out of town.

Right Man for Alabama

It seemed inevitable that Bryant would eventually become Alabama's head coach. He had coveted the job, as he had the Arkansas job, at various times throughout his career, and it had been offered to him twice while he was at Kentucky. However, the timing had never seemed right before.

Coach Bryant was always close to his grandchildren. Page 36: He gets a Christmas hug from granddaughter Mary Harmon Tyson, circa 1960. Right: He shares potato chips with her and grandson Marc, circa 1965.

Bryant had invested more than eight years of his life in the University of Alabama as player and assistant coach, and he had a genuine love for the school because it had gotten him out of the Arkansas cotton fields. Too, he had become the best known of the numerous coaches Frank Thomas had produced as Crimson Tide head coach. Thomas himself had even wanted Bryant for the job when he retired due to illness in 1946.

Alabama not only wanted Bryant in 1957, even with his reputation as a tough and demanding taskmaster and the Texas A&M probation baggage, but it needed him. The once-mighty Crimson Tide had won only eight games in four years, and only four in the last three seasons under coach J. B. "Ears" Whitworth. The Tide had managed to win only one conference title (1953 with a 6-3-3 record under Harold "Red" Drew) since 1945, when Thomas produced Alabama's last Rose Bowl team and a perfect 10-0 record.

Bryant could not refuse his alma mater's call this time, saying it was like his "mama calling him home," and he accepted the challenge of rebuilding another team, even though he had to take a cut in pay to do it. Before he accepted the dual position of head coach and athletic director at Alabama, however, he made certain that his former coaches, Crisp and Drew, and several other loyal, long-term members of the athletic staff, were given other jobs with the school.

Although it had been rumored for weeks, the official announcement of Bryant's hiring at Alabama came on December 3, 1957. The announcement noted that he had signed a 10-year contract at a salary of $17,500 per year. Bryant is said to have set his own salary, and asked only for pay equal to that of the highest-paid professor on campus, who happened to be noted author and creative writing teacher Hudson Strode. The announcement also mentioned, in something of an understatement, that Bryant was known for his "hard-nosed" brand of football, and had a 91-38-8 career record as a head coach.

The story did not mention the fact that Texas A&M had served two years' probation for recruiting violations during Bryant's four-year tenure there. That fact had not gone unnoticed by the Alabama search committee; however, it had been only a momentary stumbling block in the hiring process. Dr. Frank Rose, University of Alabama president at the time, was a Kentucky native and past president of Transylvania College in Kentucky, and he had become a Bryant fan during Bryant's eight years as Kentucky head coach. He wanted Bryant and only Bryant, and the selection committee haggled only briefly before voting unanimously for his hiring.

UA President Frank Rose (R) chose Bryant as Alabama head coach. Bryant quickly rewarded him for his choice. From 1960-1968, under Bryant, Alabama posted a record of 84-11-4, winning national championships in 1961, 1964 and 1965.

"We have secured, in my thinking, the greatest football coach of all time," Rose said in announcing Bryant's acceptance of the Alabama post. Bryant proved him true over the next 25 years by averaging 9.3 wins per season at Alabama and becoming the winningest coach in college football history.

When Bryant arrived in Tuscaloosa in December 1957, he found Alabama football in its saddest condition ever. The athletic facilities were old, ragged and rundown, and with losing seasons and poor attendance, there was little cash in the till to do anything about it. The program needed new blood, and Bryant provided it. He brought with him from Texas A&M a team of proven winners as assistant coaches, and started immediately on a 25-year march that shattered almost every record in college football. He started out in grand fashion, too, by immediately recruiting the high school class of 1958, which would help win him his first national championship four years later.

All the pieces fell into place for Bryant at Alabama, and for Alabama with Bryant. He was the right man in the right place at the right time. The Crimson Tide's long, colorful, winning football tradition gave it a recruiting advantage which provided Bryant with the final ingredient needed to put him on top. And Bryant's intense, determined coaching style provided the man of the hour for a school hungry for a return to the glory days of its past. Together, they soared to the pinnacle of college football and remained there for a quarter of a century as Bryant made coaching history and the Crimson Tide won more football games and national championships and went to more bowls than any other team during the era.

Bryant was busy hiring, firing and coaching throughout the spring and early fall of 1958. He

Page 39: Soon after his selection as Alabama coach, Bryant gained virtual hero status because of his teams' successes.

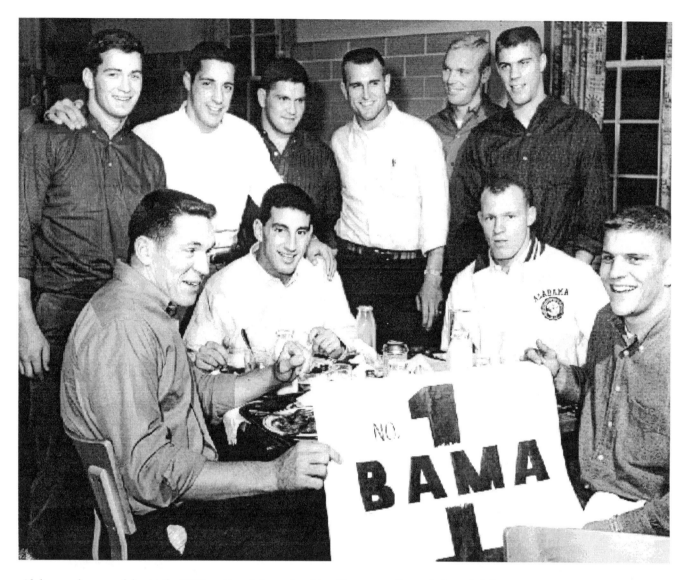

Alabama players celebrate the 1961 national championship. Shown are (front, left to right) Lee Roy Jordan, Ray Abruzzese, John O'Linger, Pat Trammell; (back, left to right) Charley Pell, Mike Fracchia, Billy Neighbors, Tommy Brooker, Butch Wilson and Bill Battle.

introduced the returning Alabama players to rugged physical conditioning and hard-nosed football, much the same as he had at Texas A&M, and found out quickly who the winners and quitters were. The winners, playing with a new, inspired intensity, in turn introduced their opponents to a new, hard-hitting, gang-tackling, blitzing, quick-kicking brand of football in the fall and produced a surprising, perhaps even shocking, 5-4-1 record. It was Bryant's only team which did not play in a post-season bowl game during his 25 years as Alabama coach. The new style of play produced wins and quickly caught the attention of the media and fans. Bryant again was an instant success.

Bryant brought Alabama's defensive tradition back to life on his return as his first Tide team allowed just 75 points for the season. It was the first time an Alabama team had held all opponents to less than 100 points since 1945. Tide teams coached by Thomas (1931-1946) allowed more than 100 points in a season only once, giving up 110 in his final season of 1946. The 1930 Alabama team, coached by Wallace Wade and winner of the Rose Bowl and a national championship, held its opponents to just 13 points, the best in school history. The 1933 Alabama team on which Bryant played as a sophomore gave up just 17 points as the second-best. Bryant learned from Thomas that defense came first, and his teams showed special pride in defense throughout his career.

Bryant's Alabama teams led the nation in scoring defense in 1961, 1966, 1975 and 1979, and the

By 1963, when this photograph of the Bryant family's Christmas dinner was taken, Coach Bryant had helped restore Alabama as a national power in football.

1961 team led the nation in total defense as well. Bryant's 1949 Kentucky team had also led the nation in total defense and scoring defense.

Alabama's 1959 team, bolstered by the sophomores of Bryant's first recruiting class, lost its opener to Georgia and the Liberty Bowl finale to Penn State, 7-0, but in between tied Tennessee and upset Georgia Tech and Auburn to finish 7-2-2 and climb into contention for the Southeastern Conference title again. Included in that 1959 season was a 19-7 victory over Tulane which gave Bryant his 100th career coaching win. The Liberty Bowl, played then in Philadelphia, started Alabama on an NCAA record streak of 25 straight bowl appearances and Bryant on his way to a record 24 straight.

The Tide went 8-1-2 in 1960, losing only to Tennessee in Knoxville. The highlight of the season came in Atlanta when Alabama fought back from a 15-0 fourth-quarter deficit to stun Georgia Tech, 16-15, with a field goal by backup kicker Richard O'Dell on the final play of the game. The kick was O'Dell's only career attempt at Alabama. That comeback victory has been remembered by many of the players on the team as the one which convinced them that they could win any game by believing in themselves and fighting until the final whistle.

1961 Team Started it All

Bryant's first national championship team in 1961 was a special one from the start. It was the first freshman class he welcomed to Alabama in the fall of 1958, and in his first meeting with them he is said to have outright guaranteed them they could win a national championship in four years if they did all that he asked them to do. He made a habit of telling each class the same thing from that time on, and most must have believed him as they delivered six times and came darn close several other times. Bryant recruited 22 freshmen classes which he coached through their senior seasons at Alabama. More than one in four (six) won national titles; another one (1966, 11-0 and the only unbeaten, untied team in the country) should have won it, and three others lost out on the championship by losing bowl games. With a lucky bounce here and there, Alabama could easily have won an astounding 10 national championships in 25 seasons under Bryant.

The 1961 team went 11-0 and won the conference and national championships, allowing just 25 points in 11 games as Bryant's stingiest defensive unit ever, prompting him to say, "They play like it's

Page 42: Coach and Mrs. Bryant board a plane for one of Alabama's several bowl trips in the 1960s.

This page: Paul Bryant Jr. and Mary Harmon Tyson, Coach Bryant's grand-daughter, unveil the building name at the dedication of Paul W. Bryant Hall on the University of Alabama campus in the mid-1960s.

a sin to give up a point." The Tide shut out six of its opponents and allowed a high of seven points. Alabama beat Arkansas, 10-3, in the Sugar Bowl, giving Bryant his first bowl win at Alabama and earning him Southeastern Conference and national coach of the year honors.

The 1961 team was a unique mixture of average talent, great leadership and even greater desire, with quarterback Pat Trammell as its catalyst. The nucleus of the team was made up of seniors, including All-America tackle Billy Neighbors, All-SEC quarterback Trammell, end Tommy Brooker, halfback Bill Oliver, center John O'Linger, linebacker Darwin Holt, guard Jack Rutledge and halfback Billy Richardson. But there were other stars on the team, too, including juniors Lee Roy Jordan, Jimmy Sharpe, Charley Pell, Bill Battle, Butch Wilson, Jimmy Wilson, Cotton Clark and Mike Fracchia.

Trammell, who tragically died of cancer in January 1969 at age 28, became an extension of Bryant on the field during his years as a Crimson Tider, and especially so in his senior season. The second-team All-America performer was a tough, determined leader who inspired and motivated his teammates, and Bryant called him the "bell cow" of the team which ranked as one of Bryant's all-time favorites.

"Pat had a great desire to win and he had a way of transmitting it to others," said teammate Lee Roy Jordan. "He would challenge you mentally or physically. He would do

The photographs of Bryant on these two pages were made during the years when he was coaching Alabama to unmatched successes in football. In 38 seasons, he coached 15 conference championships, more than any other Division I coach. He won six national championships and carried the Crimson Tide to 24 consecutive post-season bowl appearances, both college records. He was chosen National Coach of the Decade twice: in the 1960s as well as the 1970s. He was a charter member of the Alabama Sports Hall of Fame.

whatever it took to win.

"Pat was a smart player who didn't get you beat. He got the maximum from himself and helped others around him to be better. He was a great leader and teammate," Jordan added.

Bryant called Trammell "the favorite person of my entire life" in his autobiography, and their relationship was unlike that of any other between Bryant and player. "He can't run well but he scores touchdowns. He doesn't pass well but he completes them. He doesn't do anything well except win," Bryant often said of Trammell.

Football was or somehow became important to that much-alike 1961 group, and the entire roster

has become a large part of the Alabama and Bryant legends. At least five went on to play professional football and seven went into coaching, four of them becoming head coaches at the college level. And that was in the days of one-platoon football, when 18-20 players did most of the playing on both offense and defense. That 1961 team became the standard by which later Bryant-coached Alabama teams were measured, and it was special because it proved all Bryant's theories to be sound. Someone coined the phrase, "We believe," and the other championships seemed easy after that.

Alabama's 1962 team lost only one game, 7-6, to Georgia Tech in Atlanta, and the 1963 squad lost just two games by a total of six points to go 9-2.

The Tide had a 26-game unbeaten streak from October 22, 1960, until November 17, 1962, and chalked up impressive bowl wins over Oklahoma (17-0 in the Orange Bowl) and Ole Miss (12-7 in the Sugar Bowl) in 1962 and 1963, respectively, as Alabama and Bryant became the darlings of the bowls. The 1963 bowl win came on the strength of four field goals by kicker Tim Davis as star quarterback Joe Namath sat out the Tide's final regular-season win (17-12 over Miami) and the bowl game

due to a disciplinary suspension.

The Namath suspension made headline news, as did the spring suspension of quarterback Ken Stabler a couple of years later, but such action was nothing new for Bryant. His resignation at Maryland was prompted mainly because the college president, acting in Bryant's absence, reinstated a politically connected player Bryant had suspended. And at Texas A&M, a delegation of several players appealed to Bryant for the reinstatement of a suspended teammate only to end up getting the boot themselves just for butting in.

Despite his rapid and overwhelming success, Bryant's early tenure at Alabama was not without controversy.

The first came in the early sixties as Bryant and his Alabama teams ransacked the Southeastern Conference during the 1958-63 seasons with a hard-hitting, gang-tackling style not played by many teams in the league. To some, it appeared that football—at least Alabama football—had become too serious, too rough. The Crimson Tide played with a relentless intensity, much like Bryant's personality. The style of play was changing rapidly, and it was shocking to some. Georgia

A Bryant Family Album

Despite Coach Bryant's national acclaim, he remained a strong family man, as shown by the family snapshots on these pages. Opposite page, top: Bryant, Bob Hope and granddaughter Mary Harmon Tyson surrounded by security, circa 1973; bottom left, Coach and Mrs. Bryant with Sugar Bowl memorabilia, 1970s; bottom right, with their grandchildren; this page, above, Bryant plays with Christmas toys as Mrs. Bryant, daughter Mae Martin Tyson and grandchildren Marc and Mary Harmon watch; right, family portrait of the Bryant clan.

Coach and Mrs. Bryant share a momemt at home with granddaughters Mae Martin, Stella Gray, and Anna Laurie and Mrs. Paul Bryant Jr., circa 1974.

Tech and Tulane, soon regularly beaten by Bryant's leaner, meaner Alabama teams, eventually decided to leave the conference.

From the start at Alabama, Bryant had found it difficult to escape the image of a tough taskmaster he had built at Kentucky and Texas A&M. In addition to beating most opponents, Bryant offended many—opponents and otherwise—with his defiant, lead-follow-or-get-the-hell-out-of-the-way attitude. Alabama fans loved him immediately because he won. Opponents' fans and out-of-town media didn't always feel the same.

When Alabama linebacker Darwin Holt broke Georgia Tech player Chick Graning's jaw with an elbow in 1961, Georgia Tech followers screamed foul, and the Atlanta papers attacked Holt, Bryant and Alabama football in general. Holt even got telephone death threats over the incident. Before it was all over, all parties were fighting mad.

A *Saturday Evening Post* article written by an Atlanta writer and published in October 1962 accused Bryant of teaching brutal, dirty football. Much of it was based on the Holt-Graning incident

and Bryant's past reputation. Bryant was angry enough to file a $500,000 libel suit over the article.

Another article in the magazine, this time a shocking one in March 1963, accused Bryant and Georgia athletic director Wally Butts of "rigging" the 1962 Alabama-Georgia game. The 1963 story claimed Butts had given Bryant inside information on the Georgia team which helped Alabama win, 35-0. The story was based on a telephone call between Butts and Bryant which was allegedly overheard by a third party.

Bryant was fighting mad by this time, and upped his suit to $10.5 million. Butts filed a $10 million suit, also, and a federal court jury awarded Butts over $3 million in damages for the rigging story in August 1963 following a sensational 12-day trial in Atlanta. Publishers of the *Saturday Evening Post* paid Bryant over $300,000, which he demanded in a cashier's check, in a settlement of his suit a few months later. The critical stories were personally painful to Bryant and his family, and he was unforgiving of those responsible, saying they had taken 10 years off his life.

From 1960-1968, Alabama posted a record of 84-11-4, winning national championships in 1961, 1964 and 1965. The 1964 team, quarterbacked by Namath, won with a 10-1 record when the final vote in both polls was taken prior to a 21-17 loss to Texas in the Orange Bowl. The final vote in the Associated Press poll was moved to after the bowl games in 1965 to avoid a repeat of 1964's fluke. Alabama lost its season opener to Georgia in 1965, but still won the AP national title when all the higher-ranked teams lost in bowl competition, allowing the Tide, led by quarterback Steve Sloan, to claim its second straight national championship via a 39-28 Orange Bowl win over Nebraska. Alabama (9-1-1) was fourth in the United Press poll in a vote taken prior to the bowl games.

Bryant often called his 1966 Alabama team, quarterbacked by future professional football star Ken Stabler and featuring All-America performers Richard Cole, Bobby Johns, Cecil Dowdy and Ray Perkins, his best ever, and it finished the season as the nation's only unbeaten, untied team with an 11-0 record, including a 34-7 romp over Nebraska in the Sugar Bowl. Still, it finished third in both the Associated Press and United Press polls as a backlash of regional prejudice and jealousy kept the Tide from a third straight title.

Racial problems in the South during the mid-sixties surely played a role in the final 1966 vote. Alabama and other SEC teams continued to field segregated, all-white teams at the time, though they often played against integrated opponents. The South was in the spotlight due to widespread civil rights violence, and Alabama governor George Wallace was one of the most outspoken seg-

Top: Coach Bryant with son Paul Jr. (R) and grandson Marc Tyson.
Middle and bottom: At a 1982 Washington party, Bryant with granddaughter Mary Harmon Moman and Charley Boswell, and with Auburn coach Pat Dye.

Above: Bryant presents President Gerald Ford an Alabama cap as Ford visits Tide practice session.

Page 50: Coach and Mrs. Bryant with Joe Namath, Dallas Cowboys coach Tom Landry and the Rev. Billy Graham at a Billy Graham Crusade service

regationists of the period. His defiant stand against integration, including personally attempting to block enrollment of black students at the University in 1963, had focused attention squarely on the school and state. There is every reason to believe the football team's national image was tarnished somewhat by the situation. And, of course, the Tide had been fortunate the two previous seasons in somewhat backing into the championships. Voters from outside the South simply refused to vote for Alabama again in 1966, and the Crimson Tide finished third in both polls.

Failure to win a third straight championship was a bitter pill for Bryant and Alabama fans to swallow, however, considering that No. 1 Notre Dame and No. 2 Michigan State had played to a 10-10 tie late in the season. To make matters worse, Notre Dame, with no bowl game to play, had chosen to run out the clock rather than try to score in the closing seconds of the game.

"I have a lot of seniors on this team," Bryant said in voicing disappointment about the final vote. "Some of them will be graduating and going on over to Vietnam, I suppose. When they get there, I just hope they don't play for a tie."

Alabama, noted for its small, quick players during the period, had the best record of any college team in the country in the sixties, going 90-16-4 and winning three national championships. But the Crimson Tide slipped slightly in 1967 and 1968, posting 8-2-1 and 8-3 records and failing to win a conference championship after claiming four of the previous six. Other conference teams had adopted Alabama's brand of football by then, too, in self defense, and were fast catching up.

Slump Rekindled Bryant Flame

Then, with almost no warning, the near impossible happened: Alabama suddenly fell into a disastrous slump, going 6-5 and 6-5-1 in 1969 and 1970, respectively. The Tide slipped from major bowl play to just barely making the bowl list, and missed the Associated Press top twenty list both seasons for the first time since 1958.

Alabama was embarrassed physically during its slide from the top by national powers Missouri (35-10 in 1968), Colorado (47-33 in 1969) and Southern Cal (42-21 in 1970) in games which signaled that the day of the small, quick players had ended. The losses also proved to many that refusing to recruit black athletes was a mistake a major football power could no longer make. The game and the times had changed. This time, Bryant and Alabama were forced to change to keep pace.

The two sub-par seasons caused considerable concern and unrest among the Alabama fans, and Bryant was fully aware of it. He could read the headlines as well as between the lines. There was unrest throughout America, for that matter, with Vietnam War protests rampant and a general anti-establishment attitude among the youth of the nation.

Bryant was aware of that, too. He had seen it on the University of Alabama campus and to some extent on his football team. Some of his players even asked to be allowed to wear long hair and be treated more like regular students.

But there was even more unrest within Bryant. He surely didn't like losing, and he didn't care much for criticism, either. And he was a man in a position to do something about the situation. He responded angrily.

"I'm through tiptoeing around and I'm through pussyfooting around," he said in a determined tone as he issued a warning to all parties following the disappointing 1970 season. "I'm going back to being Paul Bryant and anybody who doesn't like the way Paul Bryant does things can get the heck out of here."

Speaking as athletic director, Bryant promised a quick change in direction or a change in head coaches. As head coach, however, he made it clear that he had no intentions of quitting. He invited the faint-hearted to stand aside as he took stock of the situation and immediately began implementing dramatic changes that would not only return Alabama to its winning ways, but send it to even greater heights than ever before. Bryant was about to rebuild a team again—this time his own—and prove himself again in the process.

The one surprising thing he didn't do was fire everybody in sight, as some fully expected of the man said to be so hard you could strike a match on him. He did clean out a few lockers and slam a few doors and make a few changes here and there—enough to get everyone's full attention, including his own—and that alone corrected much of the problem. Bryant rededicated himself to his brand of football and his old way of doing things. He went back to hard-nosed football, both on and off the field.

Alabama had enjoyed unprecedented success during the sixties, going 85-12-3 from 1960-69 as the nation's winningest team. Bryant had won national acclaim and enjoyed the widespread attention, including tempting offers from professional football. He proved himself only human by taking a moment to enjoy it. That moment, however, was enough time for complacency to set in and for the pack at his heels to overtake him and his Crimson Tide. The experience was humbling, and he vowed to never let it happen again, and he didn't.

Bryant was ready to make drastic changes, and he had taken special notice that friend Darrell Royal's Texas Longhorns had won national championships in 1969 (both AP and UPI) and 1970 (UPI) with a new triple-option formation called the wishbone. The formation emphasized a Bryant-favored ball control offense, and Bryant was set on moving away from the pass-oriented play the Crimson Tide had drifted into during the mid-sixties with its stable of gifted quarterbacks.

Bryant borrowed a Texas coach to teach his staff the wishbone in the summer of 1971, and Alabama switched to the new offense in the fall. The move was a masterful one as the wishbone proved to be a perfect fit for Bryant's style and the Alabama personnel. With the wishbone and such stars as All-Americas Johnny Musso, John Hannah, Jim Krapf, John Mitchell, Woodrow Lowe, Wayne Wheeler, Sylvester Croom, Leroy Cook, Ozzie Newsome, Mike Washington, Barry Krauss, Buddy Brown, Marty Lyons, Jim Bunch, Don McNeal and Dwight Stephenson, Alabama returned to national football prominence with a vengeance.

Alabama also began recruiting black athletes, signing its first recruits in the spring of 1970. Mitchell, a Mobile native who had earned junior

Page 53: In the last years of his coaching career, Coach Bryant and Mary Harmon, his wife of nearly 50 years, remained close.

college All-America honors in Arizona, became the first black athlete to play for Alabama when he started defensively against Southern Cal in Los Angeles in September 1971. Wilbur Jackson, a sophomore halfback from Ozark who had been the school's first black signee, also played in the game as a new era began for the Crimson Tide. Mitchell earned All-America honors for Alabama in 1972 and later joined Alabama as an assistant coach.

Alabama managed to keep its wishbone offense secret until the opening game kickoff, and Southern Cal was obviously surprised by the new look as the Tide pulled off a dramatic 17-10 upset to give Bryant his 200th career victory. The talented Trojans were among the nation's dominant teams of the era, and the victory quickly vaulted Alabama into the national spotlight again.

Bryant, Tide Shatter Records

The Crimson Tide rebounded from that 6-5-1 mark in 1970 to go 97-11-0 over the next nine seasons and finish the seventies with a 103-16-1 mark, becoming the first team in NCAA history to win 100 games in a decade and winning more games than any other team during the period. The streak included a 12-0 record in 1979 which won the Tide both AP and UPI national championships. The decade also included six 11-win seasons and national championships in 1973 (UPI) and 1978 (AP). Alabama won the SEC championship eight times and lost only three conference games during the 1971-79 seasons as it totally dominated the league.

Alabama set record after record as the seasons passed, and along the way Bryant seemed to suddenly have a shot at Amos Alonzo Stagg's all-time NCAA Division 1-A career win record of 314, set over 58 years of coaching. By the late seventies, the run for the record began to attract national attention as Bryant appeared to be within striking distance of the mark after the 1976 season with 262 wins in 32 seasons as a head coach. Only Glenn "Pop" Warner with 313 wins and Stagg remained in his path.

"All I know is I don't want to stop coaching and I don't want to stop winning, so we're gonna break the record unless I die," he said when finally admitting at least an interest in the record in 1977. "As long as somebody has to be the winningest coach, heck, it might as well be me," he added modestly.

Alabama reeled off 11-1, 11-1 and 12-0 seasons in 1977, 1978 and 1979 to push Bryant's win total

to 296, and the pressure built with each game of each season as the media focused more and more on the record. Bryant became as much an attraction as the games themselves as fans and the media watched his every move and began a countdown toward the record. (A story even circulated during the record run that a third-stringer on a visiting team sneaked his camera onto the sideline hoping to get a photo of Coach Bryant during or after the game.)

The Tide went 10-2 in 1980, boosting Bryant's win mark to 306 and presenting a challenge to the 1981 team to win at least nine games and hand Bryant the record. His 300th career win came in a 45-0 rout of Kentucky in Birmingham.

The pressure-filled, record-breaking Alabama season of 1981 drew every eye and ear in the sports world. Bryant was wired for sound at games, interviewed at every turn and photographed from every angle as the history-making season unfolded.

The 1981 team, though not as dominating as teams of the previous few seasons, played inspired football throughout the season behind the defensive leadership of All-Americas Thomas Boyd (linebacker), Tommy Wilcox (safety) and Warren Lyles (nose guard) as it stalked the record for Bryant. The Tide had struggled to a 4-1-1 record at midseason, defeating LSU, Kentucky, Vanderbilt and Ole Miss while losing to Georgia Tech and tying Southern Mississippi. Bryant's win total stood at 310, four from a tie with Stagg and five from the record. The task appeared difficult, if not impossible, as Alabama needed five wins in five games to give Bryant the record outright, and included in those five remaining games were such rugged opponents as Penn State, Tennessee, Mississippi State and Auburn.

The Tide beat Tennessee, 38-19, Rutgers, 31-7, and Mississippi State, 13-10, in home games to give Bryant 313 wins and a tie with Warner for second place on the career-win list before heading to Penn State to face one of the nation's most talented teams of 1981. The Alabama defense was magnificent against the powerful Penn State offense throughout the game. The highlight of the game came when the Tide staged a third-quarter defensive stand to keep the Lions from scoring on seven straight plays inside the Alabama seven-yard-line. That may have been the turning point of the game, as the Tide went on to win 31-16 to give Bryant his 314th career win and a tie with Stagg as the winningest coach of all time.

"When you look back at it, it's pretty remarkable, holding that great team seven times inside our seven. But we remembered that Coach Bryant

Bryant at the 1982 Liberty Bowl, his final game. At the end of his career, his Alabama teams had the best record in college football his last five years (50-9-1), his last 10 years (103-16-1), and for his entire 25-year tenure (232-46-9).

always stressed playing well the first two minutes of the third quarter to set the momentum of the game," said Wilcox of the Alabama effort. The effort earned a special tribute from Bryant at the time, also.

"As the defensive team came off the field after those seven plays, there was Coach Bryant, three or four yards out on the field. He took off his hat and tipped it to us as we came off as if to say, 'Job well done'," Wilcox said. "When he took his hat off to us, I had goose bumps all over. At that moment, I felt bigger than a mountain," he added.

Bryant needed an Alabama win over bitter rival

Auburn in the season finale to claim the career win record, and the Tide delivered in classic fashion on November 28, 1981, by coming from behind in the fourth quarter to defeat the Tigers, 28-17. The comeback victory pleased Bryant as much as the record itself.

"It proves to our players that they have class and character," he said of the comeback.

Alabama shared the SEC championship with Georgia in 1981, but lost to Texas, 14-12, in the Cotton Bowl to finish 9-2-1 for the season. There was speculation that Bryant would retire before the next season, but he returned for an encore perfor-

It was obvious that Bryant was tired, even weary. The many years of long hours and hard work had taken their toll.

mance in 1982, adding eight more wins to his record to finish with 323 wins for his career. Included in that final season was a resounding 42-21 victory over eventual national champion Penn State. Alabama finished at 8-4 for the year, losing its last three regular-season games to LSU, Southern Mississippi and Auburn before sending Bryant out in style with a 21-15 victory over Illinois in the Liberty Bowl.

Alabama was 124-19-1 from 1971-82, following Bryant's vow to never relax again after the slump of 1969-70. The Tide won nine of 12 conference championships during the period and lost only seven SEC games in 12 seasons, averaging 10.3 wins per year. Bryant finished his career with an NCAA record six national championships as a head coach. He also played on a national championship team at Alabama (1934). No other head coach has been a part of seven national championships in his career as coach and player.

Bryant didn't save his best for last; he simply got better—and wiser—with age, learning from his mistakes and adjusting to the changes as he grew in his ability to relate to and motivate players as individuals rather than as a group, and to turn those individuals into a team.

"I've made so many mistakes that if I don't make the same mistakes over, we're going to come pretty close to winning," he once said in explaining his secret to success. Bryant's Alabama teams had the best record in college football his last five years (50-9-1), his last 10 years (103-16-1) and for his entire 25-year tenure (232-46-9).

Bryant's return for the 1982 season proved to be a smart one, too, as far as the winningest coach record goes. A decade later, researchers discovered six more wins for Glenn "Pop" Warner and pushed him into second place on the list with 319. Had Bryant retired after the 1981 season with 315, he would have been unseated on a technicality by a coach who had been dead since 1954.

Retirement Ends Era

Bryant, 69 years old, in failing health and tired from the stress of the run for the career-win record as well as the previous 37 seasons, officially announced his retirement on December 15, 1982, two weeks before the Liberty Bowl. Ray Perkins, who had earned All-America honors as a receiver for Alabama under Bryant (1963-66) and who was then head coach of the New York Giants, was named head coach as Bryant's replacement. Bryant had planned to remain as athletic director for a year to assist in the transition process.

Bryant had lightly hinted of his retirement in August, saying, "Fifteen years ago I could have won at Vasser, but I'm not a spring chicken any more." He hinted more strongly in early November following a disappointing 20-10 loss to LSU, saying, "I'm going to alert the president and anybody that wants to know, in a heck of a hurry, that we need to make some changes and we need to start at the top. When you do as we have done for the last three or four weeks, something is wrong at the top, and I'm at the top...."

Alabama fans screamed, "Say it ain't so, Bear," but the Tide then lost to Southern Mississippi, 38-29, at home, ending an NCAA-record 57-game Bryant-Denny Stadium win streak which dated to Oct. 12, 1963. Then, two weeks later, the Tide lost to Auburn, 23-22, as the Tigers ended a nine-game losing streak to the Crimson Tide. Earlier in the season, Alabama had lost to Tennessee for the first time in 11 years. All the wrong records were being broken, and Bryant was unhappier about it than anyone.

Stronger rumors of Bryant's retirement in late November identified Perkins as his replacement, and although Bryant refused to comment, the word was out. The official announcement, when it finally came, was no surprise to anyone.

"This is my alma mater. I love this school and I love the players, but they deserve better coaching than they have been getting from me, as I've said before," Bryant said as he announced his retirement. "I know I'll miss coaching and can't say enough (about) or thank enough the coaches and players that I've been associated with." Bryant added that he had hoped to coach until he was "80 or 90," but that the time had come for him to step aside.

It was obvious at that time, and even before during the season, that Bryant was tired, even weary. The many years of long hours and hard work, the worry over the wins and losses, the bad cigarettes and good whiskey, and the millions of questions and distractions had taken their toll. The inevitable physical, mental and emotional letdown from the the record-breaking 1981 season had come. Although he had seemed so for so long, Paul "Bear" Bryant was not immortal after all.

Bryant had been ill and on medication after suffering a stroke two years earlier and mild heart failure a year before that. The illnesses had been kept quiet, and Bryant had carried on when ordinary men would not have done so. He had refused to quit because of illness, but he refused to continue when the team started going downhill, though he

Bryant's style changed through the years as he became older and wiser and found better ways to win— ways that cost him fewer players and friends and caused less commotion.

admitted he found it difficult to give up the game that had been his life for so long. "I'd probably croak in a week if I quit coaching," he had ironically joked many times.

Alabama fans took Bryant's retirement hard, but reluctantly conceded that he had earned it. Perkins was chosen as Bryant's successor by then University president Joab Thomas. Bryant had nothing to do with it, and said so. It wasn't made public at the time, but Bryant had wanted Gene Stallings, who finally became Tide head coach in 1990, as his successor.

Bryant bowed out of coaching on December 29, 1982, as the emotional Crimson Tide fought off two fourth-quarter assaults by Illinois to give its outgoing coach a 21-15 victory in his final game. "The 315th was not as important as a lot of people think," Bryant said following the Liberty Bowl victory. "But this one was real important because it was the last one. It was the last time out there. It's the one that won't be forgotten."

Death Shocks, Saddens Fans

Then, after only a few short weeks of retirement, Coach Bryant died suddenly of a heart attack shortly after noon on January 26, 1983. He had been admitted to a Tuscaloosa hospital the night before with chest pains, but had not appeared in danger.

Alabama fans were stunned and grief stricken. His retirement had been difficult to accept; his death was devastating. Many watching or listening to special newscasts of his death at work or in public areas openly wept or stared teary-eyed in disbelief. Few had words to express their emotions— their feelings of lonely, helpless sorrow.

The entire sports world was in shock, and Bryant fans throughout the nation saddened. So

Bryant Retires

Opposite page—
University of Alabama president Joab Thomas with Bryant at press conference announcing Bryant's retirement and the change in coaches. Bryant's reaction to his retirement.

This page—
Top: Coach Bryant shows emotion of the moment at press conference introducing Ray Perkins as the new Alabama head coach.

Left: Perkins speaks to the press for the first time as Alabama's new coach.

Alabama assistant athletic director Sam Bailey gives the press details of Coach Bryant's death.

many former players, coaches and dignitaries attended his funeral in Tuscaloosa that several churches were equipped for sound and opened for the services. Thousands of fans and mourners lined the funeral route to bid him a final farewell as the procession passed along the streets of Tuscaloosa, past Bryant-Denny Stadium and the University of Alabama athletic complex, then along the Interstate highway to Birmingham's Elmwood Cemetery. Interstate traffic stopped, even in Birmingham, as the procession passed, and overpasses were crowded with silent, sad-faced mourners, many bearing banners proclaiming, "We love you, Bear," and other messages of admiration or remembrance.

The man who had led the University of Alabama to its greatest football glory and who had become a legend along the way was gone. An era of unequalled football success had ended.

Perkins did not endear himself to Bryant loyalists on his arrival in Tuscaloosa. He immediately dismissed all but a couple of Bryant's long-time

assistants and dismantled Bryant's practice field tower in what seemed an obvious attempt to remove Bryant's intimidating shadow of influence from Alabama football, even though Perkins himself was a product of that influence.

Although given the additional title of athletic director after Bryant's death, Perkins remained at Alabama for only four seasons—1983-1986—before returning to professional football as coach of the Tampa Bay Buccaneers. Perkins' Tide teams went 8-4, 5-6, 9-2-1 and 10-3. The 5-6 campaign of 1984 was the Tide's first losing season since 1957 and broke Alabama's 25-year bowl streak. The 19-5-1 record over the next two seasons kept Perkins in good graces with most Tide fans, but he did not fare well with the media and he failed to produce an SEC championship before his departure.

Perkins' resignation was surprising but not greatly disappointing to Alabama fans. However, the next step in the continuing drama was.

Thomas shocked the die-hard Alabama fans when he picked Bill Curry, a Georgia Tech alumnus

Bryant's funeral at Tuscaloosa's First Methodist Church attracted onlookers, faithful fans, close friends and dignitaries.

and then Tech head coach, as Perkins' replacement in January 1987. Not only did Curry come from a school which had been one of Alabama's bitterest rivals in the sixties, his record as a head coach was an unimpressive 31-43-4. Most Alabama fans angrily wondered out loud why an "outsider" was chosen when dozens of Bryant-trained Alabama graduates were available for the job. To soften the blow, Thomas hired former Tider Steve Sloan as athletic director, but the move away from Crimson-blooded coaches was not well received, and it divided Tide supporters with the majority lining up against the choice.

The hiring of Curry was seen by many as an attempt by Thomas to move Alabama a step away from the "football school" image of the past toward a more academic posture. The change came during a period when SEC presidents were taking a firmer hand in athletic matters after many powerful head coaches had long dominated the scene and often overshadowed the school presidents.

Curry quickly won the admiration of many Alabama supporters with his outgoing personality, and his record of 26-10-0 over three seasons was acceptable to most, especially in 1989 when the Tide went 10-2 and won the conference championship for the first time in eight years. Curry failed one important test, however, as his teams went 0-3 against Auburn. That, and the fact that the hallowed halls of the Alabama athletic offices were filled with coaches without Alabama ties, kept Curry from gaining full acceptance and further split Tide loyalists.

Criticism of Curry mounted, and the pressure built with each season. Meanwhile, Thomas unexpectedly resigned, and Dr. Roger Sayers was named University president in July 1989. A month later Sloan was forced to resign as Sayers began putting together his own campus administrative team. Cecil "Hootie" Ingram, a former Alabama player (1951-54) with impressive coaching and administrative credentials who had been athletic director at Florida State for nine years, was chosen as Sloan's replacement in September.

Curry was offered a new contract as Alabama head coach following the 1989 season, but chose instead to publically explore other options as the contract lay unsigned. It soon became apparent that Curry was going to accept the head coaching job at Kentucky, and his expected resignation was announced on January 7, 1990.

The hiring of Stallings as the new Alabama head coach was announced four days later.

Stallings had been dismissed as head coach of the Phoenix Cardinals in 1989 after four seasons and was conveniently available for the Alabama job. Although there was little public knowledge of the fact, the hiring of Stallings finally fulfilled Bryant's wishes as Stallings had been Bryant's choice as Alabama's head coach in 1982.

Stallings quickly assembled a coaching staff loaded with Alabama products, and the return of Stallings and the many Bryant-trained assistants ended, in a large sense, the temporary interruption of the "Bryant era" in Alabama football. It took a while, but things finally worked out just as Bryant

Although admired for his high character, Bill Curry, who replaced Ray Perkins, could never win full support from Alabama fans.

had planned.

The rapid changes in the Alabama football camp also reunited Crimson Tide partisans after several years of discord, and there has been little to complain about since. The Tide has rolled to a record of 60-13-1 during Stallings' six years on the job. Included in that mark is a 13-0 national championship season in 1992 as well as an 11-1 mark in 1991 and a 12-1 record in 1994. Stallings' six-year record is by far the best of Alabama's "big four" coaches of all time. Bryant was 50-10-5 in his first six seasons at Alabama while Thomas was 48-6-3 and Wallace Wade 45-10-3.

"All of us former Bryant players who became coaches are always kidding each other about acting like Coach Bryant," said John David Crow, now director of development at Texas A&M, in talking of Stallings' success at Alabama. "Now it looks like Stallings has all but become Coach Bryant."

With Alabama winning at a record pace and the alumni contented, and with Stallings and an Alabama-flavored staff on hand, it appears now

that the Crimson Tide program will long bear Bryant's mark.

Bryant, in the final analysis, fared much better in life than many who knew him as a youth had expected from the shy, awkward, self-conscious farm boy in overalls. The game of football provided him with respectability and a ticket off the Arkansas farm, and Bryant knew a good thing when he saw it. He devoted his life to the game, pushing himself and his teams to unprecedented achievements as he proved dramatically wrong those critics back home who had once predicted he would quit as a player at Alabama in 1931.

He claimed to have invented nothing in football, but he undoubtedly perfected many of the inventions of others, including winning. He won in the forties, the fifties, the sixties, the seventies and the eighties, adapting to the changes in the game and the players themselves over five decades. Bryant took Bobby Dodd's split T formation and beat Dodd's own Georgia Tech team when he was a young coach at Kentucky in the fifties. He borrowed Wally Butts' passing game and won more games than any other coach in the sixties. Then he took Darrell Royal's Texas wishbone offense and won more than 100 games in the seventies. The only ingredient he added that the other coaches didn't have was Bryant.

Bryant was a center-stage headliner from beginning to end. He made the most of life's opportunities by working to make himself better each day, even in his later years, as a poem he carried in his wallet suggested. He was closer to the preacher his mother had wanted him to be than he might have known as he inspired and helped make others about him better, too, in his own way.

Here was a man who wrestled a bear as a daring 12-year-old, courageously played football against Tennessee with a broken leg, played on an Alabama national championship Rose Bowl team; then turned to coaching and won more games and more national championships and carried his teams to more bowls than any coach in history. And he did it all with a style all his own.

That style changed through the years as he became older and wiser and found better ways to win—ways that cost him fewer players and friends and caused less commotion. He learned from his mistakes, and in his later years he wistfully wished he had known more earlier in life.

"I'd do things differently now," he lamented. "I failed some of them, but it was all I knew at the time." He could not tolerate half effort, and pushed some prospects too far in his practice-field gut checks through the years. He was more than

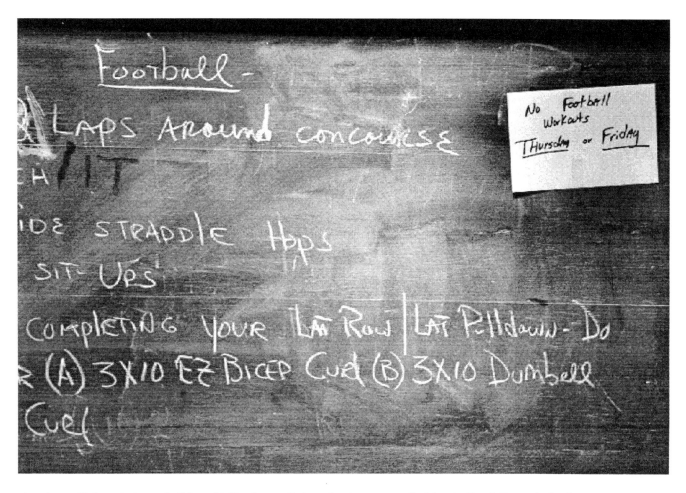

A note on Alabama's team chalkboard tells players that workouts are cancelled due to Coach Bryant's death.

halfway through his coaching career before he truly realized that football wasn't the only thing in life for everyone else as it was for him.

Bryant, as both player and coach, added significantly to the Alabama football tradition and to the lore and legend of the game itself, joining and surpassing such notable predecessors as Rockne, Warner, Stagg, Wade and Thomas in the record-books.

The Alabama and Bryant tradition continues almost intact in 1996 as many of those who helped Bryant make football history as players and assistant coaches follow in his footsteps. The Crimson Tide, under a team of coaches one would think

Bryant selected himself, won a national championship in 1992. Eight members of the 1992 coaching staff, including head coach Gene Stallings, played football for Bryant. The assistants included Bill Oliver, Mal Moore, Jeff Rouzie, Jimmy Fuller, Mike Dubose, Terry Jones (strength coach) and Jack Rutledge (dorm director). Oliver, Moore, Rouzie and Rutledge were also all former Bryant assistants. Moore became an assistant athletic director following the 1993 season, but the other former Bryant pupils remained on Stallings' coaching staff through 1995.

It is easy to see why the Bryant legend lives on at Alabama.

3

He Had a Way with Words, Too

*"I'm just a plowhand from Arkansas, but I have
learned over the years how to hold a team
together—how to lift some men up, how
to calm down others, until finally they've
got one heartbeat, together, a team."*
—Paul "Bear" Bryant

BRYANT TALKS ABOUT BRYANT, FOOTBALL, ETC.

Coach Bryant was a handy man with a quote; and for most of his career, especially his 25 seasons at Alabama, almost every word he spoke made it into print—although some of it had to be dusted off a bit now and then.

Bryant attracted sports writers in much the same way he attracted football players and fans. Prior to his arrival at Alabama in December 1957, it was rare to have more than a handful of writers covering a game, and coverage of practice sessions was almost unheard of. Within a few months after Bryant's arrival, however, every practice session drew the media, and pressbox crowds became unmanageable at times as media from far and near clamored to see his teams and to hear him talk about them. The press corps was impressed by his determination and the hard-nosed play of his teams, and they were captivated by his folksy dialogue, often expressed in biting, yet humorous terms. He had a way of cutting through the rhetoric right to the meat of the matter; and, in doing so, he often gave the media ready-made headlines.

Most of the press became Bryant fans, partly because he made their work easy by providing good copy with his winning teams and salty notes and partly because they were swept up in his charm as most who knew him were.

Coach Bryant knew what it took to make news, and he usually obliged when anyone from the press called. On one such occasion, I contacted Coach Bryant for a magazine story interview prior to his return to Kentucky as Alabama coach for the first time since he had resigned as Wildcats' head coach two decades earlier.

The interview turned out to be a lengthy one, with Coach Bryant sharing his feelings about leaving Kentucky after the 1953 season and his first game against the Wildcats since. Bryant revealed a bit of his sentimental side during the interview, and we both recognized that the story had special meaning. When I thanked him on my way out, he asked me how much I was being paid to do the story.

Page 64: Bryant strikes a familiar pose at one end of Birmingham's Legion Field.

"Forty dollars," I said rather proudly.

"Hell, they've got more than their money's worth if that's all they're paying for this story," he said with a laugh.

The following pages contain Bryant comments on such topics as Bryant; the game of football; winning and losing; motivation; and his players, teams and other favorite people.

Bryant Talks About Bryant

Coach Bryant was a modest man, but he was confident, too. He was never really boastful, however, and often downplayed his own contributions to his teams' victories. At times, though, his pride and ego were revealed as he spoke or responded to questions about himself. Here are a few of Bryant's comments about Bryant.

A carnival came through and they had this little ol' scraggly bear. A man was offering anybody a dollar a minute to wrestle it. I got the bear pinned, holding on tight. The man kept whispering, "Let him up; let him up."

Hell, for a dollar a minute, I wanted to hold him 'til he died.

I still get up at 5 o'clock. I'd like to sleep later, but with nearly 40 years in this business, I find I can't. To me, it's time wasted when you sleep past six.

I'm just an ol' dumb guy who's coaching football because that's all he can do. I'm certainly not smarter than anybody. If I were, I probably wouldn't be coaching.

As long as someone has to be the winningest coach, heck, it might as well be me.

I'm no innovator. If anything, I'm a stealer, or borrower. I've stolen or borrowed from more people than you can shake a stick at.

I'm no miracle man. I guarantee nothing but hard work.

I'd like to be remembered as a winner. I ain't never been nothing but a winner.

I'm no smarter than anybody else, but I may work a little harder.

All I know is I don't want to stop coaching and I

"Some coaches have accused me of being too defense-minded, but most of those who said that have wound up being athletic directors."—Paul "Bear" Bryant

As long as I'm right, I don't give a damn what people think.

If you stick your head above the crowd, you're going to have people trying to knock it off. We've done it wherever I've been, got it up there pretty high, and they've tried, and I've had to be darned active defending myself.

The first thing a football coach needs when he is starting out is a wife who is willing to put up with a lot of neglect.

If there is one thing that has helped me as a coach, it's my ability to recognize winners, or good people who can become winners by paying a price.

I think anyone is wrong to get involved in one thing so completely all his life like I have. You get to a point when 30 minutes after the last game you start thinking about the next one. That's not all there is in life. It's ridiculous, but that's my way.

There comes a time when you need to hang it up. That time has come for me as head coach at the University of Alabama. I'm a tired old man, but I'll never get tired of football.

Bryant Talks About Football

don't want to stop winning, so we're gonna break the record unless I die.

When we're not in the running for number one, people know I haven't done my job.

Coach Bryant truly loved the game of football. He appreciated it for its physical and mental challenges, the competition it offered, and the lessons of discipline, sportsmanship, teamwork, sacrifice and life that it teaches. He often talked about football providing a special strength, that something extra that a man could reach down and find when the going gets

Coach Bryant was always the man in charge.

me—that fear of going back to plowing and driving those mules and chopping cotton for fifty cents a day....

Years later I'd go back to Fordyce just to take a walk downtown and nod and say hello and how are you and good to see you to those slickers who laughed at me as a kid on that wagon.

You can learn a lot on the football field that isn't taught in the home, church or classroom. I'm a pretty good example of that.

Only three things can happen on a pass play, and two of them are bad.

There's really nothing new in football, just new excuses for losing.

Offense sells tickets. Defense wins games.

Unfortunately there always has been a void of sorts in my life. As soon as the games are over and the singing in the dressing room has quit, I've started right away worrying about the next game. It's been this way for me, win or lose, from the start.

tough—and not just on the football field. He meant later in life, "when your wife runs off with the drummer or you lose your job." He felt that football teaches a man to get up and fight back after being knocked down; and, if his players learned no other lesson, they learned that one.

My mama wanted me to be a preacher. I told her coaching and preaching were a lot alike. I don't think she believed me.

I cried the day Knute Rockne was killed. I was a Notre Dame fan as a kid. I remember it well. I was walking by the only barber shop in Fordyce and saw the headlines in the newspaper. I wept.

Football has never been just a game to me—never. I knew it from the time it got me out of Moro Bottom, and that's one of the things that motivated

I've had a full life in one respect, but I've had a one-track deal in another respect. My life has been so tied up with football it has flown by. I wish it wasn't that way, but it has gone by mighty fast. Practice, recruiting and games; there hasn't been anything except football.

My favorite play is the one where the player pitches the ball back to the official after scoring a touchdown.

If I ever quit coaching, I'd probably croak in a week.

Football teaches a boy to win, to work for maybe the first time in his life and sacrifice and suck up his guts when he's behind. It's the only place left where you can learn that.

A familiar hat and profile of Coach Bryant

ety and better prepared for life because I think he'll learn some lessons that are very difficult to teach in the home, in the church or in the classroom. I think that by learning these lessons, he'll win.

Lessons can be taught in football that are difficult to get across in the home, church or classroom—lessons of discipline, sacrifice and teamwork. Watching a young man apply these lessons in later life is part of my pleasure as a coach.

Bryant Talks About Winning and Losing

Coach Bryant was a winner, even in his own critical eye, and that's the way he wanted most to be remembered. He wanted to win every football game he played or coached, as anyone would. He understood that winning didn't just take place on Saturday afternoons, however. He saw it as an attitude that came from full-time, 100-percent discipline and dedication by every person connected with his football program. And he understood that winning didn't just happen—someone had to make it happen.

A winner never quits and a quitter never wins.

I'm still out there because I love it. I know you can't go on forever, but just to win that next game...I'd still rather be flailing away at this than anything else in the world. It's the only thing that's left now—the only thing that's fun. I still get cold chills when it starts—when I can finally walk on that field again.

I believe a football player who comes here [the University of Alabama] and stays four years is going to be better prepared to take his place in soci-

If wanting to win is a fault, as some of my critics seem to insist, then I plead guilty. I like to win. I know no other way. It's in my blood.

If we lose, I'll be bleeding on the inside, just like always, but I'll still try to smile on the outside and congratulate the other team and coaches.

Winning isn't everything, but it beats anything that comes in second.

Southern Mississippi coach Bobby Collins greets Bryant after a Tide win over the Eagles. On his strategy for winning, Bryant said, "Don't look back, don't lose your guts, and teach your team to go out on the field and make things happen."

I used to be one of the best, but now I'm not even a good coach any more. But I know what it takes to win. I've made so many mistakes that if I don't make the same mistakes over, we're going to come pretty close to winning.

You don't win on tradition; you win on blocking and tackling on the field. But I do think tradition is important in that it gives the players and coaches something to live up to.

I think the most important thing of all for any team is a winning attitude. The coaches must have it. The players must have it. The student body must have it. If you have dedicated players who believe in themselves, you don't need a lot of talent.

Little things make the difference. Everyone is well prepared in the big things, but only the winners perfect the little things.

You've got to keep from losing before you can win.

If you believe in yourself and have dedication and pride and never quit, you'll be a winner. The price of victory is high, but so are the rewards.

Most big games are won on five to seven crucial plays. The team that makes the big plays wins the game. Lay it on the line on every play. You never know which play is the big play. Try to win on this play. When you get 11 people trying to win on every play, you'll win.

Winning is a "we" thing, not a "me" thing.

A winning attitude is built over a lifetime. It is a person's character.

You must try to win all the time, even though only a small number of things you do determine your success. The point is, you never know which

"The best motivator I know is watching the sun rise and set between the ears of a mule."—Paul "Bear" Bryant

things they are or when the chances are coming.

I don't consider it the only game in the world, or a life or death situation, but I'd rather win this game [Alabama vs. Southern Cal, 1971] more than anything next to going to heaven, I guess.

I want to have my best offensive and defensive units rested and fresh just before the half. I want them not to be worn down for the first five minutes

Coach Bryant was recognized as a master motivator.

of the second half, and I want them fresh for the last 10 minutes of the game. These are the times that football games are won and lost.

There are just three things I ever say: If anything goes bad, then I did it. If anything goes semi-good, then we did it. If anything goes real good, then you did it. That's all it takes to get people to win football games for you. I can do that better than anybody. That, and I do know a little something about winning.

I try to find out right off who the players are and who the quitters are.

Losing doesn't make me want to quit. It makes me want to fight that much harder.

We're gonna butt heads until I see what I want.

Scout yourself. Have a buddy who coaches scout your team to look for any weak points.

Everybody—and I mean coaches, players, managers, everybody—has to suck 'em up and work and scratch and pray and fight to win.

Don't look back, don't lose your guts, and teach your team to go out on the field and make things happen.

I'm not interested in moral victories. That's too much like kissing your sister. I'm interested in winning, and all this stuff about building character with a losing team is a bunch of tommyrot.

Bryant Talks About Motivation

Bryant was recognized as a master motivator, and he was that above all else. He learned directly from the master in that area, having played for Frank Thomas, who had played quarterback for Knute Rockne at Notre Dame and roomed with the fabled George Gipp. Bryant also added his own special motivational tricks, whether it was that deep, intent look in his eye, a growl, or a pat on the back. Somehow he inspired his players to perform at their best more often than their opponents did. His plea was for 110 percent effort on every play of every game. He asked his players for all they had—and just a little more. And they responded—some out of personal pride, some out of fear, some out of love for him—and the result was victory 85 percent of the time over 38 years of coaching.

If you ask me what motivates a team, what makes them suck up their guts when the going is tough, I'll tell you I don't have the answer, but I know for myself; I've been motivated all my life.

If you want an education and you want to be a great football player, this is the place for you. I know we can coach you. If you're not interested in those two things, then we have nothing in common.

Every person represents a lot of other people. When a person does his job, it shows how well these other people did their jobs, starting at home.

When the going gets tough, the tough get going.

There are three types of football players. First, there are those who are winners and know they are winners. Then there are the losers who know they are losers. Then there are those who are not winners but don't know it. They're the ones for me. They never quit trying. They're the soul of our game.

"Frankly, I'd just as soon play lousy if we could luck out and win that way."—Paul "Bear" Bryant

A long shadow precedes Bryant as he walks into Denny Stadium for one of his final appearances there.

I don't know what class is, but I can tell you when someone has it. You can tell it from a mile away.

You'd better know something about work, discipline and sacrifice in life. You'll need it.

If I knew what makes a person a winner, I wouldn't tell you. But being able to recognize one is the important thing, whether it's by the size of his shoes or what his daddy does or something.

I'm not saying we'll win ANY games, but I will say that the only thing that will satisfy us is to win 12.

After being humiliated by them [Southern Cal, 1970] last year, if we need any incentive at all we need a blood test because there's something in there that's not blood.

I hope we quit limping and frowning and petting ourselves and get ready to play.

Don't get the impression that anybody is giving up. We're not! A lot of folks have given up. I guess I should, but I still think we have a chance. And speaking as athletic director, Alabama will be back on top quick or some changes will be made.

"There's a lot of blood, sweat and guts between dreams and success."— Paul "Bear" Bryant

One player you have to shake up and get mad, but you'll break another player if you treat him like that, so you try to gentle him along, encourage him.

The thing I try to encourage in our players is to never give up on themselves. I've had some that I've given up on, but they didn't give up on themselves and they came through.

I can't define character, but it's important, especially to those who don't have that much natural ability, on the football field or elsewhere.

Expect the unexpected.

Don't chew out a third-stringer. Pick an All-America. You'll get their attention.

Make something happen.

I'm through tiptoeing around, and I'm through pussyfooting around. I'm going back to being Paul Bryant, and anybody who doesn't like the way Paul Bryant does things can get the heck out of here.

Bryant Talks About His Players

Coach Bryant gave his players credit for winning the football games, and he was sincere about it. He asked a lot of them, and he expected a lot of them. He took special effort to build a team of "oneness," a true team, with winners at every position. And he wanted his teams to have pride and class in victory or defeat. They always did, too. Here are some of the things he said about his players.

I don't want my players to be like any other students. I want special people.

I don't make a lot of rules for my players. I expect them to act like gentlemen, have good table manners, be punctual, be prayerful.
I expect them to be up on their studies, and I don't expect them to be mooning around the campus holding hands with girls all the time. That comes later, when they're winners.

I have tried to teach them to show class, to have pride and to display character. I think football—winning games—takes care of itself if you do that.

I don't know if what I did was good or bad, taking the Texas A&M team to Junction in 1954. I never will know. It was just the only thing I could have done at the time, knowing what I knew then. I wouldn't do it now because I know more than I knew then—more about resting players, letting them drink water, more about other ways to lead them. They had to put up with my stupidity. I believe if I had been one of those players, I'd have quit, too.

My football players have changed, and as a result I've changed. I don't pretend otherwise.
For example, I let them wear their hair longer now. I don't mean they go around looking like sheepdogs, but by my bowl-cut standards it's pretty darn long. Used to be I'd have jerked it out by the roots if a kid wore long hair.

We've just got some little ol' guys who like to play. I believe they would play on Sunday if anybody would get up a game.

We don't have black players, or white players. We just have players.

Leaders say let's go, not sic 'em.

You don't have to talk a lot to be a leader. Lee Roy Jordan was a great leader, and he never said a word. But if he grunted, everybody listened.

Formations don't win games, players do. You've got to have chicken to make chicken salad. The players' abilities dictate what you do.

Those little fellows look just as good to me pitching the ball to that official behind the goal line as the big ones do.

Bigness is in the heart.

Many of our teams had only three, four or five great players. I had some with only one or two. But we usually had a dozen or so guys in the fourth quarter who got to thinking they were great.

You can't treat them all equally, but you can treat them fairly.

I don't try to save the world. I just go at it one football player at a time.

I've never won a game. I've been blessed with good players who were winners.

Team picture of Alabama's victorious 1934 Rose Bowl squad. Bryant is wearing jersey No. 12 in the back row.

Bryant Recalls Trip to Rose Bowl as Player

Coach Bryant was a member of the 1934 University of Alabama football team that defeated Stanford 29-13 in the Rose Bowl on January 1, 1935. As Bryant's 1971 Alabama team prepared to open its season on Sept. 10 against Southern Cal in Los Angeles, Coach Bryant recalled his first trip to California in the following comments:

Vanderbilt was our final game of the 1934 season, and we had an idea that we might get to go to the Rose Bowl if we won.

I recall very well that after warming up in Legion Field, Coach Thomas told everybody to go back out except the starting team. Back then you played both ways and played most of the game if you were lucky.

Coach Thomas read us a telegram from Al Masters, who was the graduate manager at Stanford, which is the same as athletic director now. The telegram said that if we won decisively we would get a call that night. I don't know about the rest of them, but cold chills went up and down my back, and they still do when I think about it.

Dixie Howell and Don Hutson played a great game, as they always did, and I remember I played most of the game until the latter part of the fourth quarter, when Coach Thomas took me out. It just so happened that our band was playing "California Here I Come," and that really excited me. (Alabama defeated Vanderbilt 34-0 in the game.)

We read in the paper the next day that we had been invited to play Stanford in the Rose Bowl; so Hutson, Riley Smith and I were invited to go over to Columbus, Miss., for the weekend with Sonny McGahey, one of our teammates. Connie Brown, Johnny Mack's wife, was visiting Son's sister at the same time, and we were all delighted to meet her.

The next week we had our A-Club dance, and it was a big deal to us back then. Johnny Mack was there with Connie, and we were really flattered when she brought him around and introduced us.

I remember we went at practice for the bowl game really well. I think what really won the game was preparation, and something Coach Thomas did that might have had more to do with it than anything happened the day before we were leaving.

We went over to Denny Stadium and played a game, first team against the second team. We just wallowed around and didn't get anything done. All of a sudden Coach Thomas called time out and started head-on tackling. It seemed like we did that for a couple of hours. But anyway, finally, we survived.

We traveled by train in those days, and lots of us hadn't been on a train many times; at least I hadn't. The train was supposed to leave at 11 the next morning from down at the station in Tuscaloosa, but when Coach Thomas came in after practice, he really ate us up, and he should have.

He said, "OK, see you out in full gear in the morning at 8 o'clock."

We were out there on the practice field, and there wasn't any foolishness then, and I think that might have won the football game. I loved every minute of the trip by train. I really loved the food, of course — it was free.

Something I'll always remember is that I had worked the summer before in Houston in the oil fields. I worked for a roughneck driller, a guy named Big Boy Williams. He was supposed to be the toughest guy in the oil fields. Well, I worked hard, and Big Boy kinda like me, I guess. Hutson and I were playing baseball on the side for extra money, but I got fired from my baseball job. I was trying to con my way through, but I just couldn't play. It was during the Depression, and Hutson, who was a fine baseball player, had gotten me the job.

Big Boy kept me on the oil field job, though, and I remember telling him that I wasn't much of a baseball player, but we were going to the Rose Bowl that year and I would see him then.

Sure enough, we stopped in Houston about 7 o'clock in the morning, and it was a big thrill for me when I stepped off the train and there was old Big Boy and some of my oil field buddies.

It must have been the second night out that Bill Young had to leave the train at El Paso and have surgery for a ruptured appendix, although we didn't know it at the time because it was at night. Anyway, he had to stay there in the hospital, and he missed the game.

We had our second practice in Tucson, Arizona. I remember that we ran a lot of signals in those days, just getting off the count and running down the field. We must have run for an hour and in that altitude were about to die, at least I was.

When we arrived in Los Angeles there were a lot of Alabama people and dignitaries there to meet us. I didn't get close to many of them, but being in the group, I saw them. That was a thrill for me.

We were staying at the Huntington Hotel in Pasadena, and that was a very big thing then. Every day there would be some stars and celebrities around, usually with Johnny Mack and Connie. People like Gail Patrick from Birmingham and

Peggy Waters, who later became Dixie Howell's wife.

I remember comedian Jack Oakie, Loretta Young and Mary Brown. I remember her because she was a good looking gal. Some of them I can't remember, but I can picture them in my mind. The names just escape me.

We made a trip to Warner Bros. studio and met Mickey Rooney and Dick Powell. Powell was from Arkansas, and he had his picture made with all of our Arkansas boys; so I got in that picture. We saw a lot of things and a lot of people, and I was in hog heaven.

We practiced out at Occidental College. Freddie Pickhard was assistant coach then. He had been a standout player at Alabama earlier. Some great writers were there, too, like Granny Rice, Braven Dyer and Henry McLemore and a little cub reporter for some radio stations and small papers named Ronald Reagan, now the governor of California. He was out there every day at practice, talking with Coach Thomas.

Coach Thomas apparently didn't have practice closed because people were everywhere. Even a lot of them were right on the field, and that burned Coach Hank [Crisp] up. We were running pass patterns, and I recall he came back into the huddle and told us, "Anybody who runs over somebody gets $2."

Howell called a pass, and my pattern was to go deep. He threw it down to me, and I ran right over somebody; so Coach Hank gave me $2.

The next day, Howell wanted his dollar, and I learned a lesson right there. I said, "Why, heck, Howell, I'm the one who ran over him." He said, "Why, I threw the ball down there." I told him I just didn't know about that, and I didn't give him his dollar. Well, he didn't throw me another pass during practice; so I went back and gave him the dollar.

One day Hutson, the Walker boys, Joe Dildy, Kay Francis and I broke training and went down to the ice cream store. Coach Thomas, Coach Burnum and Coach Drew all walked in and caught us eating the ice cream.

I thought Dildy was going to faint. It scared us all. But they just left and didn't say a word.

We were all worried, but Dildy was really worried if they were going to send him home or something. A couple of days later, though, he came in and said he must have been stupid. He said he had it figured out that if they sent all of us home, they wouldn't have but one end and one center left; so he shouldn't have worried so much.

Howell, Hutson and Bill Lee were our All-

Americans and were in great demand to make appearances and speak. They were invited along with Stanford's All-Americans to some kind of luncheon, and Stanford had a big tackle named Reynolds, who was an All-American, and I was dreaming about him and having nightmares.

Hutson came back and said, "Aw, that Reynolds looks like Ichabod Crane. I wish he were playing in front of me."

Well, he was playing in front of me, and Hutson's remarks gave me a little courage, and I could sleep a little better.

Of course, when I saw Reynolds he didn't look anything like Ichabod Crane. He was about 6-5, weighed 250 pounds and had big ol' arms and hands.

During the game there were several things I remember well. Stanford had long yardage and was about on our 40-yard-line. We had the game won by then, I think. When they were back in the huddle, I looked down on the ground, and there was a bunch of money. I mean, it was a bunch to me. There was a silver dollar, two or three half dollars and some quarters. There must have been between $3 and $4. So I picked it up real fast and had it in my hand. I was planning on running to the sidelines on the next play and giving it to somebody on our bench to keep for me.

Well, lo and behold, Grayson comes running out with the ball toward my end. I had to make a decision. It was the only tackle I made the entire game, but I lost my money in the process.

After the game was like a dream to me. I remember they entertained us and fed us, then gave us something like $10 each for us to entertain ourselves for the next couple of days. Believe me, that was a lot of money to entertain yourself on back then.

That was sure a great trip. I just hope the one coming up is as enjoyable.

4

Others Realized He Was Special

"I'd like to be remembered as a winner. I ain't never been nothing but a winner."
—Paul "Bear" Bryant

A MAN OF RARE QUALITIES

Coach Bryant had rare qualities and abilities, and he worked harder at his job than almost anyone else in his field ever has. His unequalled accomplishments are proof of that. And so is the respect he commanded among his peers, and others.

A. O. "Bum" Phillips, a Bryant assistant coach at Texas A&M (1956-57) and later head coach of the Houston Oilers and New Orleans Saints, often told a story which illustrates the respect Bryant's staff displayed for him throughout his coaching career.

"We'd be in a coaches' meeting talking and Coach Bryant would stick his head in, and in the middle of a sentence, everybody in the room would stop talking and look at him. There was total silence," Phillips said.

"He'd walk in real slow, sit down, take out a cigarette, tap it on his fingernail and light it. And often as not, he'd smoke the whole damn cigarette without anybody saying a word. We'd just sit there and wait.

"He never had to say, 'Let me have your attention.' He had it. It wasn't that we were scared of him; we respected him. If he was going to say something, we damn sure wanted to hear it."

Coach Bryant was an inspirational leader and teacher. He seemed to somehow see through the muck and mazes and mysteries of life, right to the heart of the matter. His view was a little broader and more distant, clearly focused beyond the daily obstacles toward the long-term goals. He never let himself and his teams become distracted by minor setbacks, mainly because he had a plan for any and every possible situation. He knew what the next step would be, always. Whatever the down, whatever the score, whatever the game—whatever.

Once, contemplating all the possible consequences, including an unlikely loss, in an important game with one of Alabama's bitterest rivals, Bryant said:

"If those country [expletive deleted] beat us there'll be more whiskey bottles in brown sacks in the stands and gutters than you've ever seen in life."

Page 78: Coach Bryant remains calm amid sideline drama as assistants John David Crow, Dude Hennessey and Richard Williamson (L-R) display emotion.

Then, following a momentary pause, he added, to clarify:

"They keep it in brown sacks 'cause they drink cheap whiskey."

As often noted, when Bryant looked at a situation, he saw a far larger picture than most.

Those who knew Coach Bryant best recall his coaching style; motivation; discipline; loyalty to his staff, players and the University of Alabama; charisma, and contributions to the game of football in the comments found in this chapter.

He Inspired and Motivated Many

All Bryant associates agree that he could motivate his teams and individual players to perform above even their own expectations. He earned fame by taking what many considered average players and turning them into winners, if not standouts.

He motivated different players (and staff members) in different ways, of course. Some he pushed, some he pulled, some he ignored. Some feared him, others respected him. Some loved him, others may well have hated him at some given time. But all who played for him did just that—played for *him*—because they believed in what he said and what he stood for.

He urged his players to perform for their mamas, daddies, girlfriends and themselves and for their school, but never for him. Most admit, however, that they played for him, or for his approval or rare praise. Some admit, too, that fear provided their greatest motivation. They feared his anger, and they feared being sent packing, as some were.

Some were motivated by his Wednesday night sermons on class and pride in team meetings. Some were motivated by his locker room exhortations which challenged each player to give 110 percent on every play. Some were motivated simply by his presence.

Whatever the means, Bryant seemed to find a way to reach and inspire most of those who knew him, even from a distance. Their comments about him reveal much about his character, motivation and methods.

Coach Bryant was a great motivator. He could get you to play. And everything he said, you could apply to life. I use the tools he gave me every day.
—*John Mitchell*
Alabama player, 1971-72, and assistant coach, 1974-76

Coach Bryant was the best at getting the most

Bryant's 323 wins as head coach are most in Division I NCAA history.

and best out of his people—including players, coaches, secretaries, the media, etc.—that I ever saw. He could get people to do what he wanted them to do through motivation or manipulation or whatever, and he had a great understanding of what his people could do.
—*Bill Battle*
Alabama player, 1959-62, and former Tennessee head football coach

Coach Bryant had the ability to get to know his players in a special way and to inspire them to win. He prepared them thoroughly for every game. His players knew he was talking fact, not just theory,

because he had been there and done it himself.
—*Fred Sington*
Alabama All-America tackle, 1927-30, long-time SEC football official and active Alabama alumnus

Coach Bryant never worried about a player's size. All he wanted to know was the size of your heart.
—*Darwin Holt*
Texas A&M player, 1957; Alabama player, 1960-61

Coach Bryant was a great motivator in the sense of mental preparation for a game. It was later that we discovered that at the same time he had prepared us for life's day-to-day battles.
—*Cecil Dowdy*
Alabama All-America tackle, 1963-66

He didn't treat every game alike. He knew how to bring the team to a peak with practice schedules and planning. He knew how to prepare for the big ones. He had a knack for doing those things.
—*Bill Oliver*
Alabama player, 1958-61, and assistant coach, 1971-79, and 1990-1995

Coach Bryant knew how to handle people. He either knew what to do, or found a way, to make a player give his best. He sold them on the idea that if they'd do what he told them, and a little more than that, that they could be champions.
—*Clem Gryska*
Alabama assistant coach and assistant athletic director, 1960-82

Coach Bryant prepared himself, and he motivated everybody to give their best because they knew he was going to give his best.
—*John Mitchell*
Alabama player, 1971-72, and assistant coach, 1974-76

Coach Bryant had an uncanny knack for reading people—knowing what made each person tick—and when to pat them on the back or kick them in the rump. He had a sixth sense, a gift, for knowing what motivated each person.
—*Gary White*
Alabama football manager, graduate assistant coach, athletic dorm director and athletic department administrator, 1957-82

Frank Broyles, former University of Arkansas head football coach and close friend of Bryant, said of him: "I'd say he was the most self-motivated person I've ever met. A lot of coaches can get their teams to a peak effort once in a while, but Bear Bryant could get a combined peak more often than anyone who ever lived. He could make the average player play like a champion."

Coach Bryant used techniques of motivation that I don't think he realized he used. He was a master at it. Some of the methods he used might have been in psychology books, but I don't think he had read about it. He just did it.
—*Jim Goostree*
Alabama athletic trainer and assistant athletic director, 1957-82

Coach Bryant knew people. He knew how to pick them and what made them tick. He knew when to push and when to pull back.
—*Bill Oliver*
Alabama player, 1958-61, and assistant coach, 1971-79, and 1990-1995

Coach Bryant had rare abilities. He surrounded himself with successful people—winners. And he could take the average player and make them almost super human. He could take almost nothing

and make something of it.
—*Tommy Brooker*
Alabama player, 1958-61, and volunteer kicking coach, 1966-82

He was smart as heck. He had the ability to get inside your heart and extract your best. As a result, he helped you grow.
—*Charley Bradshaw*
Kentucky player, 1946-49; Alabama assistant coach, 1959-61

Coach Bryant was motivated. Like he used to say, he didn't want to ever go back to plowing that mule in Moro Bottom. And he could motivate you, too, through his own motivation. He made some great talks to teams—he could bring tears to your eyes—about what it meant to win and to be a winner, and what it meant in life.
—*Pat James*
Kentucky player, 1948-50, and assistant coach, 1951 and 1953; Texas A&M assistant coach, 1954-57; and Alabama assistant coach, 1958-63

When we lost, it wasn't very comfortable around him. I can tell you it was not a very friendly environment.
—*Gene Stallings*
Texas A&M player, 1954-56, and assistant coach, 1957; Alabama assistant coach, 1958-64, and head coach, 1990-present

Coach Bryant was a very unique person. He was one of the great motivators of all time and a master psychologist. He had an eye for talent, and he could get a team to play as one.
—*Charley Thornton*
Alabama sports information director and assistant athletic director, 1964-82

Coach Bryant could tell what was inside a person, especially his players. He could pick the ones who really wanted to play.
—*Larry "Dude" Hennessey*
Kentucky player, 1951-53; Alabama assistant coach, 1960-75

Coach Bryant used to talk to us about what it meant to win and give 110 percent when I played at Texas A&M and he'd get those tears in his eyes and that lump in his throat. I'd leave that locker room thinking he was really a great actor. But hearing it year after year as a player and then as an assistant coach and being around him and knowing him, I learned that he wasn't acting. He genuinely felt that way about football. It was a way of life to him.

Bill Battle, Alabama player, 1959-62, observed that "Coach Bryant could bring you back to earth if you got to thinking you were a star. He was by far the best at that I ever saw. And he could rattle your cage if you weren't playing as well as you ought to be, too."

It meant that much to him.
—*John David Crow*
Heisman Trophy winner as Texas A&M player, 1954-57; Alabama assistant coach, 1969-71

Early in his career as a Vanderbilt line coach in 1940 and 41, it was evident that he could infuse in football players his own competitive fire. You knew then that he was destined to be a head coach. We had no idea that he would be the winningest coach, but he had every quality to succeed.
—*Fred Russell*
Long-time Nashville Banner sports editor

In Oklahoma, they all think they win just because it's Oklahoma. In Alabama, they know why they win—Coach Bryant.
—*Larry Lacewell (1970s)*
Alabama graduate assistant coach, 1959

He had the ability to motivate everyone, even the secretaries. We'd work holidays, weekends, whatever was necessary. He did it, and everybody else did it. His enthusiasm rubbed off on everybody.
—*Rebecca Christian*
Bryant's personal secretary, 1967-82

There's something about him that demands that you fight your guts out for him.
—*Louis Campbell*
Alabama assistant coach, 1975-76, and 1980-82

There was a degree of fear motivation in his personality. It wasn't a physical fear, however; it was a fear of failing to live up to his standards or expectations.
—*Jim Goostree*
Alabama athletic trainer and assistant athletic director, 1957-82

He had a great knack for getting people to perform better than they were—coaches and players. He knew how and when to make something happen to make you get better.
—*Pat James*
Kentucky player, 1948-50, and assistant coach, 1951 and 1953; Texas A&M assistant coach, 1954-57; and Alabama assistant coach, 1958-63

Coach Bryant was an humble person. He didn't want to take credit for handling and motivating some of the great players, but they were much better because of him. And he was able to motivate the average person to do more than they ever thought they were capable of doing.
—*Gary White*
Alabama football manager, graduate assistant coach, athletic dorm director and athletic department administrator, 1957-82

Stripped down to size and talent, a lot of Coach Bryant's teams and players wouldn't have matched up well with the opponents.

But he motivated his teams so well that he made up any difference in size and talent. He motivated through confidence because he prepared us well, and we believed in him and his plan. And he motivated us by fear. It wasn't a physical fear, but a fear of letting him and the team down.
—*Danny Ford*
Alabama player, 1966-69, and assistant coach, 1972-73; now University of Arkansas head football coach

Coach Bryant always exposed every player to a "gut check," as he called it, at some time during the season. It was done with the purpose of taking the

player to the brink of failure and leading him through that to show him that he could succeed.
—*Jim Goostree*
Alabama athletic trainer and assistant athletic director, 1957-82

He had the ability to judge and motivate people to perform at 100 percent. He got everything out of everyone.
—*Jack Rutledge*
Alabama player, 1958-61, and assistant coach, 1966-82

Coach Bryant always had winners at every position, not stars. The chemistry of his teams is what won championships, and he created that chemistry.
—*Pat Dye*
Alabama assistant coach, 1965-73, and former Auburn head football coach

Bryant was selected as Southeastern Conference Coach of the Year 10 times.

Coach Bryant had a rare ability. I don't know how, but he could connect with each person in a special way. He just seemed to know how to get people to respond in a positive way.

He knew every guy and just what to say and when to say it to get that positive response.
—*Sylvester Croom*
Alabama player, 1971-74, and assistant coach, 1976-82

You could never guess what Coach Bryant might do. If you ever expected something, he'd do something different.

Sometimes, he'd do things differently just to keep you awake.
—*Larry "Dude" Hennessey*
Kentucky player, 1951-53; Alabama assistant coach, 1960-75

Coach Bryant had a knack for handling people, teams, coaches, everyone. He knew when to push, pull, work, ease up or back off.

He wasn't perfect. He would be the first to tell you he lost some (players) he pushed too hard too long. Yet he made outstanding players out of a lot of players who wouldn't have been third stringers

on other teams. He did it by making them do things they didn't realize they could do.
—*Pat Dye*
Alabama assistant coach, 1965-73; former Auburn head football coach

Coach Bryant could do two things better than any coach I've ever seen. No. 1, he could recognize a winner. No. 2, he could get more out of everyone—players, coaches, managers, bus drivers and everyone else connected with the program—than they thought they had in them.
—*Danny Ford*
Alabama player, 1966-69, and assistant coach, 1972-73; now University of Arkansas head football coach

He was a super salesman. He made people believe.
—*Jim Goostree*
Alabama athletic trainer and assistant athletic director, 1957-82

He Preached—and Practiced—Discipline

Coach Bryant practiced what he preached, and one of the lessons he preached was discipline. That discipline translated into hard work, concentration on priorities and the patience to teach and master the small tasks as well as the large ones.

Discipline was evident from top to bottom in his program; in his staff and players; on the field, and on the scoreboard. Because of that discipline, he rarely allowed himself to be distracted from his goal of winning football games.

Bryant suspended Alabama quarterbacks Joe Namath and Ken Stabler, both future Super Bowl stars, for breaking his rules. Such a message on discipline is hard to ignore.

Coach Bryant operated on Biblical principles.

Some he knew, some he didn't. It was just the way he was raised. He talked about fairness, work, sacrifice, character, class, and many other things that I now recognize as coming from the Bible as I study it, and it blows me away. I know now that he sacrificed his life to teach those lessons through football.
—*Jimmy Sharpe*
Alabama player, 1959-62, and assistant coach, 1963-73

Coach Bryant was no con artist. He didn't manipulate people. He was straight with the players, otherwise he wouldn't have been a consistent winner.
—*Gene Stallings*
Texas A&M player, 1954-56, and assistant coach, 1957; Alabama assistant coach, 1958-64, and head coach, 1990-present

Coach Bryant was totally committed 100 percent of the time. He never lost sight of the goals and objectives he set for himself and his teams.

That kind of dedication and discipline is difficult for most people because they like to play golf or take weekends off, but he worked seven days a week, early until late, getting to where he wanted to go, and that was to be the best—to win a national championship.

He had the discipline and determination to reach his goals.
—*Lee Roy Jordan*
Alabama All-America linebacker, 1959-62

He had an understanding that players win games on the field, and he never forced a system on the players. He let the players dictate what he tried to do.

He took whatever talent he had and used it well. And he had his teams ready to play, and play relentlessly, in every game.
—*Howard Schnellenberger*
Kentucky player, 1952-53, and Alabama assistant coach, 1961-65

Coach Bryant had a knack for not letting anything interfere with what he wanted to do. He knew what he wanted to do in life, and he didn't allow himself to become distracted. He kept focused on his goals. He was intelligent enough to know what you have to do to be successful.
—*Cecil "Hootie" Ingram*
Alabama All-SEC player, 1951-54, and Alabama athletic director, 1990-1995

Coach Bryant did things that worked for him that wouldn't have worked for anyone else. No one questioned him, and no one second guessed him.

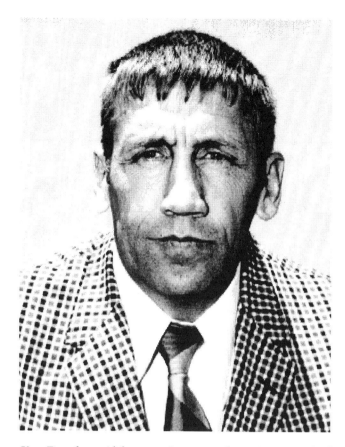

Ken Donahue, Alabama assistant coach, 1964-82, said of Bryant's work habits: "He outworked everyone else, not just Monday through Friday or August through December, but every day all year long."

Even if he made a mistake, he never admitted it; he just did something to fix it.
—*Jack Rutledge*
Alabama player, 1958-61, and assistant coach, 1966-82

Coach Bryant earned respect by what he stood for and did. He could be both tough and tender, firm and flexible. He could put the pressure on when his players needed it, and he could lift their spirits when that was needed, too.
—*Steve Sloan*
Alabama player, 1962-65, and assistant coach, 1968-70

If you went in to talk with Coach Bryant and he said something, when you went out the door you didn't have to wonder what he meant. It was clear, and he meant it.
—*Willie Meadows*
Alabama athletic equipment manager, 1965-82

We won games against people who were bigger, faster and stronger. The reason was simple: We wanted it more than they did. We wanted it for ourselves, our school, our parents. But most of all, we

Bryant chats with an admiring photographer before the 1980 Georgia Tech game in Atlanta.

wanted it for Coach Bryant.
—*Cecil Dowdy*
Alabama All-America tackle, 1963-66

Coach Bryant had discipline and a goal. He set high standards and did everything he could, legally, to be a winner.
—*Earnest G. Williams*
Chairman of search committee that hired Bryant as Alabama coach, 1957

The thing that amazed me was that he substituted every player who ever went into a game while he was coaching. The reason was that he knew how he wanted to play that game, with whom, and how long.

He also knew that different coaches have different personalities, and he wanted to control the personality of the team. He was that organized and

that much of a perfectionist.
—*Bill Oliver*
Alabama player, 1958-61, and assistant coach, 1971-79, and 1990-1995

One of Coach Bryant's many traits was that he hired good people and let them do their jobs.
—*Kirk McNair*
Alabama assistant sports information director, 1970-73, and sports information director, 1973-79

He never mellowed. He didn't do as much on the field physically during the last 10 years, but he was as tough as ever mentally, right to that final game. He wasn't tyrannical, and he had a great sense of humor, but he was always mentally tough.
—*Bobby Marks*
Texas A&M player, 1955-57; Alabama assistant coach, 1972-82

One of Coach Bryant's greatest acts, and one of the greatest in the history of football, was having the guts to change to the wishbone offense in 1971. He was good at doing things like that. That's why he could take players who were not so great and mold them into great teams.
—*Charley Thornton*
Alabama sports information director and assistant athletic director, 1964-82

He outworked everybody. He didn't know when to stop. He worked himself, the coaches and the players. His teams were always conditioned. We weren't going to be outworked or outconditioned.
—*Pat James*
Kentucky player, 1948-50, and assistant coach, 1951 and 1953; Texas A&M assistant coach, 1954-57; and Alabama assistant coach, 1958-63

Every Wednesday night during football season, Coach Bryant would talk to us five or ten minutes. He'd talk about what it meant to wear that red shirt, about looking people in the eye, about class and character, about what it takes to be a winner and to be successful in life. A lot of times there wasn't a dry eye in the house.
—*John Mitchell*
Alabama player, 1971-72, and assistant coach, 1974-76

If you ever told Coach Bryant he couldn't do something, he would do anything to prove he could.
—*Jack Hicks*
Student football manager at Alabama, 1957-63

He's the only coach I ever knew who could tell you what 22 guys were doing at one time. And if you missed your play, he got ahold of you.
—*Harry Johnsey*
Member of 1936 Union College football team

He was basically an humble person, but if he was pushed, he could let you know in his own way that he knew what was going on. He was a brilliant

The American Football Coaches Association Coach of the Year Award is named the Paul W. Bryant Award in Bryant's honor.

man, not just in football, but in every way.
—*Rebecca Christian*
Bryant's personal secretary, 1967-82

He tested players in practice. He wanted to make sure that if they were going to quit, they did it in practice, not in a game.
—*Pat James*
Kentucky player, 1948-50, and assistant coach, 1951 and 1953; Texas A&M assistant coach, 1954-57; and Alabama assistant coach, 1958-63

Coach Bryant was totally dedicated to football. That's about all he ever thought about.
—*Bill Battle*
Alabama player, 1959-62, and former Tennessee head football coach

Coach Bryant has total control. He put Joe Namath on the bench before a big game; and if he'll do that, Ozzie Newsome isn't going to come down here and raise no hell, and Ozzie Newsome knows it.
—*Ozzie Newsome (1976)*
Alabama All-America end, 1974-77

Coach Bryant recruited players to whom football was very important, and he hired coaches to whom football was very important.
—*Ken Donahue*
Alabama assistant coach, 1964-68

I always tried to do things right so I wouldn't give him the opportunity to get on me. He didn't take any prisoners when he chewed you out.
—*Willie Meadows*
Alabama athletic equipment manager, 1965-82

Coach Bryant knew in his mind the sure way. He believed in it, and he was tough enough mentally to impose his brand of football on the team. He made them do it his way.
Because of his strong belief, he never faltered in

Clem Gryska, Alabama assistant coach and assistant athletic director, 1960-82, said of Bryant: "He always told the players and coaches to keep their heads up and smile. 'I want to see a smile on each and every one of you,' he'd say. 'If there's any frowning to be done, I'll do it.'"

the tough situations, and his teams drew strength from him.

He and his teams all believed in what they were doing. And even when we lost, he didn't give in or make changes. He didn't sway.
—*Mal Moore*
Alabama player, 1958-62, and assistant coach, 1965-82

He was very demanding, and he could be mean if he had to be. He always challenged you to do your best. By doing that, he gave you tools to use later in life.
—*Charley Bradshaw*
Kentucky player, 1946-49; Alabama assistant coach, 1959-61

Coach Bryant handled losses well. He got most upset when you didn't play well against a team you should beat, but he always took the blame himself in front of the press and on his television show.

With the team, however, he told them what mistakes were made. He was truthful, and you always knew where you stood.

He kept the players striving to please him. He kept a team coming all the time. He was never satisfied.
—*Mal Moore*
Alabama player, 1958-62, and assistant coach, 1965-82

If we were playing Tennessee, he worked the players' brains. If we were playing Podunk U., he worked them physically.
—*Bobby Marks*
Texas A&M player, 1955-57; Alabama assistant coach, 1972-82

From the first day I met him as a teammate at Alabama, Paul always knew what he wanted to do. He wanted to coach.
—*Young Boozer*
Bryant teammate at Alabama and long-time friend and business associate

Coach Bryant liked to talk about being a country psychologist and not a great coach, but he was a terrific coach, and I think it's been forgotten how good a coach he was.
—*Scott Hunter*
Alabama player, 1967-70

Coach Bryant loved the University of Alabama. He reminded us often that the University was bigger than any and all of us and would be here long after we were all gone.
—*Jeff Rouzie*
Alabama player, 1969-73, and assistant coach, 1977-81, and 1991-present

He looked people in the eye and he asked them to look him in the eye. When you did, you knew what he said was the gospel.
—*Gary White*
Alabama football manager, graduate assistant coach, athletic dorm director and athletic department administrator, 1957-82

Coach Bryant wasn't greatly concerned with the X's and O's, but he knew the players and the temperament of the team. He made all the decisions on who played.
—*Bobby Marks*
Texas A&M player, 1955-57; Alabama assistant coach, 1972-82

Probably nobody really knows how much Coach Bryant loved the University of Alabama. He loved the University and he couldn't do enough for it as far as he was concerned.

He always stressed to the coaches and players

Bryant was named national coach of the year three times.

that we should never do anything to embarrass the University of Alabama from that first meeting on.

He never put himself above the University. He remembered what it did for him.
—*Larry "Dude" Hennessey*
Kentucky player, 1951-53; Alabama assistant coach, 1960-75

He had a genuine love for the people around him. It was sincere, and anyone around him for any length of time felt that.
—*Jeff Rouzie*
Alabama player, 1969-73, and assistant coach, 1977-81, and 1991-present

He Was More Different Than Most

Each person is different in his or her own way, of course. But Coach Bryant was more different, more unusual, more everything, than most.

He was unique. He was confident but not cocky.

He was proud yet often humble. He was tough and rugged but courteous and gentle. He came from the cottonfields of Arkansas but was sophisticated and well mannered. His personality was magnetic.

He seemed to see inside people. Somehow he knew—really knew—what you were thinking or feeling. He was tall, but he seemed taller. He gave simple words larger meanings. Eyes followed him closely, studying him and learning from him. People listened—and listened closely—when he spoke.

He had class, or charisma, or maybe something yet undefined. But he had something. He was truly special. Former associates reveal Coach Bryant's unique qualities in the following comments.

Coach Bryant had a presence about him that very few people have. Whether it was a bank boardroom, the locker room or a cocktail party, when he opened the door, it had a special squeak.
—*John David Crow*
Heisman Trophy winner as Texas A&M player, 1954-57; Alabama assistant coach, 1969-71

He had something nobody else I've ever been around had. Certain people have that special something—call it charisma or whatever—but he had it.

Before you saw him, you knew he was in a room because when he came in you could hear a pin drop. He dominated a room, a football stadium, or wherever he was. He was absolutely a unique person, and there'll never be another like him.
—*Kirk McNair*
Alabama assistant sports information director, 1970-73, and sports information director, 1973-79

He was the least pretentious celebrity in his field that I have ever known. He was a person of genuine humility—the simple virtues. He was one of a kind.
—*Fred Russell*
Long-time Nashville Banner sports editor

I've been around a lot of people who wanted to win and be on top, but none as much as Coach Bryant did.
—*Pat James*
Kentucky player, 1948-50, and assistant coach, 1951 and 1953; Texas A&M assistant coach, 1954-57; and Alabama assistant coach, 1958-63

He was smarter than we all thought, and he could pick winners. He had that ability, and it was his greatest asset.
—*Jack Hicks*
Student football manager at Alabama, 1957-63

When I first saw him, I thought, "This must be what God looks like."
—*George Blanda*
Kentucky player, 1946-48

I never had many heroes, but he was one of them. It was not because of his being a great coach, but because of the kind of person he was. He was as great a person as he was a coach.
—*Jack Kubiszyn*
Alabama baseball and basketball player, 1954-58

Some of the most tender and thankful, sincere prayers I've ever heard were prayed in an athletic setting by Paul Bryant.
—*Jim Goostree*
Alabama athletic trainer and assistant athletic director, 1957-82

He was a Dr. Jekyll and Mr. Hyde. Off the field, he was just like you and I; but on the field, he was something else.
—*Harry Johnsey*
Member of 1936 Union College football team

Paul Bryant has the personality to put over his program, and his apprenticeships seem solid enough as far as coaching ability is concerned.... He doesn't appear to be the type who will miss on his opportunity.... The 32-year-old youth appears to be a comer, not this season, but before his contract is over.... Keep an eye on him.
—*Arthur Daley (1946)*
Long-time New York sports writer

Kentucky is most fortunate in obtaining the finest young football coach in America today...Paul Bryant has every qualification of a great grid master. He was the most fearless football player I ever knew. He has a thorough knowledge of football. He has a flair for imparting the know-how to players. Bryant is a tireless worker. He has the patience to rehearse a play 100 times. He not only knows how to handle players on the practice field but off the practice field. No coach has more personality.... Coach Bryant was schooled under one of the greatest teachers football has ever known—Frank Thomas...As a recruiter—and a football coach nowadays must know how to get material—Paul Bryant is in a class by himself. He could sell gold bricks to bankers and they would like it.... Paul

Bryant was the first coach in NCAA history to win 100 games in a decade (Alabama was 103-16-1 in the 1970s).

Bryant is a man of action.... Paul Bryant is home folks, destined to become one of the great coaches of football.
—*Zipp Newman (1947)*
Long-time Birmingham sports writer

When Coach Bryant walked into a room, you wanted to stand up and applaud.
—*George Blanda*
Kentucky player, 1946-48

It is not surprising that Coach Bryant won more football games than any other coach. You knew he

was going to do it. If you ever shook his hand or looked him in the eye, you knew it.
—*John David Crow*
Heisman Trophy winner as Texas A&M player, 1954-57; Alabama assistant coach, 1969-71

He almost never mis-spoke. He knew, or seemed to visualize as he was speaking, how what he was saying would look in print or sound on radio or television.
—*Kirk McNair*
Alabama assistant sports information director, 1970-73, and sports information director, 1973-79

I can't ever remember hearing anyone talk back to Coach Bryant. That was something you just didn't do.
—*Steve Sloan*
Alabama player, 1962-65, and assistant coach, 1968-70

Whenever you see Bear standing around some place, he's always grave and dignified. I'm always expecting him to say, "Let us pray."
—*Frank Broyles (1970s)*
Former University of Arkansas head football coach

Bryant was inducted into the National Football Foundation College Football Hall of Fame in 1986.

Everybody who knows him is surprised out of their head every time Bear loses.
—*A. O. "Bum" Phillips (1970s)*
Texas A&M assistant coach, 1956-57

Paul Bryant is one of the ablest, most colorful, most controversial mentors. Fans either love Bear Bryant or despise him—which makes him excellent box office.
—*Lloyd Gregory (1960)*
Texas sports writer

He had a certain charisma—a presence. Wherever he went—to a pep rally, a meeting, or wherever he walked into a room, when he spoke, every eye and every ear was tuned in to him.
—*Jack Rutledge*
Alabama player, 1958-61, and assistant coach, 1966-82

Coach Bryant had a lot of outstanding coaches on his staff through the years. He won the respect and admiration of those coaches and the other outstanding head coaches of his time and kept it.
Even the coaches who were on his staff and

around him every day respected him to the end. That says a lot. I don't ever expect to see another man like him.
—*Sylvester Croom*
Alabama player, 1971-74, and assistant coach, 1976-82

I don't know what he had, but he had a lot of it. He knew what to do and when to do it.
—*Bobby Marks*
Texas A&M player, 1955-57; Alabama assistant coach, 1972-82

He was special in a lot of ways. His physical stature, his eyes, his delivery, how and what he said, and when he said it.
—*Jim Goostree*
Alabama athletic trainer and assistant athletic director, 1957-82

Coach Bryant had a tremendous influence on the University—an influence that extended far beyond the athletic fields. He was an inspiration and a model as an innovative teacher and as a motivator of people. His most significant contribution, however, was in setting the very highest standards and expectation levels for his players, his staff, and for himself. Anything short of national championship performance was substandard. I hope we can profit from that most important lesson and establish similar standards and goals throughout the University.
—*Dr. Joab Thomas (1983)*
Former University of Alabama president

He can take his and beat yours, and he can take yours and beat his.
—*Jake Gaither*
Former Florida A&M head football coach

We've done a lot of leg-pulling in our time, but we always have had a fine relationship. Personally, I think Bryant is the best coach in the country. Just look at the number he's lost; it ain't many.
—*Ralph "Shug" Jordan (1970s)*
Long-time Auburn coach and Bryant rival

Every night I say a little prayer of thanks that Paul Bryant is still winning and still loves football. It's selfish on my part. If he ever got tired of football and got into politics, I wouldn't stand a chance.
—*Alabama Governor George Wallace (1970s)*

Coach Bryant had more facets than the normal person. He had something extra that ordinary people don't have.
—*Cecil Dowdy*
Alabama All-America tackle, 1963-66

I think that's the best tag you can put on a man—that he's a Bryant man.
—*Gene Stallings*
Texas A&M player, 1954-56, and assistant coach, 1957; Alabama assistant coach, 1958-64, and head coach, 1990-present

Paul Bryant was the most soft-hearted man I've ever known, but he didn't want his boys to know about it.
—*Jim Goostree*
Alabama athletic trainer and assistant athletic director, 1957-82

Everyone had a lot of respect for Coach Bryant, but most were fearful of him, too.

Most folks will bark at you now and then, but they won't eat you. With Coach Bryant, you weren't sure he wasn't going to eat you.
—*Sang Lyda*
Alabama student manager, 1964-67; assistant trainer, 1968-1982

He Always Had a Plan, and He Stuck to It

Perhaps no coach ever spent more time thinking, talking and living football than Coach Bryant. It was his life. It gave him his place, his time, his purpose, his being. He believed in the game of football as a means of teaching life's lessons for success, and he devoted himself to it.

He spent tedious hours thinking and talking football off the field, preparing himself, his staff and his teams. He planned over and over in minute detail each practice session and each game, preparing for every possible situation, every player substitution, every position on the field, everything one can imagine. He wanted no surprises for his players, and regularly warned them to "expect the unexpected" during games.

Bryant didn't wait for things to happen, and he didn't count on luck. He had a plan for everything, a plan to make things happen, and the record shows that he and his teams did just that.

He always had a plan, and he worked at sticking to it. Coach Bryant's attention to detail is revealed in the following comments.

Bryant served as president of the American Football Coaches Association in 1972.

I always thought he was the luckiest guy in the world, the ways things always fell into place for him. But now I know he had it all laid out. He knew what he was doing the whole time. It wasn't luck.
—*Bill Oliver*
Alabama player, 1958-61, and assistant coach, 1971-79, and 1990-1995

Coach Bryant believed in defense first, but his coaching style wasn't necessarily conservative. It was intelligent.
—*Clem Gryska*
Alabama assistant coach and assistant athletic director, 1960-82

Coach Bryant was really teaching the whole time he was coaching. The sad thing is that we players were too young to recognize it. An example is his expression, "Expect the unexpected." That means something different to everybody, but it means be prepared for anything, have a plan, and not just a plan for the next game but for life.
—*Tommy Brooker*
Alabama player, 1958-61, and volunteer kicking coach, 1966-82

He kept up with the times and adjusted to them. He always got input from others and didn't often make snap decisions. We'd talk about things a lot, but when he finally said we're going to do it this way, it was over.
—*Jack Rutledge*
Alabama player, 1958-61, and assistant coach, 1966-82

Coach Bryant was light years ahead of other coaches. He had a good, sound imagination, and he had more imagination offensively than people ever gave him credit for.

He established a reputation as a defensive-minded coach because the game was a close perimeter game when he came to Alabama, but you have to know a lot about offense to coach defense.

He did a great job of planning offensively and defensively because he was six to eight years ahead of everybody else. It seems everything he did, offensively and defensively, was copied in some way later by other coaches.
—*Bill Oliver*
Alabama player, 1958-61, and assistant coach, 1971-79, and 1990-1995

He had a plan for everything. He never took anything for granted. We went through things a hundred times. He always told the players to expect the unexpected. And as a result, I don't remember a time when some unusual situation came up in a

Bryant was a master at dealing with the press. Sports reporters seemed to be in awe of him.

game that we hadn't worked on in practice.
—*Clem Gryska*
Alabama assistant coach and assistant athletic director, 1960-82

Coach Bryant never made excuses for losing, and more than anybody I've ever seen, he tried to benefit from each loss.

As a player (1959-61) and assistant coach (1971-79), the most we ever lost was three games, but he used each one as a stepping stone. His reaction depended on which loss it was, whether it was early in the season or whatever, but he did a great job of analyzing the loss to figure out why and how to avoid the same mistakes again rather than complain or make excuses.
—*Bill Oliver*
Alabama player, 1958-61, and assistant coach, 1971-79, and 1990-1995

Coach Bryant never mandated that an injured player come into a full-speed practice. He might ask

for an explanation about an injury, but he never argued with the explanation or made anyone play when he was injured. He might, however, use his comments to some of them or to the press or on television as a motivational tool to encourage them to get well.
—*Jim Goostree*
Alabama athletic trainer and assistant athletic director, 1957-82

He mellowed intelligently during his coaching career, but his philosophy never changed.

I was gone nine years (1962-1971) from the time I played until I came back as an assistant coach, and there was a big difference in the way he coached. He had learned to let the assistant coaches do more rather than trying to do so much himself.

I sometimes wonder how much longer he might have lived if he hadn't worked himself so hard the first 20 years of his career.
—*Bill Oliver*
Alabama player, 1958-61, and assistant coach, 1971-79, and 1990-1995

One of the things Coach Bryant was best at was allowing his coaches to teach, and teaching them to teach things the way he wanted them done. All the coaches were taught the same methods and techniques so they would all be teaching the same thing for every position, in every situation and in the same language. He made sure there was never any confusion.
—*Jim Goostree*
Alabama athletic trainer and assistant athletic director, 1957-82

He knew what got you beat, and he emphasized not making those mistakes. His theory was that if you kept your mistakes to a minimum, you always had a chance to win the football game.
—*Scott Hunter*
Alabama player, 1967-70

> ### *"You have to have good players to win, and Coach Bryant always had a knack for having good players. He had a knack for picking out guys who could win."—Gene Stallings, Alabama head coach, 1990-present*

A lot of people, when they enjoy success, stop listening to people. They start thinking they know

Jeff Rouzie, Alabama player, 1969-73, and assistant coach, 1977-81, explained that "Coach Bryant surrounded himself with good people, and he could recognize the qualities he wanted. First he looked for loyalty, and secondly he looked for someone not afraid to work."

everything.

But Coach Bryant, no matter what the problem, would ask for advice and input from everyone concerned, then make his decisions. He got all the information he could before making any decision.
—*Gary White*
Alabama football manager, graduate assistant coach, athletic dorm director and athletic department administrator, 1957-82

Coach Bryant always said you're only as good as the people around you, and he placed as much emphasis on a good custodian or groundskeeper as he did a good coach or player.
—*Sang Lyda*
Alabama student manager, 1964-67; assistant trainer, 1968-82

Coach Bryant was a stickler for having a plan and sticking with it.

He had a plan for every possible game situation; he had a plan for a halftime talk for every possible situation, whether his team was ahead, tied or

behind, and he had a post-game talk for every situation, too, to get the team ready to move on to the next game. He was always prepared, and he had his teams prepared, for any situation.
—*Lee Roy Jordan*
Alabama All-America linebacker, 1959-62

If I used Coach Bryant's scale for rating players—he always says he has only about five—then we wouldn't have any.
—*Paul Davis (1962)*
Alabama assistant coach, 1981-82, and former Mississippi State head football coach

Coach Bryant was a strong field position man. His priorities were kicking game, defense and offense, in that order.

His plan was to always have a tough running game, not make mistakes and beat yourself, and to always punt the ball to the opponents, never give it up on a turnover.
—*Mal Moore*
Alabama player, 1958-62, and assistant coach, 1965-82

A Man of Compassion

The University of Alabama athletic program prospered under Coach Bryant, mainly because his winning teams produced bowl and television revenue as well as sellout crowds at most football games.

Coach Bryant, as athletic director, used part of that revenue to set up a program through which the athletic department reimburses the University the full cost of student athlete scholarships, even at the out-of-state rate when applicable.

University sources say only a handful of athletic departments in the country do that. In addition, Bryant set up a program to contribute a percentage of athletic department revenues to the University to offset indirect expenses of the University related to athletics.

He also personally set up a number of endowments and scholarships, including one for children of his former players, in excess of a million dollars.

His loyalty to the University of Alabama and to those who had played for him are visible in those and many other similar actions and show clearly that he was concerned with much more than winning football games.

Without fanfare, he took care in repaying past debts, with interest. The following comments touch on Coach Bryant's compassion for others.

Jimmy Sharpe, Alabama player, 1959-62, and assistant coach, 1963-73, said of Bryant's compassion for other people: "Coach Bryant was an important part of my life, and he still is today. It's not only because I spent 16 years with him as a player and coach, but also because he sincerely cared about people. He cared about you, me, everyone. He helped people, including me, many, many years after I left Alabama, because he cared."

Coach Bryant enjoyed children. He enjoyed being around them and talking with them. He was always nice to them and took time to sign autographs and visit with them.
—*Jimmy Hinton*
Close Bryant friend and business associate

No matter what, once a player was gone, Coach Bryant considered him a star. He would brag on you like you were All-America and do anything for you.
—*Allen "Bunk" Harpole*
Alabama player, 1964-67

The thing that stands out most about Coach Bryant to me was his commitment to his players long after football.

No matter what you did after you left the University, he was always proud of you. It didn't matter what line of work you went into or your sta-

Bobby Marks (Texas A&M player, 1955-57, and Alabama assistant coach, 1972-82) said of Bryant: "He was the fairest and most honest person with the players and coaches that I've ever been around."

tion in life, as long as you were giving your best effort he was behind you.
—*Lee Roy Jordan*
Alabama All-America linebacker, 1959-62

I never realized the tremendous influence Coach Bryant would have on my life after college. I imagine if you asked all of his former players, they would admit that he passes through their thoughts almost every day. He is still very much involved in my thoughts and daily life.
—*Darwin Holt*
Texas A&M player, 1957; Alabama player, 1960-61

When football was over, the players could still count on Coach Bryant to help them, even ten years after they had graduated.
—*Ken Donahue*
Alabama assistant coach, 1964-82

Coach Bryant was often accused of playing a big role in bowl team selections in his last decade of coaching, and I think that's true. He had tremendous influence. He knew all the bowl selection committees and conference officials, and they thought a lot of his judgment. He carried a lot of weight on the bowl selections for several years.
—*Fred Sington*
Alabama All-America tackle, 1927-30, long-time SEC football official and active Alabama alumnus

There have been a lot of things that he was involved in and did for a lot of his players that they'll never know about.
—*Jim Goostree*
Alabama athletic trainer and assistant athletic director, 1957-82

Coach Bryant won at Maryland, Kentucky and Texas A&M, but when he got to Alabama, with its Rose Bowl and national championship tradition and talent as good or better than anyone, he won big.
—*Howard Schnellenberger*
Kentucky player, 1952-53, and Alabama assistant coach, 1961-65

Coach Bryant instilled in a lot of men something they couldn't have gotten anywhere else and from anyone else. They were better people when they left than when they came because they knew what it took to get somewhere.
—*Larry "Dude" Hennessey*
Kentucky player, 1951-53; Alabama assistant coach, 1960-75

Paul felt the same about the University of Alabama as I do. He felt a great obligation to it because he knew that every good thing in his life

Two Football Greats Comment on Bryant

John David Crow, Heisman Trophy winner: "Coach Bryant was one of the toughest people to ever come across the face of this earth, but he was also kind, fair and tender hearted. He genuinely cared about people."

A. O. "Bum" Phillips, former NFL coach and Bryant assistant: "Coach Bryant didn't coach football; he coached people."

could be traced to the University. That's why he came back as head coach, and that's why he gave so much of himself and his money to it.
—*Young Boozer*
Bryant teammate at Alabama and long-time friend and business associate

He wrote a lot of letters of recommendation for his players and other people, and when he really wanted to compliment or praise someone, he would say they had class. He always talked about class.
—*Rebecca Christian*
Bryant's personal secretary, 1967-82

You could always count on what Coach Bryant said. I don't ever recall a time when he told me or the team anything that he didn't follow through on.

So many people have good intentions but fail to follow through. He never failed to follow through. You always knew you could count on him.
—*Jeff Rouzie*
Alabama player, 1969-73, and assistant coach, 1977-81, and 1991-present

It's impossible for me to summarize what Coach Bryant meant to me, to Alabama football, to the University of Alabama, to the state of Alabama, to this country, and to the game of football. There just aren't enough words to do it.
—*Gary White*
Alabama football manager, graduate assistant coach, athletic dorm director and athletic department administrator, 1957-82

Coach Bryant always did what he said he was going to do. He never failed to take care of whatever he said he would, whether it was return a telephone call or handle a disciplinary matter. He always remembered, and he always stuck to his guns on discipline.
—*Lee Roy Jordan*
Alabama All-America linebacker, 1959-62

He gave more of himself to those around him than anyone I've ever known. Everyone had the utmost respect for him because of that.

I don't think anyone in football has touched more lives in a positive way than Coach Bryant.
—*Jeff Rouzie*
Alabama player, 1969-73, and assistant coach, 1977-81, and 1991-present

Death Brings Tributes and Tears

Coach Bryant's death on January 26, 1983, stunned his millions of fans throughout the world. It froze, for a few days, Alabamians and football fans nationwide just as President John F. Kennedy's death on November 22, 1963, had frozen the nation.

Bryant's death was untimely, unexpected, unbelievable. He had coached his final game less than a month before when his Alabama team defeated Illinois, 21-15, in the Liberty Bowl on December 29, 1982. The announcement of his impending retirement just a few weeks before the season ended had shocked and saddened his followers. His death was crushing, heartbreaking, unbearable news.

Tributes poured forth from all corners, praising Bryant for his contributions to football and for his personal standards of excellence. Mourners crowded the funeral route from Tuscaloosa to Birmingham. Traffic stopped along the Interstate highway. Tears and banners and saddened faces said goodbye to a maker of miracles, a modest hero, a compassionate teacher, a challenging taskmaster and a winner. He left much of himself with so many, however, and his legacy lives on. Here is a sampling of tributes offered to him at that time:

In many ways, American sports embody the best in our national character—dedication, teamwork, honor, and friendship. Paul "Bear" Bryant embodied football. The winner of more games than any other coach in history, Bear Bryant was a true American hero. A hard but beloved taskmaster, he pushed ordinary people to perform extraordinary feats. Patriotic to the core, devoted to his players and inspired by a winning spirit that never quit, Bear Bryant gave his country the gift of a legend. In making the impossible seem easy, he lived what we all strive to be.
—*President Ronald Reagan*

The country has lost an authentic hero—not in terms of the victories his teams won on the football field, but the inspiration and ideals he imparted through generations of young Americans. Paul Bryant was more than a great coach. He was a great teacher.
—*Vice President George Bush*

He was the greatest football coach of all time, one who not only was a great coach but a great human being.
—*Vince Dooley*
Former University of Georgia head football coach

There's no telling how many young men Bryant put into coaching, and how many he put out by beating them so often.
—*A. O. "Bum" Phillips*
Texas A&M assistant coach, 1956-57

He was a winner. He was honorable and he won with good, clean ball clubs.
—*Woody Hayes*
Former Ohio State head football coach

Perhaps no one has meant more to the University and to this state than Coach Bryant. I wouldn't

trade anything for the learning experience I had under him. He taught me values that will always have a lasting impact upon my life. He taught us how to fight and be victorious with discipline and hard work. In victory and defeat, he always emphasized that we show our class and be gentlemen in all endeavors....

He touched a lot of lives. That meant a lot more to him than winning a large number of football games.
—*Ray Perkins*
Alabama player, 1963-66, and head coach, 1983-86

What made Coach Bryant great was his originality and his personality, his penetrating observation on life and people. He was truly one of our profession's best ever.
—*Mike White*
University of Illinois head football coach, 1982

Coach Bryant was the epitome of college football, and there will probably never be another man to have the impact on the college football scene as he had. He was one of America's heroes.
—*Emory Bellard*
Former Mississippi State head football coach

He was a monumental figure in intercollegiate athletics, a man who set standards not easily attainable by men.
—*Joe Paterno*
Penn State head football coach

He has probably forgotten more about football than all of us young coaches will ever learn.
—*Jackie Sherrill*
Alabama player, 1962-65; now Mississippi State head football coach

In my opinion, college football has lost the greatest coach of all time.
—*Bob Devaney*
Former University of Nebraska head football coach

Page 99:"He is going to be missed by so many people because he helped so many. That was his main goal in life—to help people."—Danny Ford (1983)

5

Stories Keep His Spirit Alive

"My mama wanted me to be a preacher. I told her coaching and preaching were a lot alike. I don't think she believed me."
—Paul "Bear" Bryant

HIS PERSONALITY WAS UNIQUE

There are literally thousands of "Bear Bryant stories" still being told and retold today by his former players, assistants and close associates. These stories illustrate Coach Bryant's unique personality as they capture a special, memorable moment or humorous situation for those involved. And most of them are actually true.

Some, though true, simply aren't told—at least not for print. As former Alabama student manager Jack Hicks once told a New York writer when asked if he knew any funny Bryant stories, "I know some, but I don't tell them because I want to keep living in Alabama." Still, a few amusing Bryant stories are told now and then.

Butch Lambert, a former Southeastern Conference football and basketball official from Tupelo, Mississippi, often told a story about Coach Bryant's pride in his defensive strategy.

It seems Lambert and fellow official Harold Johnson were driving to Tuscaloosa to work an Alabama-Miami game in the early sixties, and the subject of the extraordinary success of Bryant's smaller players against larger opponents came up.

"Butch, I'll bet Coach Bryant could take a midget and teach him to guard Wilt Chamberlain [7-2 professional basketball star]," Johnson said. "I laughed and we went on talking and driving," Lambert said.

"When I went into the Alabama dressing room the next day before the game, I stopped and spoke to Coach Bryant, as I always did. I remembered what Harold had said, so I told Coach Bryant that I had heard a great compliment on him from Harold Johnson."

"What did he say, Butch?" Coach Bryant asked.

"He said he believed you could take a midget and teach him to guard Wilt Chamberlain," Lambert said.

"Hell, Butch, I don't know anything about basketball," Bryant responded modestly in brushing the compliment aside.

"I went around the dressing room visiting with the other coaches and checking for special plays or

Page 100: Coach Bryant is surrounded by a jubilant crowd following an Alabama victory.

special padding Alabama might be using, and ended up in a corner talking with Dude Hennessey a few minutes," Lambert said.

"Dude suddenly went silent, and I felt a tap on my shoulder. I turned around and there was Coach Bryant, towering over me," the somewhat dramatic Lambert added.

"But that ain't to say, Butch, that that big so-and-so can't be guarded," Coach Bryant said confidently, then walked away.

That incident actually happened, and it illustrates Bryant's reaction to any challenge he faced. He simply could not refuse one.

The stories that follow in this section are shared to help keep his spirit alive, and to illustrate some of the qualities that made him a winner. They reveal his many moods and many faces as well as his discipline and dedication to excellence.

He Was a Master Motivator

Coach Bryant is known widely for his ability to motivate his players to perform above their own expectations, but he could also motivate the press about as well as he could his football teams. The amount of favorable publicity he generated for himself and his teams through the years is proof of that.

He knew how to handle the press, as he did most people. He held an annual golf tournament for several years, and was, in addition to producing exciting, winning football teams about which to write for the media, always available for a story. With the exception of an out-of-state story now and then, he pretty much got what he wanted from the media.

In fact, he utilized the media regularly to help send messages to his players (and often to opponents); therefore, he kept a close watch on what was written or said about him and his players. He could become a bit irritated by anything that was critical or unflattering about him, his teams, and especially a player. He usually let the offending party know about it, too.

"I don't want to tell you what to write, but the way I look at it, you're either with us or against us," was his standard challenge.

Few chose to line up on the "against" team.

Former Bryant associates recall Bryant in the following stories:

The one thing you could predict about Coach Bryant was that he was unpredictable. You just couldn't figure him out.

Coach Bryant (center front) with the Bear Bryant Classic golfers, circa 1971.

A good example is our game against Georgia Tech in Grant Field in 1960, my sophomore year. We were behind, 15-0, at halftime, and when we went into the dressing room, there was a mad scramble for the back of the room. It was a big game for us, and we were scared and expecting the worst from Coach Bryant.

He came in the dressing room whistling and laughing and clapping and patting us all on the backs, telling us what a good job we were doing and that we had them right where we wanted them. He said we were going to win the game, and we did, 16-15, on the last play.

That was a very different approach for Coach Bryant, and it probably won the game for us.
—*Bill Battle*
Alabama player, 1960-62; later head coach at Tennessee

I was head manager my senior year at Alabama, and during spring practice we had a lot of visiting coaches from all over the country. One particular day the coaches were all over the place, standing around the drills, and I knew that any minute Coach Bryant was going to call me over to the tower and chew me out if I didn't get them out of the way.

Pretty soon he did call me over, too, and told me that it looked like an Arkansas picnic on that practice field and to get those people off the field. The first one I grabbed was Darrell Royal [head coach at Texas at the time], but I got them off the field.

I was worried about what kind of trouble I'd gotten into by letting them get onto the field in the first place, but Coach [Sam] Bailey told me to forget about it, that Coach Bryant probably would forget it also.

But the next day he called me in and mentioned it. He said, "You know how I want things done. You do it that way and we'll be okay."
—*Sang Lyda*
Alabama student manager

There's a story—and it's a true story—about an assistant coach going in to ask Coach Bryant for a pay raise. Coach Bryant listened to his argument and told him he'd do what he could to get him that pay raise.

The next day Coach Bryant called the assistant in and said, "I've got you that raise; it's with 'such-and-such' " a team on the West Coast, and that coach was gone.
—*Jeff Rouzie*
Alabama player, 1969-73, and assistant coach, 1977-81, and 1991-present

I know exactly when the ground-level foundation for Alabama's winning tradition under Coach Bryant was set. It was during the 1960 season, and it started with us playing Tennessee in Knoxville.

We were behind, 14-0, at the half; and Coach Bryant came through that dressing room door like a maniac. He was ranting and raving and slamming doors and kicking things. I was sitting on the floor, and when he walked by I tried to pull my feet back slowly without drawing his attention. I was scared to death and didn't know what he might do.

He got our attention, and we came out in the second half and outplayed Tennessee, but we still

Bryant-coached teams won because he instilled great confidence in his players—he believed they could win, and so did they.

lost the game, 20-7.

Four weeks later we went to Grant Field in Atlanta to play Georgia Tech, and we were behind, 15-0, at halftime. It was the same situation. I was a sophomore, and I was still scared. You played for Coach Bryant out of fear until you understood what it was all about.

The dressing room at halftime was totally silent. The coaches were backed up against the wall, trying to become a part of it. No one was moving around. We were waiting for Coach Bryant, and we thought we knew what to expect. All of a sudden, he comes in and says, "Hot dog, we've got them right where we want them." He patted us on the backs and handed out cokes and towels and told us we were going to win the game, and we believed him. We won it, 16-15, on the last play of the game.

Those two games, as far as I'm concerned, set the foundation for Coach Bryant at Alabama. They proved to us that we could win. We believed in Coach Bryant and ourselves from that time on.
—*Jimmy Sharpe*
Alabama player, 1959-62, and assistant coach, 1963-73

I was coaching high school football in Florida in 1977 and Mal Moore [Alabama assistant coach] was

down there. He asked me if I was interested in coming back to Alabama as an assistant, and I said I sure was.

I was really excited after talking to Coach Bryant and getting a job. I came up in the summer with my brother to look for a house and stopped by Coach Bryant's office to ask Rebecca [Bryant's secretary] what my salary was before I signed a lease.

Rebecca said, "Jeff, you're not going to like this," and told me it was $5,000 for the rest of the year. I was stunned. I didn't dare tell my wife. We ended up getting a house practically rent free and living mostly off our savings.

Somehow we made it until December, when Coach Bryant called me in and gave me a raise.

I never mentioned it to him during that time either. No way. I was just happy to be here.

I guess that was just his way of seeing how serious I was about coaching for him.
—*Jeff Rouzie*
Alabama player, 1969-73, and assistant coach, 1977-81, and 1991-present

We [Alabama] were leading Memphis State 14-7 late in the game in 1959 and had held them at the one-foot line to take the football. We moved the ball out to the two-yard line and lined up to punt on third down.

I was the punter, and I was backed up to the end line to kick, just hoping to kick it out of the end zone. The snap and blocking were perfect, and I got off an 81-yard punt that is still in the record book [fifth longest in school history].

I thought, "I've won the game; maybe I'll be on Coach Bryant's television show," as I ran off the field. My head had really begun to swell, and I was running toward Coach Bryant so he could hug me and congratulate me.

When I got close to him, he muttered an expletive because I was so excited, and I veered off and went to the bench and sat down.

Later, he came over to the bench and patted me on the back and said, "Good kick, Little Buddy."

He let me know that what I had done was nothing more than what he expected of me. In the heat of a game, he knew how to keep you down to earth.
—*Tommy White*
Alabama player, 1958-60

I may be the only player to have played for Coach Bryant at two different schools. I was a freshman at Texas A&M in 1957, and after Coach Bryant left to become head coach at Alabama, I left Texas A&M and transferred to Alabama about a year later.

I did it for one reason: I wanted to be with a winner, and I'd seen enough of him at A&M to know he was a winner.

The thing that attracted me to Coach Bryant was that he never asked me to gain a pound. He didn't base my football grant on my size, and he never backed down, even though I graduated from high school weighing 152 pounds.

Coach Bryant didn't worry about your size; he just wanted to know the size of your heart. I came to Alabama and played at 167 to 168 pounds.

—*Darwin Holt*
Texas A&M player, 1957; Alabama player, 1960-61

I went to a Texas A&M practice just the other day [October 1993] and those kids had more fun out there in 15 minutes than I had in four years as a player at A&M.

It was hard work back in those days [1954-57]. The game was changing. We had hard, blood-and-guts practices and played 60 minutes in every game. For us, it was a matter of survival. We just wanted to make it through the practices to the games, then we wanted to make it through the games. I don't remember having much fun at it.

I think about it now and Coach Bryant was truly amazing in that he coached through that era of tough play and through all the changes in the game and used a variety of formations and remained successful. The game and the players changed, but he kept on winning.

He did it because he surrounded himself with good coaches, demanded hard work from the players and coaches, and because he motivated people.

—*John David Crow*
Heisman Trophy winner as Texas A&M player, 1954-57; Alabama assistant coach, 1969-71

I remember one of those Wednesday night meetings when Coach Bryant looked at me and Charley Pell and Jack Rutledge and talked about the big players we were going up against in the game on Saturday. The three of us wouldn't make one of those big defensive guys from Georgia Tech or whoever we were playing.

"Everybody says you can't do it," he said. "I don't know how you're going to do it myself, but I'd bet

Much of Bryant's success can be attributed to the fact that he surrounded himself with good coaches, demanded hard work from his players, and motivated his entire staff and team.

my life you'll do it."

I'd have given my life for him at that minute, and we went out on Saturday and blocked those big guys, too.

—*Jimmy Sharpe*
Alabama player, 1959-62, and assistant coach, 1963-73

My brother Bill [Rice] was eating lunch in the athletic dorm one spring, 1960 or '61, when Coach Bryant came over and sat down with him.

They talked about spring football practice and plans for the fall and other things, and as Coach Bryant was about to leave, he said, "Oh, by the

Bryant was best known as a great motivator.

way, Bill, your eight o'clock class professor tells me that you've missed a lot of classes lately."

"Yes, sir," Bill said. "Spring practice has been tough, and I'm having a hard time getting up in the mornings."

"Well, if you're not getting up for class, you're not getting up for these nourishing breakfasts we have for you and you're not eating right and you can't do your best in class or in practice," Coach Bryant said.

"I get to the office each morning at five. I want you to meet me there starting in the morning and you can study and be up and ready for that eight o'clock class," Coach Bryant said.

Bill was waiting on the steps the next morning when Coach Bryant came to the office at five, and as Coach Bryant was unlocking the door, he turned to Bill and said, "Bill, do you own a suit?"

Bill said he did; so Coach Bryant sent him back

to the dorm to shave and dress in his suit and tie and then come back and study at the conference table in Coach Bryant's office.

This went on for about two weeks before Bill went to Coach Bryant one morning and asked how long this particular routine was going to continue.

Coach Bryant asked him why, and Bill said, "Well, I've got a big test coming up and I need to study."

"Well, what the hell have you been doing in here every morning?" Coach Bryant asked him.

"Well, it's kinda hard to study in here with you coughing and smoking and grunting and groaning. I just can't concentrate," Bill said.

Coach Bryant laughed and said, "Well, get on out of here, but if you miss another eight o'clock class, you'll be in some serious trouble."

Bill never missed another class.
—*Bobby Rice*
University of Alabama director of athletic facilities

Coach Bryant is the reason I came to Alabama to play football. My family was all Florida fans, and I grew up as a Florida Gator fan. I'd never been to the state of Alabama, and I didn't know a single person in Alabama.

But I had seen Coach Bryant on the sidelines on television, and I could tell I wanted to play for him.

When it came time to decide, my heart was leaning to Florida and my head was pointing to Alabama, because I wanted to play on the best team and for the best coach possible. I was really having a hard time deciding.

One night about 11 p.m. my mother woke me up to tell me Coach Bryant was on the telephone. I didn't know what to think.

"I know it's late," he said, "but I'm making my plans for the next four years, and I need to know if I can count on you."

I said yes, and that was it. He had read me right and challenged me and I picked Alabama, and it was the best decision I've ever made.
—*Jeff Rouzie*
Alabama player, 1969-73, and assistant coach, 1977-81, and 1991-present

I was lucky enough to grow up in Tuscaloosa and

was close friends with Hugh Thomas from junior high school on. Because of that, I was around Coach Frank Thomas [Alabama head football coach, 1931-46, and for whom Coach Bryant played] a lot.

When I got to know Coach Bryant, I was head coach at Brookwood High School [1958-59], and it was kind of frightening to hear the same words come out of Coach Bryant's mouth that I had heard from Coach Thomas.
—*Cecil "Hootie" Ingram*
Alabama All-SEC player, 1951-54, and Alabama athletic director, 1990-present

Coach Bryant was really big on family values, and he tried to reinforce what the players had learned at home. He always wanted his players to honor and respect their parents.

The first thing he would do when the team came in for fall practice was tell them to write home to their mamas and tell them how they were doing. And when he met separately with the freshmen, he strongly encouraged them to write home. I've heard him say it a hundred times.

And when we were getting ready to play a game, on Friday or Saturday, he always reminded his players to go out there and make their mamas and daddies proud.

He showed his feelings for his own mother in a telephone commercial he did once where he encouraged people to call their mamas, then added, "I sure wish I could call mine." You could tell he meant it.
—*Gary White*
Alabama football manager, graduate assistant, athletic dorm director, and athletic department administrator, 1957-82

John Mitchell was one of Alabama's first black players and Bryant's first black assistant coach. He says he learned the valuable lesson of perseverance from Bryant.

Coach Bryant used different ways to motivate different people. I remember a couple of examples that involved me.

During my senior year I was headed for practice one day when Coach Bryant pulled me aside and told me that he had just voted for me for All-America.

"I'm not sure you've earned it, but you got my vote," he said.

I went out there the rest of the season trying to kill people to prove to him that I'd earned his vote. Of course, if you knew Coach Bryant, you know he wouldn't have voted for me if he hadn't thought I'd earned it to begin with.

And once during my junior season, we had a bad practice, and Coach Bryant told us to be there at 6:15 the next morning for a scrimmage. Somehow during the scrimmage my man slipped by me and made the tackle on a play. Coach Bryant gave me a kick in the seat of my pants that really shocked me. I was having a good year and was a starter, but that was his way of getting everyone's attention, including mine.
—*Cecil Dowdy*
Alabama All-America tackle, 1963-66

I had a terrible week of practice before our 1971 game with Ole Miss, and I knew it. We won the game big [40-6], but I didn't play well, and I knew Coach Bryant would notice. I was expecting to hear from him in some way.

Sure enough, he called me into his office on Monday, and I had spent all weekend trying to think of an excuse for my poor play. All I could think of was that I was thinking about quitting, that things just weren't going well.

"If you quit this time, you won't even think about it the second time," he said.

I didn't quit, of course, but he put me on the scout team for about eight days to get my attention and make me prove myself.

That has stayed with me to this day, and I never think about quitting anything. I'd rather die than quit, and I tell all the players I coach the same thing Coach Bryant told me.
—*John Mitchell*
Alabama player, 1971-72, and assistant coach, 1974-76

We were getting ready to play Mississippi State my senior year [1974] and I felt pretty good about myself at that time. I felt I'd earned my stripes by playing on a national championship team [and earning all-conference honors].

We had a team meeting on Monday to get the scouting report on State and Coach Bryant came

Hayden Riley coached three sports at Alabama.

right out and said, "We can't win this game if Sylvester can't block Harvey Hull."

Now, I wasn't a rookie. I had played against some of the best in the country, so I took what he said almost as an insult. It challenged me. It was like the whole game was on my shoulders.

I thought to myself, "If that's the only question, this game is won."

We won the game [35-0], and I don't think I've ever played a game like that. I had one minus in the whole game. I think I'd have done anything short of killing Harvey Hull that day.

Just having Coach Bryant question whether I could handle him got me ready to play. He knew what button to push on me.
—*Sylvester Croom*
Alabama player, 1971-74, and assistant coach, 1976-82

Everyone knows Paul [Coach Bryant] played one of his best games against Tennessee with a broken bone in his leg, but he also had a serious rib cage injury once and was in so much pain I had to help him lie down in bed at night. But he didn't miss a practice or a game with that either.

Later when he was coaching, he had a player

hurt with a rib cage injury, and I saw where he said he knew the player had too much pain to practice. I can tell you he knew that from experience.
—*Young Boozer*
Bryant teammate at Alabama and long-time friend and business associate

We were working on punt coverage in practice one day, and the offensive linemen kept telling me in the huddle not to kick it so far. Finally, I yelled back at them that I didn't mean to kick it that far.

Suddenly my feet came off the ground as Coach Bryant jerked me up and said, "What did you say?"

I said, "I didn't mean to kick it that far to the left."

He grinned and said, "Quick thinking," but he got his point across, and I kept kicking it as far as I could.
—*Tommy White*
Alabama player, 1958-60

Coach Bryant told our class [freshmen of September 1958] the first time he ever met with us that if we'd do certain things he outlined and do what he told us, that he would guarantee that when we were seniors we'd win a national championship. He guaranteed it.

We didn't realize what a national championship meant at the time, but we did when we won it as seniors in 1961. The celebration wasn't anything like the 1992 celebration, but Dr. Frank Rose [UA president] declared a one-day school holiday, and that had never been done before.

Our group might not have had the ability to win a national championship, but he convinced us that we had it, and we won because we believed in him.
—*Tommy Brooker*
Alabama player, 1958-61, and volunteer kicking coach, 1966-82

I accompanied Paul [Coach Bryant], Dr. Frank Rose [UA president] and Pat Trammell [quarterback] to New York after Alabama won the 1961 national championship. The occasion was the presentation of the MacArthur Bowl to Alabama as national champion.

General Douglas MacArthur presented the trophy to Paul, and I remember his words well. He said, "It is a privilege and an honor to meet you because you are one of the few remaining men among us who knows what discipline is and how to teach it."

He went on to say, "If we don't get back to discipline, I don't know what this country is going to come to." I think about that often as I see the direction our society is headed, and I know how right

Jack Rutledge was a long-time Bryant player and assistant.

General MacArthur was about Paul believing in discipline.
—*Young Boozer*
Bryant teammate at Alabama; long-time friend and business associate

Coach Bryant always did his homework, and he had apparently made up his mind to hire me as a recruiter before ever talking to me about it.

I was coaching at Coffee High of Florence, and was in Tuscaloosa for the state basketball tournament in the spring of 1958, just after Coach Bryant had taken over as head football coach at Alabama.

I was paged over the Foster Auditorium speaker, and when I went down to answer the page, Coach Bryant was waiting for me and asked me to come to his office for a visit.

I had first met Coach Bryant in 1939 when I played in the state tournament in Tuscaloosa and he was an assistant football coach, but I had seen him only once or twice since then. I didn't know him well, but he seemed to know a lot about me.

"You have been recommended to me as knowing

Bryant is swarmed by fans and members of the press as he leaves the field after the final game of his career.

more people in Alabama and the Southeast than anyone," Coach Bryant said when he started our discussion. "I've got a job on my staff, mainly recruiting, and it involves a lot of travel. Are you interested?" he asked.

I asked how long my contract would be, and he said, "One year. But if you do a good job, I'll take care of you. If not, I'll fire you."

He said he had to have an answer by three o'clock the next day, and to make certain I made a quick decision, he said: "If you don't want the job, there is a high school coach in Arkansas with two big ol' tackles who does."

He didn't know it, but he already had me sold, and as soon as I could finish the school year at Coffee, I came to work for him at Alabama.

Not long after arriving in Tuscaloosa, I heard from a friend of mine who was principal at Excel High School in South Alabama, and he told me he had a boy down there he thought we should look at.

He was the first prospect I ever heard about or visited.

I went down and spent the night with the principal and watched a practice in the fall, and Lee Roy Jordan was the player. You know what he meant to Alabama, so my contract lasted a lot longer than one year, of course.

—Hayden Riley
Alabama assistant coach, assistant athletic director, head baseball and basketball coach, 1958-75

Coach Bryant had a way of getting your attention. Some people he never said two words to, and others he'd crawl all over. He knew who could take it, and what it took to get you going.

When I came to Alabama the second time [1973], I was given the job of coaching the offensive line in spring practice. It was the first time I'd coached the offensive line, and I was a little slow getting started.

One day in practice, Coach Ken Donahue's defense was killing the offense. All of a sudden, everybody froze and this big shadow fell over the huddle. I knew something bad was about to happen.

Coach Bryant stuck his head in the huddle and said, "Coach Powell, that's the worst job of coaching an offensive line in the history of football."

I learned how to coach the offensive line a lot faster after that.

—*Dee Powell*
Texas A&M player 1954-56; Alabama assistant coach, 1964, and 1973-82

I had been All-Southern and All-State at Woodlawn High School and averaged over nine yards a carry and scored all these many touchdowns as a fullback on two state championship teams before coming to Alabama as a freshman in the fall of 1958.

After only a day or two of practice, I was moved to the offensive line. I wasn't fast, but I was strong and weighed a little over 200 pounds, and I think I could have played fullback, given a little time.

This was Coach Bryant's first year at Alabama, and the coaches were growling and frothing at the mouth and promoting fights between the players. The practices were rough. They were trying to make people tough and get rid of those who weren't.

My first day on the line I was lined up against Jim Blevins, an ex-Marine with a battleship tattooed on his big ol' chest. He had knocked out four of someone's teeth in practice the day before. I knew I was going to have to fight for my life, and I did.

But I didn't question the move from the backfield to the line. I just did what Coach Bryant said.

There was never a question by anyone about being moved. You just wanted to be sure your name was still on that list every day, never mind where.

—*Jack Rutledge*
Alabama player, 1958-61, and assistant coach, 1966-82

Alabama's teams under Coach Bryant were always disciplined. No matter who they played, they played every play like it was a matter of life or death. The same was true on every play in practice, too.

When a team does that all year in every game and you're up against Penn State for the national championship in the Sugar Bowl in the last game and the game is on the line on one play, you know they'll play it like it's life or death.

I was around a number of other teams and

Bryant's assistant coaches and his players recognized that he knew how to get the best out of them.

coaches and saw a lot of programs, but I never saw the discipline I saw under Coach Bryant at Alabama.

—*Wayne Reed*
Alabama football manager, 1978-81

We were playing Penn State in State College, Pa., in November 1981, and we were struggling a little [7-1-1] going into the game that year. Penn State had a lot of great players, including four All-Americans, I think, and a great offensive team.

It was one of the most important games in Coach Bryant's career. If we won, it would give him a tie with Amos Alonzo Stagg as the winningest college football coach ever with 314 wins.

We went in there and played great football and got a big lead at halftime, but Penn State came back in the second half and drove right down the field to a first down at about our seven-yard-line. We held them on a couple of runs, then they threw

a pass on third down and we were called for interference, giving them a first down at our three.

They rammed at us four times from the three, but we stopped them four times and held, and we went on to win, 31-16. That goal-line stand kind of took the wind out of their sails.

When you look back at it, it's pretty remarkable, holding that great team seven times inside our seven. But we remembered that Coach Bryant always stressed playing well the first two minutes of the third quarter to set the momentum of the game.

As the defensive team came off the field after those seven plays, there was Coach Bryant, three or four yards out on the field. He took off his hat and tipped it to us as we came off, as if to say, "Job well done." People said he'd never done that before.

When he took his hat off to us, I had goose bumps all over. At that moment, I felt bigger than a mountain.
—*Tommy Wilcox*
Alabama All-America defensive back, 1979-82

Bryant had high expectations at the beginning of every football season. He told all of his players that their goal should be to win the national championship.

We were at a party in New York in the sixties when Paul was honored as a member of *Sports Illustrated*'s Silver Anniversary team, along with Bud Wilkinson and Vince Lombardi.

Coach Lombardi [Green Bay Packers coach at the time] came walking across the room and grabbed Paul's hand and said, "I've been wanting to meet you. You know what makes this game [football] go.

"Everybody thinks we win at Green Bay because of Hornung, Taylor and Starr, but we win because we stop the other team. And that's why you win—

Page 112: Bryant was known nationally for his hound-stooth hat, but he wore a variety of hats and clothing over the years.

you stop the other team."
—*Young Boozer*
Bryant teammate at Alabama; long-time friend and business associate

I first met Coach Bryant in January 1958. I bumped into him in the men's dressing room and asked, "Coach, don't we need to talk?" He said, "Yes, come on down to my office."

I followed him to his office. He sat on the corner of his desk, but he still towered over me. He said, "I know more about you than you know about me. So if I like you and you like me after spring practice, you've got a job at Alabama as long as you want it."

For some reason, I blurted out, "I've got 50 percent of that whipped already, so I'd better get out of here and go to work on the other half," and I left.

State troopers Robert Miller (L) and Red Nichols escort Bryant off the field following a 34-16 Alabama victory over Auburn.

That was my contract and job interview with Paul Bryant when he came to Alabama. It was about a 15-second deal.

In June of that year, after spring practice, I went to his door and knocked, and he was reading the Wall Street *Journal.* I asked him if I was going to be with him.

"I sure as hell hope so," he said.

I didn't wait around for him to change his mind. I went on my way, and I was a member of his staff every day he was at Alabama.

—Jim Goostree
Alabama athletic trainer and assistant athletic director, 1957-82

We were playing Georgia Tech in 1960, and it was the first year on the staff for me and Dude Hennessey. We were behind, 15-0, at halftime, and we were scared to death when we went into the dressing room.

Dude and I got a coke and went way up in the back of the dressing room as far away as possible. We expected the worst, because we were supposed to be pretty good that year, and if we were going to have a good team and a good year, we needed to win this game.

Everybody was a little tight as we waited for Coach Bryant to come in. He finally came in, got a

coke and lit a cigarette and smoked it a while. It seemed like 30 minutes went by, and all the time the tension got a little thicker in the locker room. You could have heard a pin drop.

Then he said, "We've got them right where we want them. Just keep it up and we'll win. We'll wear them down and we'll win."

And we did win, 16-15, on a last-second field goal by Richard O'Dell, and we finished the season 8-1-2.

—Clem Gryska
Alabama assistant coach and assistant athletic director, 1960-82

During my years as an assistant coach under Coach Bryant at Alabama, assistant coaches were assigned teams to scout and prepare game plans for, and they'd get their names in the paper now and then, particularly after an impressive win.

My job was mainly recruiting, but I kept wanting to be assigned a team to scout and game plan to prepare, and I'd go in every year or two and ask Coach Bryant about it.

I'd sit down on the sofa in his office and he'd be behind that big ol' desk, silhouetted against that window in that big chair, and he'd look ten feet tall. He's smoke on a cigarette and he'd say, "Hell, I can get a dozen coaches to do that; they're a dime a dozen. I can't get a good recruiter. I need you out there recruiting."

I'd leave that office sky high, feeling like I was the most important coach on the staff, and I'd be fine a year or two, then I'd go back again and we'd do it over again.

He knew how to get the most out of people, including me.

—*Clem Gryska*
Alabama assistant coach and assistant athletic director, 1960-82

Coach Bryant sent letters to his players each summer as all coaches do, encouraging them to return to school in the fall in top physical condition, set goals for next season and the like.

The following letter is one such letter, and it is typical of his summer communication to the players:

"Dear—

"You will be expected to report for football practice August 17. We will expect you to arrive in the afternoon and our first meal will be served that evening at the dorm.

"On the 18th, you will take your physical, including the mile run, get your room and locker assignments and participate in photographer's day in the afternoon. Our first practice will be on the morning of the 19th.

"I am expecting you to report in top physical condition, clean-cut, smiling, bright-eyed, bushy-tailed and raring [sic] to go. Also, I am expecting you to be prepared to run, hit, pitch, kick, catch, sweat, smell and enjoy it. There are no easy ways but there are ways to enjoy the journey and we must find them.

"I am also expecting you to work hard, eat well, sleep well, play well, display a winning attitude at all times, be a leader and help me to sell the squad on what it takes to win and enjoy the journey.

"I hope you will share your problems with me whether it be at home, at the dorm, in your school-work, with teammates, with coaches, with training regulations, self-discipline, or even flying a kite. If you do that, I will try to help you and if I can't, I'll recommend you get a job, join the Army, or join the Foreign Legion, but in any event, to reside in another state.

"Nothing's too good for the winners. I want to love you, pat you, pet you, brag on you and see you hoot, run and shout and laugh, pray, hug, kiss and win with humility.

"If we lose, I want all of us to be unhappy, no one to have any fun, and expect only what is reserved for losers but take it with dignity while

Pat Dye was a Bryant aide for nine years.

planning to come back.

"Please remember us to your family and make your personal plans on how you are going to reach your goal—the NATIONAL CHAMPIONSHIP.

"Sincerely,

"Paul Bryant"

He Was Known Far and Wide

Coach Bryant was one of the most recognizable people in the country, and even the world for that matter. His many appearances on television, his familiar houndstooth hat, his distinct features, his mannerisms and imposing size stood him apart.

I was fortunate enough to have been included as a member of Coach Bryant's party one night in New Orleans prior to an Alabama Sugar Bowl game. The party was held at an exclusive club surrounded by

Wherever Bryant went, crowds recognized and gathered around the legendary Crimson Tide head coach.

an iron fence with guards at the gate. Coach Bryant, Paul Jr., and I were being driven to a party for Sugar Bowl coaches and bowl committee members by a New Orleans police officer.

Our car stopped at the security gate, and the security officer immediately recognized Coach Bryant and waved our car through. As we moved away, the car just behind us was stopped and seemed to be having difficulty getting past the gate.

Our driver, looking back, quickly recognized the mayor of New Orleans as a member of the party in the other car, and backed up to help identify the mayor. As he did, Coach Bryant lowered his window and simply told the gate security to let the car through. The guard stepped back and waved the mayor's car through without question, acting only on Coach Bryant's word.

That incident proved once again that Coach Bryant was not only recognizable, but that not even a gatekeeper at an exclusive club in New Orleans questioned his authority.

When Coach Bryant was nominated for the *Sports Illustrated* Silver Anniversary team, I wrote a few things for them about Bryant being interested in the welfare of his players and coaches, his compassion, etc. I got a call a few days later from someone at *Sports Illustrated* asking if I had made some kind of mistake. They said it didn't sound much like the same Bear Bryant they'd heard about. Of course, they were just joking—I think.
—*Jeff Coleman*
Longtime University of Alabama executive

I remember once I was on a trip and played golf at a club in Palm Springs, California. A clubhouse worker saw my bag had "University of Alabama" on it and said, "Oh, you're from where the coach is from."

He didn't say which coach; he said "The Coach." That's how people felt about Coach Bryant all over the country. He had an aura about him—a charisma—that attracted people to him no matter where he went.
—*Sang Lyda*
Alabama student manager

We were in New York where Coach Bryant was going to speak to the Associated Press convention, and were driving to the hotel with one of the top AP executives.

Our host, sounding somewhat apologetic, said to Coach Bryant that he might find that some of the people in New York didn't know him quite as well as those down South.

About that time we drove up to the hotel and as soon as Coach Bryant got out of the car the first man he met on the street said, "Hello, Bear, how are you doing?"
—*Charley Thornton*
Alabama sports information director and assistant athletic director, 1964-82

The University of Alabama bought a second airplane back in the seventies, I think, and while I was in the process of registering it, I thought about giving it a special number.

I asked Coach Bryant what his number was when he played football at Alabama, and he said he'd had three, but his favorite had been 34. He asked me why I wanted to know, but I didn't tell him at the time.

I found that registration number 34UA was not assigned, so I registered the new plane as that number. When Coach Bryant saw his number on the side of the plane the first time he flew in it, he literally beamed.

As a footnote to that, four or five years ago, I was on a trip to Canada and stopped for fuel in Morgantown, West Virginia, when I heard the controller give instructions to [plane] 34UA on the radio. I checked to verify that it was the plane the University had owned, and when I did, the controller had to hear the story about how the plane came to be registered as 34UA. He was a big Alabama and Coach Bryant fan and really enjoyed the story.
—*Woody Hatchett*
University of Alabama pilot, 1964-82

Coach Bryant always maintained a distance

Bill Oliver, a Bryant assistant, knew first-hand of the respect the Alabama coach commanded.

between himself and his assistant coaches, but we got to be closer friends after I left Alabama, and we maintained that friendship to the end.

I kept in contact with him while I was at East Carolina and Wyoming, and even later at Auburn. I valued his opinions and we talked often. After I came back to Auburn, we played a little golf, hunted some, and visited at the conference meetings.

Once we were on a bird hunt at a lodge and were all outside visiting when Coach Bryant received a call. A few minutes later he walked out of the lodge and said nonchalantly, "Well, we just signed Jon Hand today."

It was no surprise that Alabama signed Jon Hand, and Coach Bryant wasn't really bragging; but he said it in a way that let us all know he was still in charge in Alabama.
—*Pat Dye*
Alabama assistant coach, 1965-73, and former Auburn head coach

Coach Bryant had to be in Birmingham at nine o'clock in the morning to do his television show, and we always tried to leave Tuscaloosa at eight to make it. He usually got stopped in the lobby or at

Bryant reviews his team's play on the field with Mal Moore, an assistant coach from 1965-82.

the door signing autographs or having his picture taken with some youngsters, and we were always late getting away.

Once, we didn't leave Tuscaloosa until 25 minutes until nine, and I was moving up the highway when I met a State Trooper. I watched him and saw him turn around in the median and come after us. I stopped and waited for him and as soon as he walked up with his ticket pad I asked him if I could stop on the way back in a couple of hours and take care of the paperwork, because I had to get Coach Bryant to the television studio as quickly as possible.

He looked in the back seat and saw Coach Bryant and said just two words: "Follow me." He turned on the lights and led us all the way to the television studio on Red Mountain.

—*Billy Varner*
University of Alabama policeman who served as Coach Bryant's security and driver for many years

No One 'Janked' Coach Bryant

Coach Bryant struck fear, or at least extreme respect, in the hearts of most who knew him. It could be said that no one "janked" Coach Bryant, meaning, of course, that he didn't play—not even the radio—to coin an old phrase.

A good example can be found in the trick

Alabama players in the sixties frequently played on assistant coach Carney Laslie, a close Bryant friend and assistant at Maryland, Kentucky, Texas A&M and Alabama.

Like Bryant, Laslie wore a hat, and some of the players made a game of crushing Laslie's hat when the team came together in a tight pre-game huddle on the sidelines.

The hat-crushing assignment was passed around and usually went to a third-stringer, just in case, and the players always got a good laugh out of Laslie's fiery reaction often just after he had led the team in a prayer.

It was interesting to me, however, that never once did Coach Bryant's hat get crushed in that huddle, not even by accident.

Paul Davis, a former head coach at Mississippi State, assistant at Auburn and later an assistant at Alabama, once complained about the officiating following an Alabama-Auburn game while he was at Auburn.

"Paying officials what we pay, one out of six ought to see it," Davis moaned. "Officials are not dishonest; it's just a psychological thing. They're just scared to make the master [Bryant] mad."

Bill Oliver, a former Bryant player and assistant at Alabama and current assistant at Alabama, once told a story which illustrates that "extreme respect" also. Oliver and Alabama assistant basketball coach Wimp Sanderson were roommates at a two-day golf outing hosted by Coach Bryant at Lake Martin in the early seventies. As Sanderson showered after the day's round, he discovered their bathroom had no towels.

"Run next door and grab a couple of towels," Sanderson shouted to Oliver.

"Do you know who's staying next door?" Oliver shouted back.

"No, who?" Sanderson responded as he dripped in disgust and displayed his usual patient demeanor.

"Coach Bryant!" Oliver exclaimed.

"Forget it then; we've got plenty of toilet paper," Sanderson said matter of factly.

The following memories illustrate the respect Coach Bryant commanded from his associates.

During a two-a-day practice session at Texas A&M one year, the coaches were getting dressed after the morning practice. Coach Bryant was already dressed and had started out the door. As he left, he said, "Jim Stanley was the best football player on the field this morning."

I sort of answered in agreement by saying, "I'll go along with that," as he went out the door. He

Dude Hennessey coached for 17 years at Alabama.

stuck his head back in the door and said, "I don't give a damn whether you go along with it or not."

After a minute or two of silence, I looked out in the hall to be sure he had gone and went back in the dressing room and whispered to Elmer Smith, "When I get home I'm going to get in the closet and cuss that SOB out."
—*Pat James*
Kentucky player, 1948-50, and assistant coach, 1951 and 1953; Texas A&M assistant coach, 1954-57; and Alabama assistant coach, 1958-63

I was fortunate enough to win the Heisman Trophy while playing for Coach Bryant at Texas A&M [1957], but I really think Coach Bryant won it for me.

He came out before they voted and said if I didn't win it they ought to stop giving it. He had a reputation of not complimenting too many people or players, so that statement got a lot of attention.

They couldn't stop giving it, so I won. They darn sure had to do what he said.

I've always been especially proud of that trophy, not only because it is the Heisman Trophy, but because I was the only one of Coach Bryant's play-

ers to ever win it.

I didn't lead the nation in rushing or scoring that year. Heck, I didn't even lead the Southwest Conference in rushing; I gained just over 500 yards. But I did play 60 minutes a game at left halfback on offense, safety on defense, returning kicks, blocking, pass receiving or whatever.

One thing Coach Bryant said that helped me was that I had "led the nation in opposing players run over." That's when he said, "If John David doesn't win it, they ought to stop giving it."

Later on, he said he had coached a lot greater athletes than I was, but he called me his best football player. That meant a great deal to me, coming from Coach Bryant. It's still special to me.
—*John David Crow*
Heisman Trophy winner as Texas A&M player, 1954-57; Alabama assistant coach, 1969-71

Ohio State coach Woody Hayes with Bryant at Sugar Bowl press conference

Alabama was playing Ole Miss in Jackson one year when Steve Sloan was coaching over there, and our offense had taken a lot of criticism for being conservative, as I recall.

We took the opening kickoff, ran three plays and punted. The Ole Miss offense was on the field and our offense was at the blackboard looking at the pictures and getting ready to go back onto the field.

It was a bright, sunny, hot afternoon, about 1:40 p.m., and Coach Bryant had his hat pulled down close over his eyes to keep the sun out. He looked out from under his hat and cut his eyes at me and said, "Now, Mal, I want you to throw one before it gets dark."

On the next series, we threw a pass to Bart Krout for about a 50-yard touchdown.

I wanted to lean over and ask if that's what he had in mind, but I didn't.
—*Mal Moore*
Alabama player, 1958-62, and assistant coach, 1965-82

Coach Bryant came into my office [sports information] twice during my nine years at Alabama, and the first time nearly scared me to death.

It was lunch time and I was in the office alone, working at my desk, when he stuck his head in the

door. I jumped up abruptly, knocking several things off the desk, and said, "Yes sir, what can I do for you?"

He said, "Nothing at all, I was just stall-walking and thought I'd see what you folks are up to."
—*Kirk McNair*
Alabama assistant sports information director, 1970-73, and sports information director, 1973-79

We had just beaten Auburn and were leaving Legion Field after a game in the early seventies. There was a big crowd around as always, and I was close to Coach Bryant, walking through the crowd toward our dressing room. Suddenly someone grabbed Coach Bryant's hat and ran into the crowd and headed across the field.

What made me maddest about the whole thing, I guess, was that the guy had really long hair. It was halfway down his back.

I took off after him, weaving through the crowd like a maze, and caught him as he was climbing over the fence at the 50-yard-line on the Auburn side of the field. He was wearing Coach Bryant's hat. I grabbed the hat with one hand and a hand full of his hair with the other and jerked him backward off the fence. About that time, the police arrived and the whole thing was over.

I took the hat into the dressing room and gave it to Coach Bryant, and he just said, "Thank you, Jack."

That hat was a big thing with Coach Bryant. He had a favorite hat he liked to wear, a favorite shirt, a favorite coat. He even placed his shoes in a certain way in his locker. It was all like a ritual with

Bryant had a favorite houndstooth hat, favorite shirt and favorite coat. His clothing became a ritual to him.

This page and page 122: Although their teams were bitter rivals, Bryant and Auburn coach Shug Jordan were close friends and often worked on fundraising efforts together.

him. That hat was important to him, and that made it important for me to get it back for him.
—*Jack Rutledge*
Alabama player, 1958-61, and assistant coach, 1966-82

Coach Bryant was famous for teaching blocking and tackling on the practice field by getting in on the contact himself to demonstrate just how it should be done. He was also famous for the discipline he had learned at home and in the military, and some of his players found it hard to take at times.

Bob Gain, an all-conference tackle at Kentucky under Coach Bryant, finally decided he wasn't going to take it any more, and was bragging around how he was going to whip Coach Bryant to get even for some of the things he had said and done in practice.

Gain popped off to a bunch of the players at the football house, and pretty soon he had talked himself into a corner where he had to put up or shut up. A couple of carloads of players went over to Coach Bryant's house, and Gain went up to the door and knocked.

Coach Bryant came out in the dark and said, "Gain, what the hell do you want?"

Gain hesitated a minute and finally said, "Coach, I was just wondering if I could go home for Christmas this year."

Not only did Gain not try to whip Coach Bryant, I don't know anyone who ever did. Coach Bryant could motivate a player to get tough and want to fight, and that's what he was trying to do, but I don't think he ever motivated one to the point the player would take him on.
—*Larry "Dude" Hennessey*
Kentucky player, 1951-53; Alabama assistant coach, 1960-75

We had a terrible practice one day back in the sixties, and Coach Bryant kept everybody out on the practice field until well after dark.

When we finally came in, he chewed out the coaches pretty good and told us all to be in the office at five o'clock the next morning for a meeting.

Things were a little hot around there at that time, so I didn't take any chances on being late for the meeting. I slept on the floor in my office that

Bryant had a special place in his heart for his quarterbacks. Here he poses with 1980 quarterback candidates Michael Landrum (12), Alan Gray (14), Greg Haynes (17) and Dan Jacobs (5).

night. I wanted to be darn sure I got to that meeting on time.
—*Larry "Dude" Hennessey*
Kentucky player, 1951-53; Alabama assistant coach, 1960-75

A national television reporter was in Tuscaloosa for background information on an upcoming Alabama TV game once, and he was really confident in the sports information office, saying "Bear this" and "Bear that" before we went to Coach Bryant's office.

When he went into Coach's office and sat down on that low, soft couch and sunk down to just about floor level, with Coach Bryant towering over him from behind that big desk, he stammered and stuttered, but he said "Coach Bryant this" and "Coach Bryant that." He was scared to death.

When we left the interview, he said, "I've never

been so intimidated in my life."

That happened to just about everyone who sat on that couch, though, including me.
—*Kirk McNair*
Alabama assistant sports information director, 1970-73, and sports information director, 1973-79

I was a third-stringer during my freshman year, and we were having a goal-line scrimmage, trying to take the ball in for a score against the defense during spring training.

The offense tried several times but kept failing to score. Suddenly, we heard the chain gate on Coach Bryant's tower rattle and there was total silence. Everybody tightened up as he came into the huddle and let out a few expletives.

"Put 15 people on defense!" he yelled. The offense ran a couple of plays and didn't move the ball, so Coach Bryant put 22 men on defense.

Bryant with close friend Bob Hope and former Alabama quarterback Joe Namath.

We tried to score for 15 or 20 minutes more and finally he chewed us out and said nobody was blocking except Dowdy and told us to go to the dressing room but not dress.

After all the spectators were gone, he locked the gate and sent us back out for another scrimmage for 30 or 45 minutes, but it seemed like two hours with the coaches screaming and pushing and pulling us around.

The funny thing about that was that when we started back out, he told Jimmy Fuller he could stay in because he had been doing a good job earlier. He had forgotten that I was the one he had bragged on earlier, but I wasn't about to remind him.
—*Cecil Dowdy*
Alabama All-America tackle, 1963-66

The University had one airplane back in 1965, and we were about to have it repainted. Alabama had just won the national championship in football, and I had the idea of changing the registration number to 1UA.

The number was already taken, but I did some checking and found out who had the number and

was able to get them to transfer the number to the University. The University has had a plane with that number since, and the jet the school has now is still registered as 1UA in honor of Alabama's 1964 national championship.
—*Woody Hatchett*
University of Alabama pilot, 1964-82

It was tough at Junction that first year Coach Bryant came to Texas A&M [1954], probably as tough as everyone has heard. It was hot and we worked hard.

It wasn't a lot rougher than teams have it today, but it was tough on us because we weren't used to it. It came at a time when football was in a transition to hard-nosed, kill-or-get-killed football.

We lost a lot of players [more than 100 went to the pre-season training camp and only 27 returned]. Those who couldn't take it left. I don't know why I didn't leave, except that I didn't want to disappoint Coach Bryant. I didn't want to be a quitter.

Those of us who stayed learned something about character and heart. We didn't do much winning that first year [1-9] with those few who were left,

Mal Moore (L), Alabama assistant from 1965-82, said, "Coaching for Coach Bryant was an experience. He changed the way football was played in the Southeastern Conference, and it was a time in college football that will long be remembered."

but we fought hard. We put some knots on some heads, and we laid the ground work for some good teams the next three years [24-5-2].
—Dee Powell
Texas A&M player, 1954-56; Alabama assistant coach, 1964 and 1974-82

I didn't know what to expect when I came to Alabama as one of the first black players on the football team. I remember when Mom and Dad and I met with Coach Bryant the first time, we talked about it.

He said he couldn't promise me there would be no problems, but he said that if there were any, he wanted me to come to him first with them.

He never treated me any differently than anyone else, and I never had a single problem on the field or anywhere else in my career at Alabama. I never heard a racial comment, and there was never a single incident.

I had a white roommate, Bobby Stanford, from

Georgia, whose family treated me like I was a member of their family, and we had a great group of players during my years there.

I think Coach Bryant's stature, and the way he always talked about class and character, probably prevented any problems. If there had been one, they would have had to deal with him.
—*John Mitchell*
Alabama player, 1971-72, and assistant coach, 1974-76

I worked at Missouri for a year, and I remember the first team meeting I attended. When the head coach walked into the room, everybody just kept on talking.

At Alabama, there was instant silence when anyone even glanced toward the door as if Coach Bryant might be coming down the hall.
—*Wayne Reed*
Alabama football manager, 1978-81

I don't know whether Coach Bryant ever knew it, but some of us gave him the nickname "Britches" when I was an assistant coach at Alabama [1958-63].

Several of us coaches and staff were in the dressing room talking about this and that one day when Finus Gaston or B. W. Whittington or someone asked why we did a certain thing a certain way.

Coach Bryant wasn't there at the time, of course, but his locker was open and his khaki pants were hanging there in full view. I pointed to those pants and said, "I'm gonna do whatever the guy who wears those britches says."

After that, he was known as Britches among several of us. But again, I never called him that to his face, and I don't know if he ever knew it.
—*Pat James*
Kentucky player, 1948-50, and assistant coach, 1951 and 1953; Texas A&M assistant coach, 1954-57; and Alabama assistant coach, 1958-63

When Coach Bryant died, I remember feeling bad and being sorry that he died, but I remember feeling worst for all the people who weren't going to meet him and know him, or even see him.

He was that great a person. It was everybody else's loss when he died.
—*Wayne Reed*
Alabama football manager, 1978-81

I was coaching in high school in the fifties when Pat James called me and told me about a job that paid more than I was making. It was a head coaching job in Texas.

Pat asked if I was interested, and I said yes. He

Jim Goostree served as a Bryant aide for 25 years.

said he'd talk with Coach Bryant [then head coach at Texas A&M] and call me back. After a few days, I called Pat to see what was going on, and he said he had talked to Coach Bryant about it.

Pat said Coach Bryant had said, "We don't know if he [Dude] can coach or not. Let's see if he can coach first, then we'll get him a job."

I said, "Well, that's fine with me. Whatever Coach Bryant thinks is fine with me." And it was, too. That's how much I respected Coach Bryant's opinion. Of course, he was right.

About four years later [1960] he hired me as an assistant coach at Alabama. I guess I had proven I could coach, and when he called and offered me a job, I didn't even ask what the pay was. I just packed up and came to Alabama.
—*Larry "Dude" Hennessey*
Kentucky player, 1951-53; Alabama assistant coach, 1960-75

Kentucky All-America tackle Bob Gain [1949] told me before his induction into the College Football Hall of Fame that while he was a soldier in Korea, he had written Coach Bryant a letter just before going into a big battle.

"I told him that at Kentucky I hated his guts,

but that tonight, I love you for what I used to hate you for," Gain said.

—*Fred Russell*
Long-time Nashville Banner Sports Editor

He Was Quick to Lend a Hand

During the early seventies, Coach Bryant and Coach Ralph (Shug) Jordan of Auburn were co-chairmen of a statewide drive to raise funds to build a chapel at Partlow State School in Tuscaloosa. The drive was successful, of course, and Bryant and Jordan were on hand for the ground-breaking ceremonies.

Later, during construction, one of the residents of the institution approached one of the construction workers on the job and asked if he knew Bear Bryant.

"Yes, I know him," said the worker.

"Well, where is he?" asked the resident excitedly, looking about the worksite.

"He's at the University down the road coaching the football team. He isn't out here," the worker responded.

"That's what I figured," the resident said in disgust. "They told us Bear Bryant was going to build us a chapel, and he comes out here and turns one shovel full of dirt and we ain't seen his — since."

Maybe Coach Bryant didn't do any brick and mortar work on the chapel, but he asked the people of Alabama to contribute funds to build it, and they did. He was a hard man to say no to. He was great at lending a helping hand, too, and rarely did he wait for a call before taking action.

He used his connections and influence to get jobs for many of his former players, including many who followed him into coaching.

Jeff Rouzie was one of those, of course, but he also recalls another time when Coach Bryant stepped in without being asked.

Rouzie was one of Alabama's outstanding players in 1971, but was seriously injured in an automobile accident in February 1972.

"Coach Bryant was the first one in that hospital room every morning," Rouzie, now an Alabama assistant, said. "He helped me, and my family, during that situation.

"But that wasn't unusual. That's the way he was. He helped everyone any way he could, any time," Rouzie added.

Coach Bryant received thousands of fan letters each year, but one particular letter in 1973 was from a young girl, maybe 10 or 12 years old, writing from Florida to ask for his help.

"...I am having problems with my parents. It seems they don't love me any more.... It seems I'm always doing something wrong that they can fuss at me for....

"I don't know why I'm telling you my problems, but even though my parents don't love me, I hope you do, because I love you."

The letter was signed, "Someone who needs to be loved."

Coach Bryant handled the letter personally, and encouraged the youngster to talk with her parents.

"I am certain your parents love you, although they may be too busy sometimes to show it," he wrote.

The following memories illustrate Coach Bryant's concern for others and his willingness to lend a helping hand at any time.

Coach Bryant had special relationships with his quarterbacks [five made All-America, nine all-conference]. He ate meals with them, took walks with them on game days and spent time talking with them about practice, leadership, game situations, etc.

He made a special effort to make them feel comfortable with him. Everybody was scared to death of him. He wanted to give them a secure feeling, to take the pressure off them so they would go into the game and play, not worry.

He also did it for another important reason, too. That was to build respect for the quarterbacks with the other players. He wanted the other players to look up to the quarterbacks because they were close to him and were the leaders.

He was such a dominating figure, and everyone had great respect for him and what he stood for. Some of that respect transferred to the quarterbacks because they were "in" with him.

—*Mal Moore*
Alabama player, 1958-62, and assistant coach, 1965-82

I first met Coach Bryant in early 1965 in Washington, D.C. He was there to accept the Washington Touchdown Club award for the 1964 national championship, and I was there to accept an award as the outstanding service football player.

I had played against his teams in 1959-60 while at Georgia, and I knew a lot of his former players from service ball, but I'd never met him. Later, I wrote him a letter and asked about a job on his staff. He responded right away with a nice letter, but I didn't get too excited about it.

I got out of the Army in June 1965 and was

Coach Bryant poses with Tennessee cheerleaders prior to a Tide-Volunteer clash.

headed for Canada to play professional football, but Coach Bryant called me four days later and we talked. I visited with him a few days later, and he hired me.

He put me on the payroll effective the first day we talked by telephone, and I was an assistant coach with him at Alabama for nine seasons.

If I hadn't been a winner before in high school and college and in service football, I don't think I would have had the opportunity to coach at Alabama. I didn't learn to win at Alabama, but I learned a lot about handling people and a winning football philosophy from Coach Bryant.

I believed in his philosophy. That's why I wanted to coach at Alabama under him, and I tried to absorb as much about the game and the organization of his program as I could. Learning football from him was like getting a PhD. in business from Harvard.

—Pat Dye
Alabama assistant coach, 1965-73

I was visiting with Coach Bryant in his office once about my future and plans and such. I was a

sophomore at the time and had had a knee injury and wasn't practicing and had contributed zero to the Alabama program. I had even been told that my football career was over.

Rebecca [Bryant's secretary] stuck her head into the room and said, "Coach, I have the White House, Bob Hope and the head of ABC sports all on hold."

Coach Bryant said, "I'll be with them in a minute"; then he turned to me and asked, "What are you doing this summer?"

He made me feel like the most important person in the world at that moment. He could do that; it was a gift he had.

I've tried to carry that same practice over to 1200 kids, and not a day goes by that in some way I don't use his influence to influence others, even subconsciously.

He has affected hundreds of thousands and continues to do so through those who played for him, and I have a chance to do that with all these children. I can't think of a higher tribute to him.

—John Croyle
Alabama player, 1971-73; founder and director of Big Oak Ranch

LSU mascot greets Coach Bryant before game.

Coach Bryant was instrumental in helping me get my first coaching job, and that says a lot about him because I didn't play for him.

Alabama recruited me hard, but I went to Vanderbilt instead, and we were lucky enough to beat Alabama once while I was there. When I graduated, Pat Dye was leaving Alabama as an assistant coach to become head coach at East Carolina.

Coach Dye hired me as an assistant based on recommendations from Coach Bryant and Coach Steve Sloan (Vanderbilt head coach).

Several times through the years I called Coach Bryant to ask his advice or to talk about other coaching jobs, and he always helped me.
—*Watson Brown*
Head football coach, UAB

A while after I graduated, I was living at home in Mobile and thinking about my future. I thought I might go to law school, so I called Coach Bryant and asked him about a possible part-time job somewhere in the athletic department to help me work my way through school.

He was very short with me on the telephone, and simply said, "I don't want to talk with you about this on the phone. Why don't you come up here and sit down with me and let's talk about it."

I drove up to Tuscaloosa on a Wednesday morn-

ing, planning to drive back home that afternoon, and I really wasn't expecting too much. But when I went in to see Coach Bryant, I had no more than sat down on his couch when he said, "I have a full-time job for you on our coaching staff if you want it."

I didn't know how to say no to Coach Bryant, so I said okay. He said, "Go over to the athletic dorm and move into a room there; you start this afternoon."

He wouldn't even let me go home for more clothes. I worked three days before I had a chance to get back to Mobile and move to Tuscaloosa. That was July 1973, and I've been in coaching since that day.
—*John Mitchell*
Alabama player, 1971-72, and assistant coach, 1973-76

I was already in graduate school when I finished my football eligibility, and I asked Coach Bryant about a job after my final season.

I wasn't thinking about coaching. I was just thinking about any job on a part-time basis while I went to school. Several weeks later, I heard that Coach Bryant wanted to see me.

When I went to his office, he sort of tossed a scrap of paper on his desk with a telephone number on it and said, "Call this number. Jim Sweeney wants someone to help him teach our system."

I called the number collect, and the local operator had a very distinct Southern accent. She said, "I have a collect call from Mal Moore for Coach Sweeney," and there was a long silence on the other end of the line before Coach Sweeney said, "My, I can just smell the magnolia blossoms."

I spent a year with Coach Sweeney at Montana State, then came back to Alabama as an assistant and was with Coach Bryant until his retirement.

Coaching for Coach Bryant was an experience. He changed the way football was played in the Southeastern Conference, and it was a time in college football that will long be remembered.

He gave his players a sense of pride and confidence. His teams always felt like they could win, and his players felt like they had been with the best, and could pass it on. That's why so many of us went into coaching. And he helped a lot of them get into coaching, just like he did me.

—*Mal Moore*
Alabama player, 1958-62, and assistant coach, 1965-82

I was living in a farmhouse with five little boys in January 1975, trying to start Big Oak Ranch with no money and a dream.

I went to see Coach Bryant and asked for three things: a letter of endorsement, him to serve on the advisory board, and $70,000 for a house.

"I'll answer them one at a time," he said. "Yes, yes, and let's wait and see."

At the time he died in January 1983, he had collected $70,000 in donations for us, and had personally made a sizeable contribution of his own, added to that $70,000.

The last donation we got through him was interesting in that a man offered Coach Bryant $1000 for his autograph on a shirt after the Liberty Bowl game in Memphis, his last game.

Coach Bryant said, "It's a deal; make the check out to Big Oak Ranch."

—*John Croyle*
Alabama player, 1971-73; founder and director of Big Oak Ranch

I grew up in Birmingham and really wanted to go to the University of Alabama, but I knew the only way I could go was to get a scholarship of some kind.

I went to Tuscaloosa and applied for an athletic hostess tuition scholarship, but I had no connections of any kind, and I was told that I was not selected.

I was really disappointed, and it looked as if I was going to have to stay at home and go to UAB.

My dad told a friend of his about my situation, however, and the friend said he knew Coach Bryant and would tell him about me.

The next day I got a call from Coach Clem Gryska telling me I had a scholarship. I was a hostess for four years and head hostess my senior year.

—*Dee Thompson Riley*
Alabama athletic hostess, 1972-76

I went with Dr. Frank Rose [University president] to Houston to meet with Coach Bryant when Alabama decided to offer him the head coaching job at Alabama during the 1957 season.

The thing that impressed me most during our discussions was Coach Bryant asking what would happen to Coach Hank Crisp [then athletic director] and Coach Red Drew [assistant football coach] if he took the job at Alabama.

Coach Crisp had signed Coach Bryant and brought him from Arkansas to Alabama, and Coach Hank and Coach Drew had been his coaches at Alabama. He wanted to make sure they were set up in a job before he would agree to take the job as head coach and athletic director.

—*Fred Sington*
Alabama All-America tackle, 1927-30, long-time SEC football official and active Alabama alumnus

I remember clearly the first time I ever laid eyes on Coach Bryant. I had heard a little about him, but I had no idea who he really was.

He called all the managers into his office when he first arrived at the University in January 1958, and about 20 or 30 people showed up, some I'd never seen in my life, and I'd been on the football field all season as a manager for Coach [J. B.] Whitworth in 1957.

Coach Bryant looked at us and said, "There are a lot of people here, and as of right now, you're all fired. You have between now and fall to prove yourselves, and the ones who work, we'll keep."

I nearly killed myself that spring and summer. I worked. By that fall, there were only two managers, myself and Bert Jones, and we went on scholarship.

I found out then that when Coach Bryant said something, that was the way it was. You didn't have to go back and check or remind him. He was a man of his word, and he took care of the people who worked for him.

—*Gary White*
Alabama football manager, graduate assistant coach, athletic dorm director and athletic department administrator, 1957-82

Coach Bryant kept in touch with his former players for years after they graduated, and he helped them in any way he could. He even helped their kids go to college.

And if one of his former players—even from the Kentucky or Texas A&M days—wasn't doing just right and Coach Bryant heard about it, he'd write him a letter and tell him to get off his butt.

Coach Bryant cared about his players and coaches, and the players had great respect and loyalty for Coach Bryant because they knew that.

—Larry "Dude" Hennessey
Kentucky player, 1951-53; Alabama assistant coach, 1960-75

About a year before he broke the record for most wins, Coach Bryant called me and asked me to ride with him to dinner, and as we drove along, he said he was concerned with the safety of his staff.

"There are a lot of crazy things going on in the world," he said. "As I get closer to this record, someone could kidnap a child or some member of my family or my staff to get to me. I want you to keep a close eye on your family."

Here he is, bigger than life, worried about his staff and their families. He did that sort of thing over and over, all through the years. And he did so much for so many that went unknown.

—Gary White
Alabama football manager, graduate assistant coach, athletic dorm director and athletic department administrator, 1957-82

As a freshman manager on the football team in 1978, I was assigned the job of sitting on the gate at Denny Stadium one day during our final scrimmage before the opening game with Nebraska.

This particular practice was closed to everyone, and Coach Bryant had wanted the gates locked when the players got inside. I had to be there at a specific time, but was riding with another manager and ended up being a little late. When I arrived, I checked the stadium to see that no one had gotten in, but as I did that, I bumped into Coach Bryant and Pat Thomas, the head manager.

Bryant was often seen holding his familiar "to do list" on the sideline.

As I walked toward them, Pat pointed to me and said, "There he is, Coach." Coach Bryant looked at me and said two words to Pat as he turned and walked away. All he said was, "Fire him."

I was really upset. Here I was a Tuscaloosa native and the biggest Coach Bryant and Alabama fan in the world and a freshman manager on the team, just as I'd dreamed, and I was being fired before the first game.

Pat told me to stick around and he'd see what he

could do, so I waited in the tunnel the whole practice, worried sick. Pat apparently talked with Coach Goostree [trainer Jim] and Coach Goostree talked with Coach Bryant during practice, and after practice Pat told me that Coach Bryant had said he could keep me, "but put someone on the gate who'll be there."

I stayed on the gate the entire season, but I was never late again. I was a manager four years, and head manager my senior year. I met with him every day to go over practice plans, and I would round up players for him to meet with.

He never mentioned the time he fired me, and neither did I.

—*Wayne Reed*
Alabama football manager, 1978-81

He Had a Humorous Side, Too

As a sports editor covering Alabama football for several years, I had many opportunities to talk with Coach Bryant alone. On one particularly casual occasion, I asked him what he would change about the the game of football, given the chance.

I sat poised with pen in hand, ready to write something profound, like "eliminate the forward pass," or "add 20 yards to the length of the field," or something of that magnitude.

Coach Bryant thought briefly but intently, then said without a hint of a smile, "Make Auburn quit cheating."

He wasn't joking, I later learned, but he had a sense of humor that often enabled him often to turn difficult situations into lighter moments, and in doing so he usually made a point.

He did so at Grant Field in Atlanta one Saturday in the sixties by wearing a football helmet as he walked past the student section prior to an Alabama game against Georgia Tech.

The Alabama-Tech football series grew into an intense rivalry during the early sixties, due in part to an injury to a Georgia Tech player during one game and in part due to newspaper and magazine stories out of Atlanta critical of Bryant and his coaching style.

During one game in Atlanta, the Alabama sideline was pelted by debris, including whiskey bottles, thrown by the Tech students. Some of the players and coaches were actually struck by some of the objects.

Two years later, when Alabama returned to Grant Field, Coach Bryant stunned the Tech fans by wearing a helmet as he strolled past the student section as the team walked onto the field prior to the game.

"He wore Louis Thompson's helmet. I remember that very well," said former assistant coach Clem Gryska. "The team was taking its pre-game walk around the field in street clothes, and as Coach Bryant turned toward the Alabama bench right in front of the Tech students, he put the helmet on," Gryska said.

"He knew what he was doing. He got their attention, and they [the Tech student section] even cheered him," Gryska added.

Bryant was almost hit by a bottle two years before, and afterward was asked what he thought when he saw the bottle at his feet.

"I noticed the label," he said, "and saw it was Ancient Age. I thought, 'That sure is cheap whiskey.'"

Following are some of the stories illustrating Coach Bryant's more humorous side.

When Alabama played Penn State in Pennsylvania in 1981, the officials made a questionable call which gave Penn State seven downs on one series inside the Alabama 10-yard-line, but Alabama still managed to win the game, 31-16, even after having two touchdowns called back in the first half.

The clock went out in the last quarter, and it took an hour to play the last five minutes. Papa [Coach Bryant] got onto the officials about the game lasting so long, and one of them said, "You shouldn't be worried, Coach, you've got the game in hand."

Papa said, "What you're telling me is that we're going to play 'til they score." And they kept the game going until Penn State scored.

During a late timeout, one of the officials approached Papa to shake his hand and said, "Coach Bryant, I just want you to know what an honor it is to work one of your games."

Papa shook his hand, smiled and said, "And I just want you to know that this is the worst officiated game I've ever been involved in."

—*Paul Bryant Jr.*

I introduced Paul [Coach Bryant] at an alumni banquet in Dothan shortly after he returned to Alabama as head coach, and in my introduction I told about his football accomplishments and mentioned that he had "attended" the University of Alabama.

Later on, he got me aside and said, "Next time you introduce me, be damn sure you say I graduated from the University."

He was proud of that degree, although he didn't get it until he was an assistant coach a year or so after he finished playing football. I think Mary Harmon [Mrs. Bryant] made him get it, but I know he was certainly proud of it.
—*Young Boozer*
Bryant teammate at Alabama; long-time friend and business associate

Bear and I were coaching opposing teams in the Texas High School All-Star game in 1951 and we got together before the game and made a deal with each other that if one team got 14 points ahead, the other one would give a signal to call off the dogs so the winner wouldn't make the other one look bad.

I was coaching at Clemson at the time, and Bear was coaching at Kentucky.

When we played the game, Bear's team got ahead, 14-0, and kept pouring it on; and I kept trying to get his attention across the field, but he kept looking the other way. It got to be 21-0, and I was hollering and waving my hat, and he just kept looking the other way. I think his team finally won about 35-0, and afterwards I asked him about our deal and how come he couldn't see me over there waving the white flag. He said he couldn't see me because the sun was in his eyes.
—*Frank Howard*
Alabama player, 1928-30; Clemson head coach

We were in New York just before Coach Bryant broke the record for most wins, and he was going on all the talk shows, like Dick Cavett and the *Today Show.*

Cavett asked him a couple of dumb questions, and when we left Coach turned to me and said, "You know, I don't think that guy knew who the hell I am."
—*Charley Thornton*
Alabama sports information director and assistant athletic director, 1964-82

While he was recognized as a tough coach, Bryant was also known to have a sharp sense of humor.

I was all set to go to Marion Institute in the fall of 1958 and was working out with the Livingston High School team when Coach Sam Bailey stopped by practice one day and spotted me and talked with me about going to Alabama.

Coach Bailey said if I could get my release from MI to pack my bags and get ready to come to Alabama, and that I should call Coach Bryant the next day at 10 a.m. sharp and let him know that I was coming.

I got my release and called the next day at 10 o'clock, and got Coach Bryant on the phone. I told him who I was and said I'd gotten everything done and was ready to come to Alabama.

"You are?" he asked. I repeated what I'd said, and he asked again, "You are?" The same thing happened a third time, and I froze. I finally called my mama to the phone and she explained to him what had transpired. As it turned out, Coach Bailey hadn't told him about me.

I ended up signing a baseball grant, which was legal at the time and playing football and baseball.
—*Bill Oliver*
Alabama player, 1958-61, and assistant coach, 1971-79 and 1990-1995

I was playing golf with Joe Namath, Coach Bryant and two or three others once and I had a three or four-foot putt to tie the hole.

As I was lining up my putt, Coach Bryant mumbled something about how slow the greens were, and I hit the ball 30 feet off the green.

Needless to say, I wasn't on Coach Bryant's team.
—*Jack Hicks*
Student football manager at Alabama, 1957-63

Coach Bryant rarely said anything that would offend or inspire an opposing team, but sometime before the Alabama-Auburn game of 1972, he said something about Auburn being a "cow college," or something like that.

Alabama was favored in the game, but Auburn blocked two punts late in the game and won, 17-16. I don't think his "cow college" remark had anything to do with Auburn winning, but he didn't forget it.

The following spring, after practice one day, he was talking about how the players had performed and said, "We looked like a cow college out there today." Then he took a long puff on his cigarette and said, "Change that to barber college."

—*Kirk McNair*
Alabama assistant sports information director, 1970-73, and sports information director, 1973-79

I was in New York with Joe Namath one summer when Coach Bryant came to town and went to see Joe in a play.

After the play, several of the cast members went to dinner and Coach Bryant sat across the table from Joe and the female lead in the play. The female lead kept leaning over to Joe and they kept whispering back and forth during dinner.

Coach Bryant, finally realizing that Joe was having to repeat to her everything that he said, responded, "Joe, tell her I also teach diction at Alabama."

—*Jack Hicks*
Student football manager at Alabama, 1957-63

Coach Bryant and I got on an elevator in New York once, and Robert Redford got on with us. As we rode up, Redford reached out and shook hands with Coach Bryant and said he was a fan of his.

After Redford got off, Coach looked at me and said, "That fellow looked kinda familiar; who is he?"

I told him it was Robert Redford, and Coach couldn't wait to get to his room to call Mrs. Bryant and tell her whom he had met. When he called her and told about it, she said, "Aw, Papa, you wouldn't know Robert Redford if you did meet him."

—*Charley Thornton*
Alabama sports information director and assistant athletic director, 1964-82

We [Alabama] were playing Houston in Denny Stadium one year and they had the veer offense. We were having a hard time stopping them, and they were having a hard time stopping us. There was a lot of scoring in the game.

We had the ball and were backed up pretty deep, running the wishbone. We kept running and moving a little. Coach Bryant said out loud that their off-side linebacker was making all the tackles and we should run a reverse.

We ran a couple more plays and Coach Bryant said the same thing again. Finally we had a first down somewhere around the 20-yard-line, and

Coach Bryant took me by the arm firmly and told me to run a reverse.

I called the reverse to David Bailey, and their defensive end nailed him for about a 15-yard loss.

Coach Bryant looked at me and said, "I meant the other way."

—*Mal Moore*
Alabama player, 1958-62, and assistant coach, 1965-82

Several of us were visiting with Coach Bryant and Mrs. Bryant after the Alabama Sugar Bowl game with Ohio State.

Some television reporter was interviewing Coach Bryant and asked him what he thought of Woody Hayes.

Coach Bryant heaped the praise on Woody, saying what a great person he was, what a great coach he was and on and on. He couldn't have built him up any higher. Then he added, "And you know what, I ain't too bad myself."

—*Pat Dye*
Alabama assistant coach, 1965-73

Our Kentucky football team was in Knoxville in 1946 to play Tennessee, and we were having our pre-game meal in the hotel when Coach Bryant asked the waitress for a second cup of coffee.

The waitress, thinking he was a player because he looked a lot younger than most of the players on the team, refused to give him more coffee. He was 33, but most of the players were ex-servicemen, like myself, and looked a lot older.

Coach Bryant turned to one of the players who looked a lot older and asked for permission to have another cup of coffee, and the player said, "Aw, let the boy have his coffee," and the waitress got him the coffee.

—*Charley Bradshaw*
Kentucky player, 1946-49, and Alabama assistant coach, 1959-61

Coach Bryant was a guest on the *American Sportsman* television show with Curt Gowdy back in the seventies, and a crew was shooting film while Bryant and Gowdy hunted birds at Sedgefield, a hunting reserve in South Alabama.

The photographers were having a difficult time getting good film of the kills because there was poor light early and late in the day when they found birds, and few birds in the middle of the day when the light was good.

One day Coach Bryant got a double [two kills on one flush] and he was really beaming when he turned around toward the cameraman.

"I'm sorry, Coach," the cameraman said. "I didn't have any film in the camera. I wasn't quite ready for that shot and I missed it."

Coach Bryant proceeded to give that guy a lecture about his purpose for being out there and how he'd better be prepared to get those shots in the future. As you know, Coach Bryant believed in being prepared. He made plans and thought things through in anything he did.

It turned out that the cameraman did have film in the camera after all, and had gotten the shot of the double. He was just joking with Coach Bryant about not filming his double, but he got a pretty good Paul Bryant lecture before he could explain that it was just a joke.

—*Jimmy Hinton*
Close Bryant friend and business associate

Coach Bryant was visiting in New York once and joined fellow Alabama graduate Mel Allen on his New York Yankee's television interview show. The show was sponsored by a cigar company, and when time for a commercial came along, Allen handed Bryant a cigar, said "Have a smoke," and began lighting his own cigar.

Bryant recoiled and pushed the cigar back at Allen, stammering, "That thing would make me as sick as a dog."

Allen tried frantically to recover, making it look like a joke and trying again to hand Bryant the cigar.

"I'm telling you the truth," Bryant reiterated, "that thing would make me as sick as a dog." Thus ended the interview.

—*Fred Russell*
Long-time Nashville Banner Sports Editor

We used to have chair drill on Fridays before games to keep our legs fresh. We did it for all the games.

We'd sit in chairs and when the coaches called a play, we'd point to our assignment. The coaches would watch us to be sure we were correct.

When we [Alabama] played Penn State in the Liberty Bowl in Philadelphia in 1959, the press and everybody up there made a big to-do of it because they'd never seen it before.

Coach Bryant had a little fun with the press with it, too, by calling it a lazy man's way to prepare for a big game. The paper ran a big picture of it and called it a sitdown drill, but it was something we did for every game back then.

—*Tommy Brooker*
Alabama player, 1958-61, and volunteer kicking coach, 1966-82

Coach Bryant did a lot of flying while he was

coaching at Alabama, of course, but he had apparently been scared in a plane sometime before I came here [1964] as a University pilot. It usually took him a little while to get at ease on a plane trip.

I recall that I regularly flew him to Montgomery each Sunday for his television show back in the sixties. Once, he told me he wouldn't need me on a particular Sunday morning because he was flying down with someone else in their plane.

As I watched his playback show that afternoon, I heard Coach Bryant mention the flight down and the bad weather they had gone through. He said something about it being a little scary. I knew right then he'd be calling me to come and get him and bring him back, because I knew he had confidence in me.

Sure enough, as soon as his television show was over, he called and told me to come pick him up and bring him home.

—*Woody Hatchett*
University of Alabama pilot, 1964-82

Coach Bryant had a special dislike for Tennessee, first born in his playing days at Alabama and fully grown during his coaching days at Kentucky when his Wildcats were beaten regularly by the Volunteers.

While coaching at Kentucky, Bryant visited Army posts in Europe with several other coaches. Knowing full well that many of the troops were familiar with past Kentucky-Tennessee scores, particularly Tennessee's latest victories, Bryant would start off his talk by asking, "Are there any good folks from the old Bluegrass State here?"

Lots of hands would go up, with mingled cheering.

Then Bryant would ask, "Are there any of those Tennessee - - - - -s here?"

That would bring down the house.

—*Fred Russell*
Long-time Nashville Banner Sports Editor

While I was an assistant coach at Alabama [1968-70], I worked with the offense, handling the sideline telephone, relaying messages from coaches in the pressbox to Coach Bryant.

We were ahead in one particular game, but the other team was driving, and our defense couldn't seem to do much about it. We made adjustments, but they didn't work.

Coach Bryant wasn't the mildest of men when something like that was going on, and I heard him holler, "Get Durby in there!"

I knew Ron Durby had graduated three or four years before, and I didn't do anything. I went on

Bryant was gracious even in defeat. Here, he shakes hands with Mississippi State coach Emory Bellard after a 6-3 State win.

talking to the coaches in the pressbox.

All at once, I'm almost falling to the ground. Someone has almost jerked my head off with the wire to the headset. It was Coach Bryant.

"Dammit," he yelled, "I said get Durby in there!"

"Yes, sir," I said. I knew Durby had graduated; the other coaches knew Durby had graduated; the players on the bench knew Durby had graduated; but we all darn sure went looking for him.

—*Steve Sloan*
Alabama player, 1962-65, and assistant coach, 1968-70

There was one year, I think about 1961, when the Rose Bowl didn't have a contract with the Big Ten Conference, and they were looking at outside teams, and Alabama was one of the teams being considered.

Coach Bryant got word in advance that we wouldn't be invited, so he called a meeting of the team, and the team voted to go to the Sugar Bowl, turning down the Rose Bowl, in effect.

We had a press release on it and everything; so before the Rose Bowl could turn us down, he figured out a way to get the jump on them and turn the Rose Bowl down.

—*Gary White*
Alabama football manager, graduate assistant coach, athletic dorm director and athletic department administrator, 1957-82

I was quarterback in 1969 when Alabama outscored Ole Miss, 33-32, in the wildest football game I've ever been involved in. Archie Manning completed 33 of 52 passes for over 400 yards for Ole Miss, and I completed 22 of 29 for 300 yards for Alabama.

Coach Bryant stuck a cigarette in his mouth in the third quarter, but things were happening so fast, and he was giving orders left and right that he forgot to light it. It stayed there for the entire second half without him ever lighting it.

Ole Miss led us, 32-27, late in the game; and Alabama had a fourth and 10 at the Ole Miss 15. I called time out and went over to the sideline and asked Coach Bryant what he wanted to do.

He turned to Coach Jimmy Sharpe and asked him what he wanted to do. Sharpe said, "I don't know; I'll ask Steve," and he called Coach Steve Sloan, who was in the pressbox, but he didn't get an answer.

The official came over and said, "Captain, your time is up." Coach Bryant said, "Well, call 56X, that's your best pass." I called it and threw complete to George Ranager, and Alabama won, 33-32.

I asked Coach Sloan later what had happened when he didn't answer the phone in the pressbox and he said, "When I saw you call time out and go to Coach Bryant and ask him what to do, and then I saw him turn to Sharpe and ask him what to do, I pulled off the headphones and said, 'Lord, what should we do?'"
—Scott Hunter
Alabama player, 1967-70

I wish I had a cartoon of a little mouse standing up on its back feet chasing a big bear backward. That would depict one really amusing incident involving Coach Bryant.

Coach Bryant had flown to Mobile on a recruiting trip to visit Scott Hunter, and when he came back to the plane, I stood aside at the door to let him enter first, then I followed.

He had just stepped into the plane when he came backing out as fast as he could, yelling, "Rat! Rat! Rat!" He must have jumped six feet off that plane when he finally got turned around.

He then ordered me to get in the plane and get that rat out of there, so co-pilot Cliff Atkins and I went into the plane and looked for it. We never could find it. I'm sure it was afraid to come out after all the commotion.

Coach Bryant finally got back on the plane so we could return to Tuscaloosa, but he put his feet up in the seat in front of him and flew all the way home that way, afraid to put his feet down because of that rat.

When he got off the plane in Tuscaloosa, he told me to find that rat and get it off that plane. Cliff and I put out two traps with peanuts on them that night, and the next day we had a little mouse about four inches long, tail and all, in one of them.

I put the mouse in a plastic bag and took it to Coach Bryant to show him what we'd found. When he saw it, he smiled and said, "I told you there was one in there."
—Woody Hatchett
University of Alabama pilot, 1964-82

Coach Bryant made a lot of commercials during

Present Alabama coach Gene Stallings was one of Bryant's favorite players at Texas A&M.

his last few years as Alabama head coach, and he often recorded them on tape and listened to them to see how he sounded.

One day he discovered that he had left his portable recorder at home and sent Billy Varner back to get one. Billy went to Coach Bryant's house and came back with a small recorder in each hand, and stepped into Coach Bryant's office holding them out.

"Coach, I've got both recorders, but neither one of them works," Varner announced.

Coach Bryant was reading the paper or something, and turned his eyes toward Billy, looking over his glasses.

"Do I look like Radio Shack?" he asked.

Billy didn't say a word. He just turned and sprinted to Radio Shack to have them repaired.
—Gary White
Alabama football manager, graduate assistant coach, athletic dorm director and athletic department administrator, 1957-82

Smokey Harper was Bryant's trainer at Kentucky and Texas A&M and later joined him at Alabama for a time as film manager.

When Harper first reported to work at Kentucky,

he asked Bryant what his job assignment was.

"Just go somewhere for coffee every morning and tell the folks what a great coach I am," Bryant responded.
—*Fred Russell*
Long-time Nashville Banner Sports Editor

When I was a player at Kentucky [1946-50], Coach Bryant took the first 22 players and a few coaches to a Boy Scout camp before the 1950 [11-1, Southeastern Conference championship] season to "get some oneness."

We didn't work out in pads, but we had a football and we practiced twice each morning and watched films at night. During the afternoons we'd go fishing or swimming or play softball.

One morning I went fishing between the early practice and the late practice, and the fish were biting and I ended up being late for practice. When I got there, I jumped right in and took my spot and my turn like nothing had happened, and nobody said anything at the time.

After practice was over, Coach Bryant said, "Hold it a minute. One of our men was late for practice and we need to address that."

He looked at me and said, "Patricia, I took up for you, but the other players held a kangaroo court and decided that you need to cover up all those cow piles out there in the pasture." So I got a bucket of sand and covered up all the cow piles after practice.

The next morning, the trainer or somebody failed to wake up Coach Bryant, and he was about 30 minutes late for practice. Some of the players kept riding me, saying I should get on him for being late.

So after practice, I said, "Hold it a minute." I looked at Coach Bryant and said that the team had held a kangaroo court and decided he needed to pick up all the cow manure in the pasture and throw it over the fence for being late. He went out there and did it, too.
—*Pat James*
Kentucky player, 1948-50, and assistant coach, 1951 and 1953; Texas A&M assistant coach, 1954-57; and Alabama assistant coach, 1958-63

Coach Bryant got a letter once criticizing his coaching, and in one game in particular. It was a long letter that went on and on, pointing out what the writer thought was wrong with the Alabama program.

Coach Bryant wrote back and thanked the writer for his interest and comments, and added:

"I am sorry that you did not include the nature of your work so I could help you with your business as

much as you have helped me with mine."
—*Rebecca Christian*
Bryant's personal secretary, 1967-82

We were practicing one fall, and Coach Bryant was watching from his tower. We had a scrimmage under way, and it was hot and we had gone on and on and on and Coach Bryant hadn't blown the whistle to quit.

We were all about to drop—coaches and players—and we kept looking up at the tower after every play and yelling and hustling, trying to impress him so we could go in, but he didn't move a muscle.

It started to get dark, so we finally decided to send a manager up on the tower to see about him. We figured he was mad as hell about something or dead.

The manager went up the tower cautiously, planning to ask Coach Bryant if he wanted some water or something, and found him sound asleep.
—*Hayden Riley*
Alabama assistant coach, assistant athletic director, head baseball and basketball coach, 1958-75

He Seemed to Know Everything

Coach Bryant had a habit of going for a drive with anyone he really wanted to talk with privately. That way he escaped the telephone and other interruptions. Also the victim was not as likely to make a run for it.

Once, Coach Bryant heard through the grapevine that one of his top assistants had been offered a job at another school; so he asked the assistant to go for a ride with him the next morning.

Coach Bryant drove and chatted about the weather and practice and family and whatever for a long time before cleverly steering the conversation to the school in question, never letting on that he knew the assistant was considering a move.

He casually mentioned that the coach at the other school wasn't in the best of graces with the administration, and that he could be in trouble. He then steered the conversation to other matters as he steered the car back toward the athletic offices.

Needless to say, the assistant didn't leave Bryant's staff, and the other head coach was fired at the end of the season.

Coach Bryant had a way of knowing such things, and of handling such matters.

His associates agree that he seemed to be all-

In his latter years, Bryant often surveyed the football practice field from his golf cart.

knowing and all-seeing. They also agree that he left no detail to fate, no loose end untied. The following comments capture Coach Bryant's eye for detail.

Coach Bryant seemed to know everything. He kept everybody on their toes because he knew what was going on.

One day after a practice session he asked me how a particular player had done. I said I thought he looked pretty good, but all the time I figured he had me in a lose-lose situation. He liked to set you up like that.

"That's amazing," he said. "We were watching the same player, and I didn't think he played worth a damn."
—*Bobby Marks*
Texas A&M player, 1955-57; Alabama assistant coach, 1972-82

Coach Bryant was Lt. Commander Bryant in 1945 at the Navy's Pre-Flight school at Chapel Hill, N.C., when he was hired as head football coach at Maryland. He took 15 of the players off the military team with him to Maryland and posted a 6-2-1 record in his first year as head coach.

Bryant resigned abruptly in January 1946 and went to Kentucky as head coach. It wasn't so much that Kentucky was his choice. He had his eye on other possible jobs at Alabama and Arkansas, but the timing just wasn't right. Kentucky was about the only choice he had at the moment.

Bryant had been visiting in Alabama over the Christmas season, and while he was away from Maryland, the school president, Dr. Harry Byrd, had fired a Bryant assistant and reinstated a player Bryant had dismissed.

"I knew then I had to quit," Bryant said. "Dr. Byrd had coached at Maryland for 23 years. He thought he knew as much football as the coaches he hired. Maybe back then he knew more football than I did, but I didn't think so," he added.
—*Fred Russell*
Long-time Nashville Banner Sports Editor

Richard Todd was a fine quarterback for Alabama and could speak perfectly except in one particular situation: He had trouble calling the plays in the huddle, especially if the play had a "thirty" in it. He had a slight hesitation, or stutter. Outside the huddle, person to person, even in a game, he could call the plays perfectly. And he had no problem with the snap count. It was a strange thing.

Coach Bryant came up with the idea of having

Danny Ridgeway [a kicker and backup quarterback] run onto the field between each offensive play, stick his head in the huddle and call the plays, then run back off the field. That helped us get the play in quicker and have it called without any problems.

We did it all season that one year, but they changed the rule the next year and required any player going onto the field to remain in for a play.
—*Mal Moore*
Alabama player, 1958-62, and assistant coach, 1965-82

When I left football the first time to go into business, Coach Bryant told me I should give it a try while I was young. He said if I later found I couldn't live without football to call him.

He said if anyone could live without football, he shouldn't be a coach.
—*Jeff Rouzie*
Alabama player, 1969-73, and assistant coach, 1977-81 and 1991-present

When I went into professional football from Alabama, I thought everybody probably knew about the same about the game as I did, but I saw mistakes made in the pros that Coach Bryant had covered when I was a sophomore. I was amazed by how many little things I'd learned from Coach Bryant that other players and coaches from other schools didn't know or teach.

A good example is punting out of bounds on short punts. Coach Bryant always taught his punters to kick out of bounds to the left if they were right-footed kickers, never to the right. Punting to the right increases the chance of a shank going out of bounds short ten fold. I saw it happen once in the pros when our punter shanked one out for about five net yards. Later I slipped over to him and told him what I had learned at Alabama, even though I wasn't a punter, and he said, "Gee, I never heard that, and it's so obvious when you think about it."

When I was quarterback for the Atlanta Falcons, I had another experience that showed how thorough Coach Bryant was. We had a back who made a long run and was winded when he came back to the huddle, so I sent him off the field and waved his backup on.

After the game, Coach Marion Campbell mentioned it to me and said that he'd handle the substitutions, if I didn't mind. I explained that at Alabama, Coach Bryant had taught his quarterbacks to be alert for that situation, and in case the coaches missed it, to send the tired back off and get a fresh one in, and that I was just doing what I thought was the proper thing. Coach Campbell

said, "Hey, that's pretty smart," so I continued to do it.

I never knew any coach who covered the details like Coach Bryant did, and I say that after playing ten years of pro football and being around a lot of coaches and players from other colleges. He was a terrific coach who always had his teams prepared to play.
—*Scott Hunter*
Alabama player, 1967-70

I was doing some background research before Coach Bryant's 200th win [which came against Southern Cal in Los Angeles in the first game of the 1971 season], and asked Coach Bryant about the big games during his career.

He recalled maybe 35 games and talked about them, including reciting the scores all the way back to the 1945 season at Maryland, where he started out as a head coach.

When we finished, he suggested I check the scores of the games and when I checked he had missed only one score by one point and it was a Kentucky game back about 1950.

That was typical of him. He never forgot a single detail about anything, and that was one of the things that made him unique and such a great coach.
—*Kirk McNair*
Alabama assistant sports information director, 1970-73, and sports information director, 1973-79

As athletic director at the University, I have a unique perspective of Coach Bryant.

Sitting in this desk, I can see the results of his work every day. I see things he did 20 or 30 years ago that help make my job easier and our program better.

He built a solid foundation for our athletic programs, just as Coach Crisp and Coach Thomas and others had done before him.

He established principles and standards at the University of Alabama that continue to help us to be successful today.
—*Cecil "Hootie" Ingram*
Alabama All-SEC player, 1951-54, and Alabama athletic director, 1990-1995

We used to spend a great deal of time in staff meetings after practice, and a lot of that time in the days before platoon football would be spent with Coach Bryant at the blackboard.

He'd take 30-40 minutes sometimes in discussion of the best 11 players on offense, the best 11 on defense, and the best 11 players period.

Coach Bryant spent a lot of time on that because

he wanted to know and he wanted the coaches to know who to have in the games at the most critical times.
—Clem Gryska
Alabama assistant coach and assistant athletic director, 1960-82

We had a pretty good football team at Kentucky in 1950 and won the Southeastern Conference championship for the first time in the school's history [and to date].

Our first game of the season was against North Dakota; and we ended up winning it, 83-0. We knew they didn't have much of a team going into the game because when Coach Dick Holway gave his scouting report prior to the game Coach Bryant asked him what they did best and Holway said "Nothing; they don't even come out of the huddle well."

We ran up a pretty big lead in the first half, and Coach Bryant sent the first team to the practice field to run windsprints during the second half. He didn't even let us stay on the sideline and watch the rest of the game. He wanted to be sure we got a good workout since we hadn't worked too hard in the game.
—Pat James
Kentucky player, 1948-50, and assistant coach, 1951 and 1953; Texas A&M assistant coach, 1954-57; and Alabama assistant coach, 1958-63

It is difficult to capture the moment in words. You can't put into words the sounds, the smells, the feeling, the intensity of a practice session at Texas A&M in 1954 or 1955 when Coach Bryant was building our teams there.

But I remember one day I was playing defense, and I didn't quite get to the pile on a play before it was over. All of a sudden somebody hit me in the back and knocked me into the pile. It was Coach Bryant, and the next time I got there, and I got there every time from then on.
—John David Crow
Heisman Trophy winner as Texas A&M player, 1954-57; Alabama assistant coach, 1969-71

I was officiating as the offensive linemen hit the blocking sled during the mid-sixties, and I was watching for any holding violations. The rules were different then. If a player's hands got away from the body, it was holding, and I threw a flag any time a player's hands got away from his body.

Cecil Dowdy was in the group, and his hands got away from his body once as he hit the sled, but I didn't throw a flag because he had sort of slipped and had caught himself on the sled. Cecil was a great player [All-America] and had great techniques. I did mention it to Cecil, though, and about the same time I heard Coach Bryant turn on the megaphone.

"Maybe our guy won't call that, but they'll call it in the game," he said, talking to Cecil. I don't know how he saw it; we must have been a hundred yards from his tower, but that's the way he was. He saw everything on that field.
—Eddie Conyers
Alabama football practice official, 1960-82

Coach Stallings used to tell the story about Coach Bryant and the Texas A&M coaches watching a film of a high school game we [Gainesville, Texas] played against Cleburne in the mud with the temperature about two degrees above zero.

They were looking at my brother Jack, a halfback who was one of the top prospects in the state that year and who later signed with Oklahoma.

"I don't know about that Holt boy, but I'll take that number 64," Coach Bryant said while watching the film. He didn't know at the time that we were brothers. I was just a junior and played center and linebacker at 145 pounds.

I don't know what Coach Bryant saw in me on that film, but he saw something. He had a gift for that, and he also worked at it. He had a way of finding people who were self-motivated the way he was.

I don't know how he did it, looking at a piece of fuzzy, two-dimensional, black and white game film, but he could see something.
—Darwin Holt
Texas A&M player, 1957; Alabama player, 1960-61

John Mitchell was the first black player to play in a game for Alabama, starting at defensive end against Southern Cal in September 1971, in Los Angeles, and it is interesting that he played first against Southern Cal because Coach Bryant practically stole him from Southern Cal coach John McKay.

Coach Bryant and Coach McKay were at some function in Houston in December 1970, just before the Alabama-Oklahoma game in the Astro-Bluebonnet Bowl, when Coach McKay mentioned an Arizona junior college player he was going to sign the next day. McKay mentioned it because the player was from Mobile, Alabama, but he refused to tell Coach Bryant the player's name.

Somehow, before the evening was over, Coach Bryant managed to find out that the player's name was John Mitchell, and he called me and told me to track him down. Within two hours, I had Coach Bryant on the telephone with John Mitchell, and he

Coach Bryant and long-time security escort Billy Varner

talked him into holding off on signing with Southern Cal until we could talk with him.

The morning after the bowl game, Clem Gryska, Pat Dye and I and our wives were on the plane to Mobile, where we met with John and took him and his high school coach out to dinner.

We went to one of the finest restaurants in Mobile, and I doubt any blacks had been in there before, because a few people got up and left when we sat down. It was 1971, but that's the way it was then. If John went in there today, they'd line up to get his autograph.

Judge Ferrell McRae helped us recruit John, and we finally signed him, beating out Miami and Southern Cal.

We couldn't have picked a better person than John Mitchell to represent Alabama and to be our first black player. He ended up making All-America and playing in the Senior Bowl game in Mobile, and of course he was All-Southeastern Conference. He was also elected a permanent captain as a senior and later became an assistant coach at Alabama.

I've always been proud to have been a part of John Mitchell's signing with Alabama, and Coach Bryant was proud of his part in it, too.
—*Hayden Riley*
Alabama assistant coach, assistant athletic director, head baseball and basketball coach, 1958-75

Everything Paul did as a player at Alabama— every practice, every day— he gave 110 percent, just the way he always talked about it. He did

everything to the best of his ability. He gave every ounce of energy and went full speed, even if we were having dummy drills.
—*Young Boozer*
Bryant teammate at Alabama; long-time friend and business associate

I was looking forward to going to Junction in the the fall of 1954 for football practice with Texas A&M, but being a freshman, I was left behind. Only the players eligible for the 1954 season made the trip.

I watched two or three buses with over 100 players leave the campus, and two weeks later I watched one bus half loaded with players [27] come back.

I'd only been to church camps and had been disappointed that I hadn't been taken along. I learned from those players who survived and came back that Junction wasn't much like the church camps I'd been too, so I wasn't quite as disappointed after that.
—*John David Crow*
Heisman Trophy winner as Texas A&M player, 1954-57; Alabama assistant coach, 1969-71

Coach Bryant hated penalties, and he was the first coach I ever heard of that used an official at practice every day to call any penalties. He started it in about 1959, I think, and it was an everyday thing. He wanted the officials to be picky about it, too. He worked at avoiding penalties, and he wanted total discipline on the field.

I remember New York Jets coach Weeb Ewbank coming to a practice in the mid-sixties and taking note of my officiating at practice. He asked what I did and seemed to think it was a great idea.

I don't know if anyone did it before Coach Bryant, but I doubt anyone was as conscious of avoiding penalties as Coach Bryant was. It was just one of the many, many things he worked on that helped his teams win.
—*Eddie Conyers*
Alabama football practice official, 1960-82

I had been with the University of Alabama as a pilot for four years, and I had tried several times to get Dr. Frank Rose [UA president] to let me have a state car, but he had never done so.

I had a car, but it was a pretty old one, and I wasn't very proud of it, especially for special people or guests who might need a ride to or from the airport.

Once after a trip, I drove Coach Bryant home, and I apologized for my old car, saying I'd been trying to get a new one with no success.

When he got out of the car at home, he told me to come by his office the next morning at nine o'clock. When I went in to see him the next day, he told me I had a new car, and to go pick it up.

That's an example of the way he was and what he could do. He could make things happen, and it didn't take him long to do it.
—*Woody Hatchett*
University of Alabama pilot, 1964-82

I've never told this before, but I guess it's time to confess. I was a Southeastern Conference football official for 15 years, and I worked a lot of Kentucky games when Coach Bryant was head coach there [1946-53].

I worked the Kentucky-Tennessee game in about 1950, but Coach Bryant scratched me from the game the next year. We were friends, and I thought there must be some mistake, so I had someone check with him for me to be sure he didn't want me working the game.

Coach Bryant told the go-between that "Sington is a heck of an official, but he has a thousand eyes; he sees too much."

I got back on his officiating list again later, of course, and we always remained friends.
—*Fred Sington*
Alabama All-America tackle, 1927-30, long-time SEC football official and active Alabama alumnus

Most people think of Coach Bryant as just the football coach, but he was athletic director, too, and he thought about that area of his responsibility also, especially when it came to money.

A good example came on the first day of spring practice one year. I was working with the kickers, just learning their names and getting a look at each one. We had about 20 walk-ons out there that day.

Coach Bryant was riding around in his golf cart, taking a look at each group. He circled our group a couple of times, then stopped and called me over.

"You've got too many kickers," he said.

I didn't think I understood him and asked again what he had said. He said again, "You've got too many kickers. Can you imagine how much soap and water that many kickers will use?"

I got busy evaluating them and trimming the roster that same day.
—*Tommy Brooker*
Alabama player, 1958-61, and volunteer kicking coach, 1966-82

Coach Bryant had a certain instinct about games and other teams. He was very adaptable. He would change at any time if he thought an idea would help his program.

I recall a boat trip a couple of days before the 1966 Orange Bowl game. He got me over to the side and told me to forget the conventional way of calling plays. He didn't feel we could stop Nebraska, so he decided that we needed to pass on any down at any place on the field.

That was a dramatic shift from his normal philosophy. But he accurately anticipated that we would have to score a lot of points.

I opened the game offensively by throwing a tackle-eligible pass for 17 yards, and had completed 17 of 25 for 258 yards and two touchdowns for a 24-7 lead by halftime.

The wide-open offense must have made Coach Bryant a little nervous, because he sent in a substitute guard near the end of the first half with a message, and the guard's exact words from Coach Bryant were, "You don't have to pass on every down!"

I threw only four passes [three completions for 38 yards] in the second half. We won the game, 39-28, for the national championship.
—*Steve Sloan*
Alabama player, 1962-65, and assistant coach, 1968-70

Coach Bryant picked up on every little thing that might make a difference, and made sure we had it in our plans.

I remember we were playing Tulane in Mobile in 1959, and it was foggy and the lights were weak, and Billy Richardson was having trouble handling the punts.

Coach Bryant asked Billy about it and Billy said it wasn't the fog or lighting as much as it was the spin on the football because Tulane had a left-footed kicker.

On Monday morning, Coach Bryant told us to find a left-footed kicker, and that's how Goobie [Laurien] Stapp got to be our punter. Goobie was a versatile player to begin with. He was a good runner and passer, and he turned out to be an outstanding left-footed punter.

Coach Bryant was the same with the soccer-style kickers. When he saw what they were doing, he called Clem Gryska and me in and told us to

Bryant joins New Orleans jazz band on arrival for Sugar Bowl game.

start looking for one, and he said he didn't care if we had to go to Australia to get him. Coach Bryant wanted every weapon available.
—*Hayden Riley*
Alabama assistant coach, assistant athletic director, head baseball and basketball coach, 1958-75

Coach Bryant didn't miss a trick. Those tearaway jerseys in the seventies are a good example.

We [Alabama] were behind against LSU in Birmingham in 1970, and Johnny Musso was about to score what would have been the winning touchdown when an LSU player grabbed him by the jersey at the three or four-yard-line and spun him around and tackled him. We ended up losing, 14-9, and we had tearaway jerseys the next week.

We went through a lot of those for the next few years before they ruled them out because they were expensive and all the other schools couldn't afford them.
—*Willie Meadows*
Alabama athletic equipment manager, 1965-82

Coach Bryant used to have a beautiful tailor-made gray suede coat. It was one of his favorites, and I always wanted one like it.

The kids finally bought me one like it, but a cheaper brand off the rack, and a pair of red checked pants. I couldn't wait to wear them at a Sugar Bowl game for the first time.

After our pre-game warmup, just before we went on the field for the game, I was in the locker room getting ready to go up to the pressbox.

Coach Bryant was in there as I was putting on my coat and he asked, "Where are you going with that coat?" I said, "To the pressbox." He asked me again before I caught on. He thought I had his coat, and I had to show him the label before he'd let me leave with it.

Here he was, just before a Sugar Bowl game and everything happening, but he still noticed that coat. That's how he was about everything. He didn't miss much.
—*Clem Gryska*
Alabama assistant coach and assistant athletic director, 1960-82

We almost got into trouble once at Alabama by signing too many freshmen football players. Coach Bryant called me in and said we'd offered scholarships to too many, and we'd better find a way out of it.

I read the rules, and found that there was no rule against allowing a player to sign a basketball scholarship and play football, so I told Coach Bryant about it.

"Dang, that'll save us," he said. "But they'll have to dress for the basketball games, too."

Some of that group turned out to be pretty good basketball players and played some for us, but I ended up with about 30 players on basketball scholarship for a year or two.

One of the other Southeastern Conference basketball coaches asked me how I was able to talk Coach Bryant into letting me sign so many basketball players, but I didn't tell him how it actually came about.

The conference office found out about it, though, and passed a rule limiting scholarships in each sport, and requiring that anyone playing football had to be signed to a football grant.

Coach Bryant didn't break any rules to my knowledge, and he didn't allow anyone else to break any, but he wasn't against bending them now and then.
—*Hayden Riley*
Alabama assistant coach, assistant athletic director, head baseball and basketball coach, 1958-75

6

His Records Remain Unmatched

"I'm still out there because I love it. I know I can't go on forever, but just to win that next game…. I'd still rather be flailing away at this than anything else in the world. It's the only thing that's left now—the only thing that's fun. I still get cold chills when it starts, when I finally walk on that field again."
—Paul "Bear" Bryant

HIS RECORD SPEAKS FOR ITSELF

The Bryant record speaks for itself: the winningest Division I college football coach in history with 323 victories; winner of six national championships; national coach of the year three times; Southeastern Conference coach of the year 10 times; 24 consecutive bowl games; national coach of the decade twice, and winner of 232 games in 25 years (1958-82) as Alabama head coach, an average of 9.3 wins per season at Alabama and 8.5 overall. His teams won 15 conference titles in 38 seasons, and Alabama was the winningest team in the nation during Bryant's quarter-century at his alma mater.

Bryant was the center of national attention in 1981 as he surpassed Amos Alonzo Stagg's record of 314 career wins. Alabama defeated Penn State, 31-16, in State College, Pa., to give Bryant a tie and then beat Auburn, 28-17, in the final regular-season game to give him 315 wins and the record. He added eight wins to his total in 1982, his final season, for the 323 total.

In years leading toward the record, Bryant had downplayed his attempt to surpass Stagg, but finally relented and said, "I don't plan to stop coaching, and I don't plan to stop winning, so we're going to break the record if I don't die."

On another occasion he quipped, "Heck, as long as someone has to be the winningest coach, it might as well be me."

Bryant remains the only college coach to win five Associated Press national championships, and he added a separate United Press national title in 1973 when the Associated Press poll placed Alabama fourth with an 11-1 record, giving him six national championships as a head coach. He also played on a national championship team at Alabama in 1934, giving him a part in seven national titles overall.

Overall, Bryant-coached teams placed in the nation's top twenty a total of 30 times in his 38 seasons as a head coach. In his 25 years at Alabama, his teams missed the final top twenty only three times: his first year in 1958, 1969 and 1970.

Page 124: Alabama players give Coach Bryant a victory ride after the 1962 Orange Bowl win over Oklahoma.

Bryant is the winningest Division I college football coach in history, with 323 career victories.

Alabama finished in the final top ten 19 times in his 25 years as coach of the Crimson Tide.

Bryant-coached Alabama teams accounted for two of the most impressive streaks in NCAA history, going 116-15-1 from 1971-81 while winning three national titles and posting a record of 84-11-4 from 1960-68 while claiming three other national championships.

Bryant's trademark was defense, something he had learned well as a player and assistant coach at Alabama in the thirties—and a tradition at Alabama long before that. His teams normally were among the nation's best in every defensive category, and he was proud of that fact.

"Some coaches have said I am too defense-minded," he once said. "But most of those who said that have ended up as athletic directors."

Bryant's teams recorded 94 shutouts during his 38 years, with his Alabama teams claiming 61 of those in his last 25 years. His 1961 Alabama national championship team recorded six shutouts and allowed only 25 points in 11 games. The 1961 and 1962 teams combined to shut out 10 of 22 opponents and allowed no more than seven points in a game over two seasons, prompting Bryant to quip, "They play like it's a sin to give up a point."

Bryant, however, did not dominate all opponents. He was 0-4 while at Alabama against Notre Dame in some of football's most dramatic and exciting games ever, and 0-2 against Alabama while at Kentucky. He also failed to win in his only meetings against Colorado, Oklahoma State, Santa Clara and William & Mary during his career. Except for those teams and Missouri (2-2-0), Southern California (2-2-0), Texas (1-7-1), Texas A&M (1-2-0) and UCLA (1-1-0), he had a career record of more wins than losses against every other team.

Bryant's record for most wins by an NCAA Division I coach could be challenged within a few years by two active coaches with more than 200 wins each. Penn State's Joe Paterno, who was 0-4 against Bryant, has 268 victories in 28 seasons as a head coach heading into the 1995 season, and could eclipse Bryant's mark of 323 within six seasons if he continues to coach and average 9.5 wins per season. Nebraska's Tom Osborne is the only other active head coach with more than 200 victories at 219. Osborne, 1-1 against Bryant, has averaged 9.9 wins per season over his 22-year career and must keep up the pace for 10 more seasons if he hopes to climb atop the win list. Bobby Bowden of Florida State had 249 total victories, but many of those were not in Division I.

Winningest Coaches in NCAA Division I College Football History

(Minimum 10 years coaching at Division I school)

Name	Years	Record	Avg. Wins Per Season
1. Paul "Bear" Bryant	38	323-85-17	8.5
2. Glenn "Pop" Warner	44	319-106-32	7.2
3. Amos Alonzo Stagg	57	314-199-35	5.5
*4. Joe Paterno	30	278-72-3	9.3
*5. Bobby Bowden	30	259-81-4	8.6
6. Woody Hayes	33	238-72-10	7.2
7. Bo Schembechler	27	234-65-8	8.7
*8. Tom Osborne	23	231-47-3	10.0
*9. LaVell Edwards	24	214-80-3	8.9
*10. Hayden Fry	34	213-162-10	6.3
11. Jess Neely	40	207-176-19	5.2
12. Warren Woodson	37	203-95-14	5.5
13. Eddie Anderson	39	201-128-15	5.1
14. Vince Dooley	25	201-77-10	8.0

*Active 1996.

Bryant's Record as Head Coach: 323-85-17

Year	School	W	L	T
1945	Maryland	6	2	1
1946	Kentucky	7	3	0
1947	Kentucky	8	3	0
1948	Kentucky	5	3	2
1949	Kentucky	9	3	0
1950	Kentucky	11	1	0
1951	Kentucky	8	4	0
1952	Kentucky	5	4	2
1953	Kentucky	7	2	1
1954	Texas A&M	1	9	0
1955	Texas A&M	7	2	1
1956	Texas A&M	9	0	1
1957	Texas A&M	8	3	0
1958	Alabama	5	4	1
1959	Alabama	7	2	2
1960	Alabama	8	1	2
1961	Alabama	11	0	0
1962	Alabama	10	1	0
1963	Alabama	9	2	0
1964	Alabama	10	1	0
1965	Alabama	9	1	1
1966	Alabama	11	0	0
1967	Alabama	8	2	1
1968	Alabama	8	3	0
1969	Alabama	6	5	0
1970	Alabama	6	5	1
1971	Alabama	11	1	0
1972	Alabama	10	2	0
1973	Alabama	11	1	0
1974	Alabama	11	1	0
1975	Alabama	11	1	0
1976	Alabama	9	3	0
1977	Alabama	11	1	0
1978	Alabama	11	1	0
1979	Alabama	12	0	0
1980	Alabama	10	2	0
1981	Alabama	9	2	1
1982	Alabama	8	4	0
TOTAL:		**323**	**85**	**17**

Bryant's Record as Player, Assistant Coach and Head Coach

As A Player	W	L	T
1933 Alabama	7	1	1
1934 Alabama	10	0	0
1935 Alabama	6	2	1
TOTAL:	**23**	**3**	**2**

As An Assistant	W	L	T
1936 Alabama	8	0	1
1937 Alabama	9	1	0
1938 Alabama	7	1	1
1939 Alabama	5	3	1
1940 Vanderbilt	3	6	1
1941 Vanderbilt	6	1	2
TOTAL:	**38**	**12**	**6**

As Head Coach	W	L	T
Maryland (1945)	6	2	1
Kentucky (1946-53)	60	23	5
Texas A&M (1954-57)	25	14	2
Alabama (1958-82)	232	46	9
TOTAL:	**323**	**85**	**17**
Composite Totals:	**384**	**100**	**25**

Bryant Records and Honors

• Won more games (323) than any other NCAA Division I coach in history

• Won more bowl games (15) than any other coach in NCAA history

• Won more national championships (six) than any other NCAA coach in history (1961, 1964, 1965, 1973, 1978, 1979)

• Coached Alabama to a top ten finish in the Associated Press poll 19 times in 25 years

• Carried Alabama to an NCAA record 24 consecutive bowl games

• Won more conference championships (15) than any other coach in NCAA history: 13 at Alabama (Southeastern), 1 at Texas A&M (Southwest), 1 at Kentucky (Southeastern)

• Competed in more bowl games (31) as a player and coach than any other coach in college football history

• Honored as national coach of the year more (three times) than any other coach in NCAA history (1961, 1971, 1973)

• Named national coach of the decade twice: 1960s by the past presidents of the NCAA and 1970s by the Football Writers Association of America

• Chosen Southeastern Conference Coach of the Century (1970) in a regional media poll

• Named Southeastern Conference Coach of the Year 10 times: 1950, 1961, 1964, 1965, 1971, 1973, 1974, 1977, 1979 and 1981

• First coach in NCAA history to win 100 football games in a decade (103-16-1 in the 1970s)

• Averaged 8.5 wins per season over a 38-year head coaching career (323 wins, 85 losses and 17 ties)

• Averaged 9.3 wins per season over a 25-year period as head coach at Alabama (232 wins, 46 losses and 9 ties)

• Averaged 10.3 wins per season over his last 12 years as head coach at Alabama (124 wins, 19 losses and 1 tie)

• Had a combined record of 384 wins, 100 losses and 25 ties as player, assistant coach and head coach

• Had a record of 72 wins and only 2 losses at Bryant-Denny Stadium, including an NCAA record 57 consecutive home wins from October 26, 1963, until November 13, 1982

• Had a record of 25 wins and no losses in Alabama homecoming games

• Had a record of 43 wins and 6 losses against head coaches who had either played for him or coached on his staff

• Inducted into the National Football Foundation College Football Hall of Fame in 1986

• Elected to *Sports Illustrated* Silver Anniversary

Bryant received an Honorary Doctorate of Law Degree from the University of Alabama shortly before his death.

All-America team 1960

• Inducted into the Alabama Sports Hall of Fame, 1969

• Inducted into the Arkansas Hall of Fame, 1964

• Selected Kentucky Citizen of the Year, 1950

• Named Southwest Conference Coach of the Year, 1956

• Served as President of the American Football Coaches Association, 1972

• Selected University Administrator of the Year for the State of Alabama, 1973, by the American Association of University Administrators for the State of Alabama

• Presented Presidential Medal of Freedom, 1983 (posthumously), by President Reagan

• Presented the Stagg Award, 1983, by the American Football Coaches Association in recognition of his outstanding service to the advancement of football

• Served as honorary chairman of numerous charities and actively participated in fund raising

Milestone Victories in Bryant's Career

#1—Maryland, 60-6 over Guilford College, 1945
#50—Kentucky, 14-6 over Florida, 1951
#100—Alabama, 19-7 over Tulane, 1959
#150—Alabama, 24-7 over Georgia Tech, 1964
#200—Alabama, 17-10 over Southern Cal, 1971
#250—Alabama, 23-10 over LSU, 1975
#300—Alabama, 45-0 over Kentucky, 1980
#314—Alabama, 31-16 over Penn State, 1981
#315—Alabama, 28-17 over Auburn, 1981
#323—Alabama, 21-15 over Illinois, 1982

Bryant's Record Against All Opponents

Team	Record
Alabama	0-2-0
Arkansas	4-1-1
Arkansas State	1-0-0
Auburn	19-6-0
Baylor	5-1-0
California	1-0-0
Chattanooga	1-0-0
Cincinnati	7-0-0
Citadel	1-0-0
Clemson	6-0-0
Colorado	0-1-0
Dayton	1-0-0
Duke	1-0-0
Evansville	1-0-0
Florida	12-2-0
Florida State	2-0-1
Furman	2-0-0
George Washington	1-0-0
Georgia	12-5-0
Georgia Tech	10-3-0
Guilford	1-0-0
Houston	9-1-1
Illinois	1-0-0
Kentucky	4-0-0
LSU	20-5-1
Louisiana Tech	1-0-0
Louisville	2-0-0
Marquette	2-0-0
Maryland	2-0-0
Memphis State	3-0-0
Merchant Marines	1-0-0
Miami	14-0-0
Michigan State	2-0-0

Mississippi	15-7-1
Mississippi State	27-2-0
Missouri	2-2-0
Nebraska	4-2-0
North Carolina State	2-0-0
North Dakota	1-0-0
North Texas State	1-0-0
Notre Dame	0-4-0
Ohio State	1-0-0
Oklahoma	2-0-1
Oklahoma State	0-1-0
Penn State	4-1-0
Rice	3-2-0
Richmond	2-0-0
Rutgers	2-0-0
Santa Clara	0-1-0
South Carolina	4-0-0
Southern Cal	2-2-0
Southern Methodist	4-2-0
Southern Mississippi	11-1-1
Tampa	1-0-0
Tennessee	17-13-4
Tennessee Tech	1-0-0
Texas	1-7-1
Texas A&M	1-2-0
Texas Christian	6-1-0
Texas Tech	2-1-0
Tulane	8-1-1
Tulsa	1-0-0
UCLA	1-1-0
Vanderbilt	25-2-2
Villanova	5-1-1
Virginia	1-0-0
Virginia Military	1-0-0
Virginia Tech	7-1-0
Washington	2-0-0
West Virginia	2-0-1
Wichita State	1-0-0
William & Mary	0-1-0
Xavier	4-0-0

Associated Press National Champion Coaches

Five Championships
Paul "Bear" Bryant, Alabama (1961, 1964, 1965, 1978, 1979)

Four Championships
Frank Leahy, Notre Dame (1943, 1946, 1947, 1949)

Three Championships
Bernie Bierman, Minnesota (1936, 1940, 1941)

Bryant displays intensity as he encourages the Tide against Mississippi State. MSU was one of many teams over which Bryant enjoyed a winning record. Under his leadership, the Tide had a record of 27-2-0 against the Bulldogs.

John McKay, Southern Cal (1962, 1967, 1972)
Barry Switzer, Oklahoma (1974, 1975, 1985)
Bud Wilkinson, Oklahoma (1950, 1955, 1956)

Two Championships
Red Blaik, Army (1944, 1945)
Bob Devaney, Nebraska (1970, 1971)
Dennis Erickson, Miami (1989, 1991)
Woody Hayes, Ohio State (1954, 1968)
Tom Osborne, Nebraska (1994, 1995)
Ara Parseghian, Notre Dame (1966, 1973)
Joe Paterno, Penn State (1982, 1986)
Darrell Royal, Texas (1963, 1969)

One Championship
Bobby Bowden, Florida State (1993)
Paul Brown, Ohio State (1942)
Dan Devine, Notre Dame (1977)
**Paul Dietzel, LSU (1958)
Vince Dooley, Georgia (1980)
LaVell Edwards, Brigham Young (1984)
*Danny Ford, Clemson (1981)
Lou Holtz, Notre Dame (1988)
Jimmy Johnson, Miami, Fla. (1987)
Ralph "Shug" Jordan, Auburn (1957)
Bill McCartney, Colorado (1990)
Johnny Majors, Pittsburgh (1976)
Dutch Meyers, TCU (1938)
Biggie Munn, Michigan State (1952)

Bob Neyland, Tennessee (1951)
Homer Norton, Texas A&M (1939)
Bernie Oosterbaan, Michigan (1948)
*Howard Schnellenberger, Miami, Fla. (1983)
Ben Schwartzwalder, Syracuse (1959)
*Gene Stallings, Alabama (1992)
Jock Sutherland, Pittsburgh (1937)
Jim Tatum, Maryland (1953)
Murray Warmath, Minnesota (1960)

*Former Bryant player and assistant.
**Former Bryant assistant.

United Press
National Champion Coaches

(Poll Began 1951)

Four Championships
Paul "Bear" Bryant, Alabama (1961, 1964, 1973, 1979)
John McKay, Southern Cal (1962, 1967, 1972, 1974)

Three Championships
Darrell Royal, Texas (1963, 1969, 1970)
Bud Wilkinson, Oklahoma (1950, 1955, 1956)

Two Championships
Woody Hayes, Ohio State (1957, 1968)
Tom Osborne, Nebraska (1994, 1995)
Joe Paterno, Penn State (1982, 1986)
Barry Switzer, Oklahoma (1975, 1985)

One Championship
Bobby Bowden, Florida State (1993)
Duffy Daugherty, Michigan State (1965)
Bob Devaney, Nebraska (1971)
Dan Devine, Notre Dame (1977)
*Paul Dietzel, LSU (1958)
Vince Dooley, Georgia (1980)
LaVell Edwards, Brigham Young (1984)
Dennis Erickson, Miami (1989)
**Danny Ford, Clemson (1981)
Lou Holtz, Notre Dame (1988)
Don James, Washington (1991)
Jimmy Johnson, Miami (1987)
Johnny Majors, Pittsburgh (1976)
Biggie Munn, Michigan State (1952)
Bob Neyland, Tennessee (1951)
Ara Parseghian, Notre Dame (1966)
John Robinson, Southern Cal (1978)
Bobby Ross, Georgia Tech (1990)
Red Sanders, UCLA (1954)
**Howard Schnellenberger, Miami (1983)
Ben Schwartzwalder, Syracuse (1959)
**Gene Stallings, Alabama (1992)
Jim Tatum, Maryland (1953)
Murray Warmath, Minnesota (1960)

*-Former Bryant assistant coach.
**-Former Bryant player and assistant coach.

American Football Coaches Association Division 1-A Coach of the Year Award

1935-Lynn Waldorf, Northwestern
1936-Dick Harlow, Harvard
1937-Edward Mylin, Lafayette
1938-Bill Kern, Carnegie Mellon
1939-Eddie Anderson, Iowa
1940-Clark Shaughnessy, Stanford
1941-Frank Leahy, Notre Dame
1942-Bill Alexander, Georgia Tech
1943-Amos Alonzo Stagg, Pacific
1944-Caroll Widdoes, Ohio State
1945-Bo McMillin, Indiana
1946-Earl "Red" Blaik, Army
1947-Fritz Crisler, Michigan

1948-Bennie Oosterbaan, Michigan
1949-Bud Wilkinson, Oklahoma
1950-Charlie Caldwell, Princeton
1951-Chuck Taylor, Stanford
1952-Biggie Munn, Michigan State
1953-Jim Tatum, Maryland
1954-Red Sanders, UCLA
1955-Duffy Daugherty, Michigan State
1956-Bowden Wyatt, Tennessee
1957-Woody Hayes, Ohio State
*1958-Paul Dietzel, LSU
1959-Ben Schwartzwalder, Syracuse
1960-Murray Warmath, Minnesota
1961-Paul "Bear" Bryant, Alabama
1962-John McKay, Southern Cal
1963-Darrell Royal, Texas
1964-Frank Broyles, Arkansas, and
          Ara Parseghian, Notre Dame
1965-Tommy Prothro, UCLA
1966-Tom Cahill, Army
1967-John Pont, Indiana
1968-Joe Paterno, Penn State
1969-Bo Schembechler, Michigan
1970-Darrell Royal, Texas, and
          **Charles McClendon, LSU
1971-Paul "Bear" Bryant, Alabama
1972-John McKay, Southern Cal
1973-Paul "Bear" Bryant, Alabama
1974-Grant Teaff, Baylor
1975-Frank Kush, Arizona State
1976-Johnny Majors, Pittsburgh
1977-Don James, Washington
1978-Joe Paterno, Penn State
1979-Earl Bruce, Ohio State
1980-Vince Dooley, Georgia
1981-**Danny Ford, Clemson
1982-Joe Paterno, Penn State
1983-Ken Hatfield, Air Force
1984-LaVell Edwards, Brigham Young
1985-Fisher DeBerry, Air Force
1986-Joe Paterno, Penn State
1987-Dick McPherson, Syracuse
1988-Don Nehlen, West Virginia
1989-Bill McCartney, Colorado
1990-Bobby Ross, Georgia Tech
1991-Bill Lewis, East Carolina
1992-**Gene Stallings, Alabama
1993-Barry Alvarez, Wisconsin
1994-Tom Osborne, Nebraska
1995-Gary Barnett, Northwestern
     *Former Bryant assistant coach
     **Former Bryant player and assistant coach

Bryant-Coached Teams Were Regulars on Top 20 List

Penn State's Joe Paterno (L) ranks fourth on the all-time NCAA win list but was 0-4 against Bryant.

Alabama teams won national championships six different seasons during Bryant's 25-year tenure as head coach of the Crimson Tide, making him the winner of more national crowns than any other coach.

The five Associated Press titles during the period gave Bryant the all-time record for AP championships, and his four United Press titles (1961, 1964, 1973 and 1979) gave him a share of the record for most championships in that poll.

Bryant's Alabama teams finished first in both polls in 1961, 1964 and 1979; won the AP championship in 1965 and 1978, and claimed the top spot in the final United Press International (coaches) poll in 1973.

Bryant-coached teams placed in the top twenty in the final polls 30 times during his 38-year career, missing only in 1945, 1946, 1947, 1948, 1954, 1958, 1969 and 1970. Alabama missed the top 20 in the AP poll in 1982, but placed 17th in the UPI poll.

Twenty-two of Bryant's 25 Alabama teams finished in the top twenty while five of his eight Kentucky teams and three of his four Texas A&M teams finished in the top twenty.

Teams coached by Bryant finished in the top ten a total of 23 times (22 times each in both the AP and UPI polls), with Alabama teams placing in the top ten twenty times in 25 seasons under Bryant. Fourteen of his teams finished in the top five in the UPI poll and 12 finished in the top five in the AP poll.

Final Rankings of Bryant-coached Teams, 1945-1982

Year	Team	Record	AP Poll	UPI Poll
1945	Maryland	6-2-1	Unranked	No Poll
1946	Kentucky	7-3-0	Unranked	No Poll
1947	Kentucky	8-3-0	Unranked	No Poll
1948	Kentucky	5-3-2	Unranked	No Poll
1949	Kentucky	9-3-0	11	No Poll
1950	Kentucky	11-1-0	7	7
1951	Kentucky	8-4-0	15	17
1952	Kentucky	5-4-2	20	19
1953	Kentucky	7-2-1	16	15
1954	Texas A&M	1-9-0	Unrnkd	Unrnkd
1955	Texas A&M	7-2-1	17	14
1956	Texas A&M	9-0-1	5	5
1957	Texas A&M	8-3-0	9	10
1958	Alabama	5-4-1	Unrnkd	Unrnkd
1959	Alabama	7-2-2	10	13
1960	Alabama	8-1-2	9	10
1961	Alabama	11-0-0	1	1
1962	Alabama	10-1-0	6	5
1963	Alabama	9-2-0	8	9
1964	Alabama	10-1-0	1	1
1965	Alabama	9-1-1	1	4
1966	Alabama	11-0-0	3	3
1967	Alabama	8-2-1	8	7
1968	Alabama	8-3-0	17	12
1969	Alabama	6-5-0	Unrnkd	Unrnkd
1970	Alabama	6-5-1	Unrnkd	Unrnkd
1971	Alabama	11-1-0	4	2
1972	Alabama	10-2-0	7	4
1973	Alabama	11-1-0	4	1
1974	Alabama	11-1-0	5	2
1975	Alabama	11-1-0	3	3
1976	Alabama	9-3-0	11	9
1977	Alabama	11-1-0	2	2
1978	Alabama	11-1-0	1	2
1979	Alabama	12-0-0	1	1
1980	Alabama	10-2-0	6	6
1981	Alabama	9-2-1	7	6
1982	Alabama	8-4-0	Unrnkd	17

Alabama Achievements Under Bryant

Paul "Bear" Bryant did not earn the title of college football's winningest coach for his 323 wins alone. During his 25 years at the University of Alabama, the Crimson Tide was the nation's winningest team with 232 victories.

Alabama won 103 games during Bryant's last ten years as coach, and was the only team in the country to win as many as 100 during that period. During Bryant's last five years, the Tide record was 50-9-1 for an .842 winning percentage, also the best in major college football.

Alabama's standing among major colleges during Bryant's 25-year tenure as head football coach (1958-1982):

	All Games		Regular Season	
1. Alabama	232-46-9	.824	220-36-7	.850
2. Penn State	219-59-2	.786	206-54-1	.791
3. Texas	217-58-5	.784	206-49-4	.803
4. Ohio State	194-56-8	.767	190-48-8	.789
5. So. Calif.	206-61-11	.761	196-57-11	.763
6. Arizona St.	205-66-1	.756	198-65-1	.752
7. Nebraska	211-69-5	.749	199-62-5	.758
8. Oklahoma	206-67-8	.749	196-62-5	.755
9. Arkansas	198-74-7	.722	191-66-6	.738
10. Michigan	184-76-6	.703	181-68-6	.722

Alabama's standing among major colleges during Bryant's last 10 years as head coach (1973-1982):

	All Games		Regular Season	
1. Alabama	103-16-1	.863	96-13-1	.877
2. Oklahoma	98-17-3	.843	92-15-3	.850
3. Penn State	99-21-0	.825	92-18-0	.836
4. So. Calif.	94-21-4	.807	88-19-4	.811
5. Michigan	93-22-3	.801	91-16-3	.841
6. Ohio State	93-22-3	.801	90-16-3	.839
7. Nebraska	96-24-2	.795	90-20-2	.813
8. Pittsburgh	92-25-2	.782	86-22-2	.791
9. Cent. Mich.	88-19-3	.772	86-19-3	.767
10. Notre Dame	85-28-2	.748	80-27-2	.743

Alabama's standing among major colleges during Bryant's last five years as head coach (1978-1982):

	All Games		Regular Season	
1. Alabama	50-9-1	.842	48-8-1	.846
2. Pittsburgh	50-10-0	.833	47-8-0	.855
3. Penn State	50-10-0	.833	48-9-0	.836
4. So. Calif.	48-9-2	.831	46-8-2	.839
5. Georgia	48-10-1	.822	47-7-1	.864
6. Nebraska	50-11-0	.820	48-8-0	.857
7. Brig. Young	51-12-0	.810	49-9-0	.845

Alabama players hoist Bryant on their shoulders following a bowl victory. Bryant's bowl record was 15-12-2.

8. Clemson	48-11-1	.802	44-10-1	.809
9. Oklahoma	47-12-1	.792	43-11-1	.791
10. Cent. Mich.	42-12-2	.768	41-12-2	.764

Bryant Coached 29 Bowl Teams

Bryant holds the record for most bowl games as a head football coach with 29 appearances in 38 seasons. He also went to a bowl game as a player at Alabama and another as an assistant coach at Alabama for a total of 31 bowl appearances.

Bryant began his bowl string as a member of the 1934 Alabama team which won the Southeastern Conference and national championship with a perfect 10-0 record, including a 29-13 victory over Stanford in the Rose Bowl. He returned to the Rose Bowl three years later as an Alabama assistant, when the Crimson Tide lost to California, 13-0.

Counting the Rose Bowl appearances as a player and assistant, Bryant went to eight different bowls, including the Sugar Bowl nine times as a coach. His teams went to the Cotton Bowl five times and the Orange Bowl six times. His teams also played in the Great Lakes, Liberty and Bluebonnet bowls.

As a head coach, Bryant's bowl record was 15 wins, 12 losses and two ties. Alabama won seven of its last eight bowl games under Bryant as he carried the team to an NCAA record 24 straight bowl games, including a 21-15 victory over Illinois in his final game after the 1982 season.

Bryant led Kentucky to four bowl games in eight seasons (1946-53) as Wildcat head coach and took Texas A&M to one bowl (Gator, 1957) in four sea-

Alabama teams won six national championships during Bryant's 25-year tenure.

sons. He started the record streak of 24 straight at Alabama when the Tide appeared in the 1959 Liberty Bowl.

Bryant's Bowl Record as Head Coach

Season	Bowl	Result
1946	Great Lakes	KENTUCKY 24, Villanova 14
1949	Orange	Santa Clara 21, KENTUCKY 13
1950	Sugar	KENTUCKY 13, Oklahoma 7
1951	Cotton	KENTUCKY 20, TCU 7
1957	Gator	Tennessee 3, TEXAS A&M 0
1959	Liberty	Penn State 7, ALABAMA 0
1960	Bluebonnet	ALABAMA 3, Texas 3
1961	Sugar	ALABAMA 10, Arkansas 0
1962	Orange	ALABAMA 17, Oklahoma 0
1963	Sugar	ALABAMA 12, Mississippi 7
1964	Orange	Texas 21, ALABAMA 17
1965	Orange	ALABAMA 39, Nebraska 28
1966	Sugar	ALABAMA 34, Nebraska 7
1967	Cotton	Texas A&M 20, ALABAMA 16
1968	Gator	Missouri 35, ALABAMA 10
1969	Liberty	Colorado 47, ALABAMA 35
1970	Bluebonnet	ALABAMA 24, Oklahoma 24
1971	Orange	Nebraska 38, ALABAMA 6
1972	Cotton	Texas 17, ALABAMA 13
1973	Sugar	Notre Dame 24, ALABAMA 23
1974	Orange	Notre Dame 13, ALABAMA 11
1975	Sugar	ALABAMA 13, Penn State 6
1976	Liberty	ALABAMA 36, UCLA 6
1977	Sugar	ALABAMA 35, Ohio State 6
1978	Sugar	ALABAMA 14, Penn State 7
1979	Sugar	ALABAMA 24, Arkansas 9
1980	Cotton	ALABAMA 30, Baylor 2
1981	Cotton	Texas 14, ALABAMA 12
1982	Liberty	ALABAMA 21, Illinois 15

Year-By-Year Game Results of Bryant-Coached Teams

Maryland Era
1945 (6-2-1)

60	Guilford	6
21	Richmond	0
22	Merchant Marine Academy	6
13	Virginia Poly	21
13	West Virginia	13
14	William & Mary	33
38	VMI	0
19	Virginia	13
19	South Carolina	13

Kentucky Era
(8 Years, 60-23-5)

1946 (7-3)

20	Mississippi	6
26	Cincinnati	7
70	Xavier	0
13	Georgia	28
10	Vanderbilt	7
7	Alabama	21
39	Michigan State	14
35	Marquette	7
13	West Virginia	0
0	Tennessee	7

1947 (8-3)

7	Mississippi	14
20	Cincinnati	0
20	Xavier	7
26	Georgia	0
14	Vanderbilt	0
7	Michigan State	6
0	Alabama	13
15	West Virginia	6
36	Evansville	0
6	Tennessee	13

Great Lakes Bowl

24	Villanova	14

1948 (5-3-2)

48	Xavier	7
7	Mississippi	20
12	Georgia	35
7	Vanderbilt	26
25	Marquette	0
28	Cincinnati	7
13	Villanova	13
34	Florida	15
0	Tennessee	0
25	Miami	5

1949 (9-3)

71	So. Mississippi	7
19	LSU	0
47	Mississippi	0
25	Georgia	0
44	The Citadel	0
7	SMU	20
14	Cincinnati	7
21	Xavier	7
35	Florida	0
0	Tennessee	6
21	Miami	6

Orange Bowl

13	Santa Clara	21

1950 (11-1)
SEC Champions

25	N. Texas State	0
14	LSU	0
27	Mississippi	0
40	Dayton	0
41	Cincinnati	7
34	Villanova	7
28	Georgia Tech	14
40	Florida	6
48	Mississippi State	21
83	North Dakota	0
0	Tennessee	7

Sugar Bowl

13	Oklahoma	7

1951 (8-4)

72	Tennessee Tech	13
6	Texas	7
17	Mississippi	21
7	Georgia Tech	13
27	Mississippi State	0
35	Villanova	13
14	Florida	6
32	Miami	0
37	Tulane	0
47	G. Washington	13
0	Tennessee	28

Cotton Bowl

20	TCU	7

1952 (5-4-2)

6	Villanova	25
13	Mississippi	13
10	Texas A&M	7
7	LSU	34
14	Mississippi State	27
14	Cincinnati	6
29	Miami	0
27	Tulane	6
27	Clemson	14
14	Tennessee	14
0	Florida	27

1953 (7-2-1)

6	Texas A&M	7
6	Mississippi	22
26	Florida	13
6	LSU	6
32	Mississippi State	13
19	Villanova	0
19	Rice	13
40	Vanderbilt	17
20	Memphis State	7
27	Tennessee	21

TEXAS A&M ERA
(4 Years, 25-14-2)

1954 (1-9)

9	Texas Tech	41
6	Oklahoma State	14

6	Georgia	0
7	Houston	10
20	TCU	21
7	Baylor	20
7	Arkansas	14
3	SMU	6
19	Rice	29
13	Texas	22

1955 (7-2-1)

0	UCLA	21
28	LSU	0
21	Houston	3
27	Nebraska	0
19	TCU	16
7	Arkansas	7
13	SMU	2
20	Rice	12
6	Texas	21

1956 (9-0-1)
SWC Champions

19	Villanova	0
9	LSU	6
40	Texas Tech	7
14	Houston	14
7	TCU	6
19	Baylor	13
27	Arkansas	0
33	SMU	7
21	Rice	7
34	Texas	21

1957 (8-3-0)

21	Maryland	13
21	Texas Tech	0
28	Missouri	6
28	Houston	6
7	TCU	0
14	Baylor	0
7	Arkansas	6
19	SMU	6
6	Rice	7
7	Texas	9

Gator Bowl

0	Tennessee	3

ALABAMA ERA
(25 Years, 232-46-9)

1958 (5-4-1)

3	LSU	13
0	Vanderbilt	0
29	Furman	6
7	Tennessee	14
9	Mississippi State	7

Bryant gives emphatic instructions to an assistant coach. His confident, take-charge attitude was one of the key ingredients in his successful coaching career.

12	Georgia	0
7	Tulane	13
17	Georgia Tech	8
14	Memphis State	0
8	Auburn	14

1959 (7-2-2)

3	Georgia	17
3	Houston	0
7	Vanderbilt	7
13	Chattanooga	0
7	Tennessee	7
10	Mississippi State	0
19	Tulane	7
9	Georgia Tech	7
14	Memphis State	7
10	Auburn	0

Liberty Bowl

0	Penn State	7

1960 (8-1-2)

21	Georgia	6
6	Tulane	6
21	Vanderbilt	0
7	Tennessee	20
14	Houston	0
7	Mississippi State	0
51	Furman	0

16	Georgia Tech	15
34	Tampa	6
3	Auburn	0

Bluebonnet Bowl

3	Texas	3

1961 (11-0-0)
National Champions
SEC Champions

32	Georgia	6
9	Tulane	0
35	Vanderbilt	6
26	N. Carolina State	7
34	Tennessee	3
17	Houston	0
24	Mississippi State	0
66	Richmond	0
10	Georgia Tech	0
34	Auburn	0

Sugar Bowl

10	Arkansas	3

1962 (10-1)

35	Georgia	0
44	Tulane	6
17	Vanderbilt	7
14	Houston	3

27	Tennessee	7
35	Tulsa	6
20	Mississippi State	0
36	Miami	3
6	Georgia Tech	7
38	Auburn	0

Orange Bowl

17	Oklahoma	0

1963 (9-2-0)

32	Georgia	7
28	Tulane	0
21	Vanderbilt	6
6	Florida	10
35	Tennessee	0
21	Houston	13
20	Mississippi State	19
27	Georgia Tech	11
8	Auburn	10
17	Miami	12

Sugar Bowl

12	Mississippi	7

1964 (10-1-0)
National Champions
SEC Champions

31	Georgia	3
36	Tulane	6

24	Vanderbilt	0
21	N. Carolina State	0
19	Tennessee	8
17	Florida	14
23	Mississippi State	6
17	LSU	9
24	Georgia Tech	7
21	Auburn	14

Orange Bowl

17	Texas	21

1965 (9-1-1)
National Champions
SEC Champions

17	Georgia	18
27	Tulane	0
17	Mississippi	16
22	Vanderbilt	7
7	Tennessee	7
21	Florida State	0
10	Mississippi State	7
31	LSU	7
35	South Carolina	14
30	Auburn	3

Orange Bowl

39	Nebraska	28

1966 (11-0-0)
SEC Champions

34	Louisiana Tech	0
17	Mississippi	7
26	Clemson	0
11	Tennessee	10
42	Vanderbilt	6
27	Mississippi State	14
21	LSU	0
24	South Carolina	0
34	So. Mississippi	0
31	Auburn	0

Sugar Bowl

34	Nebraska	7

1967 (8-2-1)

37	Florida State	37
25	So. Mississippi	3
21	Mississippi	7
35	Vanderbilt	21
13	Tennessee	24
13	Clemson	10
13	Mississippi State	0
7	LSU	6
17	South Carolina	0

Cotton Bowl

16	Texas A&M	20

Bryant receives the 1979 Sugar Bowl trophy from Arkansas coach Lou Holtz after Alabama's 24-9 win over the Razorbacks.

1968 (8-3-0)

14	Virginia Tech	7
17	So. Mississippi	14
8	Mississippi	10
31	Vanderbilt	7
9	Tennessee	10
21	Clemson	14
20	Mississippi State	13
16	LSU	7
14	Miami	6
24	Auburn	16

Gator Bowl

10	Missouri	35

1969 (6-5-0)

17	Virginia Tech	13
63	So. Mississippi	14
33	Mississippi	32
10	Vanderbilt	14
14	Tennessee	41
38	Clemson	13
23	Mississippi State	19
15	LSU	20
42	Miami	6
26	Auburn	49

Liberty Bowl

33	Colorado	47

1970 (6-5-1)

21	Southern Cal	42
51	Virginia Tech	18
46	Florida	15
3	Mississippi	48
35	Vanderbilt	11
0	Tennessee	24
30	Houston	21
35	Mississippi State	6
9	LSU	14
32	Miami	8
28	Auburn	33

Astro-Bluebonnet

24	Oklahoma	24

1971 (11-1-0)
SEC Champions

17	Southern Cal	10
42	So. Mississippi	6
38	Florida	0
40	Mississippi	6
42	Vanderbilt	0
32	Tennessee	15
34	Houston	20
41	Mississippi State	10
14	LSU	7
31	Miami	3
31	Auburn	7

Bryant and Illinois coach Mike White at the press conference following the 1982 Liberty Bowl, his final game, in which the Tide beat the Illini, 21-15.

Orange Bowl

6	Nebraska	38

1972 (10-2-0)
SEC Champions

35	Duke	12
35	Kentucky	0
48	Vanderbilt	21
25	Georgia	7
24	Florida	7
17	Tennessee	10
48	So. Mississippi	11
58	Mississippi State	14
35	LSU	21
52	Virginia Tech	13
16	Auburn	17

Cotton Bowl

13	Texas	17

1973 (11-1-0)
UPI National Champions
SEC Champions

66	California	0
28	Kentucky	14
44	Vanderbilt	0
28	Georgia	14
35	Florida	14
42	Tennessee	21

77	Virginia Tech	6
35	Mississippi State	0
43	Miami	13
21	LSU	7
35	Auburn	0

Sugar Bowl

23	Notre Dame	24

1974 (11-1-0)
SEC Champions

21	Maryland	16
52	So. Mississippi	0
23	Vanderbilt	10
35	Mississippi	21
8	Florida State	7
28	Tennessee	6
41	Texas Christian	3
35	Mississippi State	0
30	LSU	0
28	Miami	7
17	Auburn	13

Orange Bowl

11	Notre Dame	13

1975 (11-1-0)
SEC Champions

7	Missouri	20
56	Clemson	0
40	Vanderbilt	7

32	Mississippi	6
52	Washington	0
30	Tennessee	7
45	Texas Christian	0
21	Mississippi State	10
23	LSU	10
27	So. Mississippi	6
28	Auburn	0

Sugar Bowl

13	Penn State	6

1976 (9-3-0)

7	Mississippi	10
56	SMU	3
42	Vanderbilt	14
0	Georgia	21
24	So. Mississippi	8
20	Tennessee	13
24	Louisville	3
34	Mississippi State	17
28	LSU	17
18	Notre Dame	21
38	Auburn	7

Liberty Bowl

36	UCLA	6

1977 (11-1-0)
SEC Champions

34	Mississippi	13

24	Nebraska	31
24	Vanderbilt	12
18	Georgia	10
21	Southern Cal	20
24	Tennessee	10
55	Louisville	6
37	Mississippi State	7
24	LSU	3
36	Miami	0
48	Auburn	21

Sugar Bowl

35	Ohio State	6

1978 (11-1-0)
AP Nat'l Champions
SEC Champions

20	Nebraska	3
38	Missouri	20
14	Southern Cal	24
51	Vanderbilt	28
20	Washington	17
23	Florida	12
30	Tennessee	17
35	Virginia Tech	0

35	Mississippi State	14
31	LSU	10
34	Auburn	16

Sugar Bowl

14	Penn State	7

1979 (12-0-0)
AP and UPI
National Champions
SEC Champions

30	Georgia Tech	6
45	Baylor	0
66	Vanderbilt	3
38	Wichita State	0
40	Florida	0
27	Tennessee	17
31	Virginia Tech	7
24	Mississippi State	7
3	LSU	0
30	Miami	0
25	Auburn	18

Sugar Bowl

24	Arkansas	9

1980 (10-2-0)

26	Georgia Tech	3
59	Mississippi	35
41	Vanderbilt	0
45	Kentucky	0
17	Rutgers	13
27	Tennessee	0
42	So. Mississippi	7
3	Mississippi State	6
28	LSU	7
0	Notre Dame	7
34	Auburn	18

Cotton Bowl

30	Baylor	2

1981 (9-2-1)
SEC Champions

24	LSU	7
21	Georgia Tech	24
19	Kentucky	10
28	Vanderbilt	7
38	Mississippi	7
13	So. Mississippi	13

38	Tennessee	19
31	Rutgers	7
13	Mississippi State	10
31	Penn State	16
28	Auburn	17

Cotton Bowl

10	Texas	12

1982 (8-4)

45	Georgia Tech	7
42	Mississippi	14
24	Vanderbilt	21
34	Arkansas State	7
42	Penn State	21
28	Tennessee	35
21	Cincinnati	3
20	Mississippi State	12
10	LSU	20
29	So. Mississippi	38
22	Auburn	23

Liberty Bowl

21	Illinois	15

7

Many Follow in His Footsteps

"I don't know what class is, but I can tell you when someone has it. You can tell it from a mile away."—
Paul "Bear" Bryant

A LEGACY OF SUCCESSFUL COACHES

Coach Bryant made lasting impressions on his players and associates. As a role model, he inspired many of them to imitate him or follow in his footsteps as a football coach.

In recognition of his contributions to college football, the College Football Coaches Association Coach of the Year award is named the Paul Bryant Award in his honor.

Forty-eight of his former players and/or assistants have become head coaches at the college or professional level. Many others have become high school coaches or assistants at the college or professional level. Others will likely become head coaches, pushing the number well past 50, as those wearing the Bryant brand are still in demand.

A. O. "Bum" Phillips, a Bryant assistant at Texas A&M and later head coach of the Houston Oilers and New Orleans Saints of the National Football League, once noted Bryant's contributions to the coaching ranks by saying, "There's no telling how many [young men] he put into coaching—or out of it by beating them."

There are obvious reasons why so many of his pupils went into coaching. First of all, they knew the subject well, having been taught by Bryant, who had been taught by Frank Thomas, who in turn had been taught by famed and fabled Notre Dame coach Knute Rockne. Secondly, the game of football was important to Bryant's pupils, just as it was to him. Thirdly, and most importantly, he helped many of them get started by giving them jobs on his own staff or by recommending them to other coaches. No other coach has spawned as many coaches simply because no other coach gave as much help to his former players. And finally, so many wanted to be like him because he was an admired leader.

Four former Bryant pupils have won national championships, including Gene Stallings at Alabama in 1992, Paul Dietzel at LSU in 1958, Howard Schnellenberger at Miami in 1983 and

Page 164: Mal Moore and Coach Bryant discuss offensive strategy during an Alabama game. Almost 50 of Bryant's former players and assistants became head coaches at the college or professional level.

Bill Battle, who played under Bryant at Alabama, served as Tennessee's head coach.

Danny Ford at Clemson in 1981.

Two of those national championship coaches (Stallings at Alabama and Ford at Arkansas) are still active in 1996. Jackie Sherrill at Mississippi State is the only other former Bryant pupil serving as a head coach in the 1996 season.

A number of former Bryant players and/or assistants hold prominent assistant coaching posts in 1996, however, and are poised to step into head coaching jobs. These include Bill Oliver (Auburn), Mike Riley (Southern Cal), Mickey Andrews (Florida State), Don Lindsey (Hawaii), Tony Nathan (Tampa Bay), Richard Williamson (Carolina Panthers), John Mitchell (Pittsburgh Steelers), Sylvester Croom (San Diego Chargers), Jeff Rouzie (Alabama), Mike Dubose (Alabama), Jimmy Fuller (Alabama), Curly Hallman (Alabama), Ray Perkins (New England Patriots), Jeff Rutledge (Vanderbilt), Louis Campbell (Arkansas), Jim Tanara (Eastern Kentucky),

George Pugh (Alabama-Birmingham), Neil Callaway (Houston), and Wally Burnum (South Carolina).

Bryant sent his own teams against teams coached by former pupils 49 times, winning 43 and losing just six. One of those wins came at Tennessee in 1972, when Alabama staged a shocking yet almost nonchalant comeback in the final two minutes to score two touchdowns and triumph, 17-10, over a Tennessee team coached by former Alabama player (1959-62) Bill Battle.

"Coach Bryant must know something I don't," a stunned Battle wondered out loud following the defeat. The comment prompted someone to quip, "Coach Bryant taught his pupils all they know, but not all he knows."

Bryant's Pupils Who Became Head Coaches

Name (Association): College/Professional Team

Andrews, Mickey (Player, Alabama): North Alabama, Livingston

Arians, Bruce (Assistant, Alabama): Temple

Battle, Bill (Player, Alabama): Tennessee

Blevins, Jim (Player and Assistant, Alabama): Jacksonville State

Boler, Clark (Player, Alabama): Bloomsburg State

Bradshaw, Charley (Player, Kentucky; Assistant, Alabama): Troy State

Callahan, Ray (Player, Kentucky): Cincinnati

Claiborne, Jerry (Player, Kentucky; Assistant, Texas A&M, Alabama): Kentucky, Maryland, Virginia Tech

Crow, John David (Player, Texas A&M; Assistant, Alabama): Northeast Louisiana

Cutchin, Phil (Player, Kentucky; Assistant, Kentucky, Texas A&M, Alabama): Oklahoma State

Dietzel, Paul (Assistant, Kentucky): LSU, Army, South Carolina

Dye, Pat (Assistant, Alabama): Auburn, Wyoming,

Former Bryant player Charlie McClendon later became the head coach at LSU.

East Carolina

Elias, Bill (Player, Maryland): Virginia

Ford, Danny (Player and Assistant, Alabama): Clemson, Arkansas

Fuller, Jimmy (Player, Alabama): Jacksonville State

Fuller, Leon (Player, Alabama): Colorado State

Hallman, Curley (Assistant, Alabama): LSU, Southern Mississippi

Hannah, Bill (Player, Alabama): Fullerton (Calif.) JC

Harper, Tom (Player, Kentucky): Wake Forest

Jamerson, Wilbur (Player, Kentucky): Morehead State

Kincaid, Al (Assistant, Alabama): Arkansas State, Wyoming

King, J. T. (Assistant, Texas A&M): Texas Tech

Lacewell, Larry (Assistant, Alabama): Arkansas State

Meyer, Ken (Assistant, Alabama): San Francisco 49ers

McClendon, Charles (Player and Assistant, Kentucky): LSU

McKenzie, Jim (Player, Kentucky): Oklahoma

Moore, Bud (Player and Assistant, Alabama): Kansas

Moseley, Frank (Assistant, Maryland, Kentucky): Virginia Tech

Oliver, Bill (Player and Assistant, Alabama): UT-Chattanooga

Owens, Jim (Assistant, Texas A&M): Washington

Pardee, Jack (Player, Texas A&M): Birmingham Barracudas, Houston Oilers, Chicago Bears, Washington Redskins, University of Houston, Houston Gamblers

Parilli, Vito "Babe" (Player, Kentucky): Chicago Wind

Pell, Charley (Player and Assistant, Alabama): Florida, Clemson, Jacksonville State

Perkins, Ray (Player, Alabama): Alabama, New York Giants, Tampa Bay Buccaneers, Arkansas State

Phillips, A. O. "Bum" (Assistant, Texas A&M): Houston Oilers, New Orleans Saints

Pugh, George (Player, Alabama): Alabama A&M

Riley, Mike (Player, Alabama): Winnipeg (CFL) and San Antonio (WLAF)

Robbins, Don (Player, Texas A&M): Idaho

Schnellenberger, Howard (Player, Kentucky; Assistant, Alabama): Oklahoma, Louisville, Miami, Baltimore Colts

Jackie Sherrill, head coach at Mississippi State, played for Bryant at Alabama.

Sharpe, Jimmy (Player and Assistant, Alabama): Virginia Tech

Sherrill, Jackie (Player, Alabama): Mississippi State, Texas A&M, Pittsburgh, Washington State

Sloan, Steve (Player and Assistant, Alabama): Duke, Ole Miss, Vanderbilt, Texas Tech

Stallings, Gene (Player, Texas A&M; Assistant, Texas A&M, Alabama): Alabama, Texas A&M, Phoenix Cardinals

Stanley, Jim (Player, Texas A&M): Michigan Panthers, Oklahoma State

Taylor, Loyd (Player, Texas A&M): Tarleton State

Tyler, Bob (Assistant, Alabama): Mississippi State, North Texas State

Williamson, Richard (Player and Assistant, Alabama): Memphis State, Tampa Bay Buccaneers

Wright, Jim (Player, Texas A&M): Wichita State

Bryant Helped Assistants Move Up Ladder

Bryant often gave his assistant coaches credit for their hard work and knowledge of football, and he allowed them to do a lion's share of the coaching on the practice field, especially in the last 10-15 seasons as he assumed a role he liked to call "the chairman of the board."

He recommended many of his assistant coaches for head coaching positions at other schools, helping them climb the ladder of success.

Alabama head coach Gene Stallings, a former Bryant player at Texas A&M and assistant at A&M and Alabama, is a good example of Bryant's relationship with his former pupils.

Bryant hired Stallings as an assistant at Alabama in 1958, bringing him from Texas A&M, where he had served a a graduate assistant in 1957 after playing for Bryant, 1954-56. Stallings served as an assistant at Alabama through 1964 and was then recommended for the head coaching job at A&M by Bryant. He ended up facing Bryant in the Cotton Bowl game following the 1967 season. Texas A&M defeated Alabama in the game, 20-16, and Bryant hoisted Stallings onto his shoulder after the game and gave him a brief victory ride, showing his fondness for his young protege.

"He was pleased for me, but he still didn't like it [the loss]," Stallings said of the game. "No matter who or what game, he wanted to win."

Stallings spent seven years at Texas A&M before resigning under pressure. He was about to leave coaching to enter business when Dallas Cowboys coach Tom Landry offered him a job based on a call from Coach Bryant to Landry.

Stallings spent 14 years with the Cowboys and then four seasons with the St. Louis and Phoenix Cardinals as head coach before returning to Alabama in 1990, again on the recommendation of Bryant, seven years following Bryant's death.

Bryant had approximately 100 different assistants during his 38-year career, and most of those were his own former players. Twenty-seven of those former assistants went on to become head coaches.

The following list of assistant coaches who worked with Bryant during his 38 years was compiled from media guides, programs, newspaper clippings, etc., and documents the scores of assistants who helped him become football's winningest coach. Information in parentheses indicates college and year of graduation, when available.

Gene Stallings, a player for Bryant at Texas A&M and an assistant at A&M and Alabama, is now at the helm of the Crimson Tide.

MARYLAND 1945
Carney Laslie (Alabama '33)
Frank Moseley (Alabama '34)
Ken Whitlow (Rice '41)
Al Heagy (Maryland '30)
Herman Ball (Davis-Elkins)

KENTUCKY 1946
Carney Laslie
Frank Moseley
Mike Balitsaris (Tennessee '42)
Joe Atkinson (Vanderbilt '42)
Bill McCubbin (Kentucky '40)

KENTUCKY 1947
Carney Laslie
Frank Moseley
Mike Balitsaris
Joe Atkinson
Bill McCubbin

KENTUCKY 1948
Carney Laslie
Frank Moseley
Joe Atkinson
Bill McCubbin

Ermal Allen (Kentucky '42)
Clarence Underwood (Marshall
    '38)
Ted Osborn (Ohio Wesleyan '31)
Charles Browning (Kentucky
    '48)
Bill Moseley (Kentucky '48)
Leo Yarutis (Kentucky '48)

KENTUCKY 1949
Carney Laslie
Frank Moseley
Ermal Allen
Clarence Underwood
Joe Atkinson
Ted Osborn
Bill McCubbin
Jim Brooks (Kentucky '49)
George Sengel (Kentucky '49)

KENTUCKY 1950
Carney Laslie
Frank Moseley
Ermal Allen
Clarence Underwood
Bill McCubbin
George Chapman (Georgia '35)
Richard Holway (Kentucky '50)
Unis Saylor (Kentucky '49)

KENTUCKY 1951
Carney Laslie
Ermal Allen
Clarence Underwood
Jim Owens (Oklahoma '50)
Charles McClendon (Kentucky
    '51)
Bill McCubbin
Vic Bradford (Alabama '39)
J.D. Langley (Chattanooga '43)
Pat James (Kentucky '51)
Paul Dietzel (Miami, Ohio, '47)

KENTUCKY 1952
Ermal Allen
Paul Dietzel
Clarence Underwood
Jim Owens
Phil Cutchin (Kentucky '43)
Jerry Claiborne (Kentucky '50)

KENTUCKY 1953
Ermal Allen
Jerry Claiborne
Phil Cutchin

Sam Bailey spent 28 years close to Bryant.

Jim Owens
Clarence Underwood
Pat James

TEXAS A&M 1954
Jim Owens
Phil Cutchin
Jerry Claiborne
Pat James
Willie Zapalac (Texas A&M '47)
Elmer Smith (Hendrix '31)
Tom Tipps (Sul Ross '38)

TEXAS A&M 1955
Jim Owens
Phil Cutchin
Jerry Claiborne
Pat James
Willie Zapalac
Elmer Smith
Tom Tipps

TEXAS A&M 1956
Phil Cutchin
Elmer Smith
Pat James
Willie Zapalac
Sam Bailey (Ouachita '49)
O.A. "Bum" Phillips (Stephen F.
    Austin '50)

TEXAS A&M 1957
Carney Laslie
Phil Cutchin
Willie Zapalac
Elmer Smith
Pat James
Sam Bailey
O. A. "Bum" Phillips
J. T. King (Texas '38)

ALABAMA 1958
Sam Bailey
Phil Cutchin
Jerry Claiborne
Carney Laslie
Pat James
Gene Stallings (Texas A&M '57)
Bobby Keith (Texas A&M '57)
Bobby Luna (Alabama '54)
Hayden Riley (Alabama '48)

ALABAMA 1959
Carney Laslie
Jerry Claiborne
Phil Cutchin
Pat James
Sam Bailey
Bobby Keith
Gene Stallings
Hayden Riley
Charley Bradshaw (Kentucky
    '50)
Bob Ford (Memphis State '55)
Larry Lacewell (Arkansas A&M
    '59)

ALABAMA 1960
Carney Laslie
Jerry Claiborne
Phil Cutchin
Pat James
Gene Stallings
Charley Bradshaw
Sam Bailey
Bob Ford
Hayden Riley
Clem Gryska (Alabama '49)
Dude Hennessey (Kentucky '55)

ALABAMA 1961
Sam Bailey
Phil Cutchin
Dude Hennessey
Clem Gryska
Charley Bradshaw

Gene Stallings
Carney Laslie
Pat James
Howard Schnellenberger
    (Kentucky '56)
Elwood Kettler (Texas A&M '55)
Don Cochran (Alabama '59)

ALABAMA 1962
Sam Bailey
Clem Gryska
Dude Hennessey
Howard Schnellenberger
Phil Cutchin
Pat James
Gene Stallings
Elwood Kettler
Carney Laslie
Bobby Keith
Jim Blevins (Alabama '60)

ALABAMA 1963
Sam Bailey
Howard Schnellenberger
Dude Hennessey
Ken Meyer (Denison '50)
Dee Powell (Texas A&M '57)
Jimmy Sharpe (Alabama '63)
Pat James
Gene Stallings
Carney Laslie
Clem Gryska
Jim Blevins
Charley Pell (Alabama '63)

ALABAMA 1964
Sam Bailey
Carney Laslie
Ken Donahue (Tennessee '51)
Howard Schnellenberger
Dude Hennessey
Dee Powell
Gene Stallings
Clem Gryska
Ken Meyer
Jimmy Sharpe
Richard Williamson (Alabama
    '64)

ALABAMA 1965
Sam Bailey
Ken Donahue
Mal Moore (Alabama '63)
Jimmy Sharpe
Clem Gryska
Dude Hennessey

Howard Schnellenberger, ex-Bryant pupil, has served as a head coach at Oklahoma, Louisville, and Miami and with the Baltimore Colts.

Pat Dye (Georgia '62)
Ralph Genito (Kentucky '50)
Carney Laslie
Howard Schnellenberger
Ken Meyer
Richard Williamson
Don Lindsey (Arkansas A&N '65)

ALABAMA 1966
Ken Donahue
Mal Moore
Jack Rutledge (Alabama '62)
Sam Bailey
Jimmy Sharpe
Pat Dye
Carney Laslie
Clem Gryska
Dude Hennessey
Ken Meyer
Richard Williamson
Ralph Genito
Don Lindsey
Charley Richards (Livingston '50)

ALABAMA 1967
Ken Donahue
Mal Moore
Jack Rutledge

Sam Bailey
Jimmy Sharpe
Pat Dye
Carney Laslie
Clem Gryska
Dude Hennessey
Ken Meyer
Richard Williamson
Ralph Genito
Tom Rogers (Delta State '56)
Charley Richards
Frank McGaughy (Memphis
    State)
Clayton Powers (Kentucky)

ALABAMA 1968
Sam Bailey
Mal Moore
Ken Donahue
Jack Rutledge
Jimmy Sharpe
Tom Rogers
Pat Dye
Carney Laslie
Hayden Riley
Clem Gryska
Dude Hennessey
Ralph Genito
Clayton Powers
Charley Richards
Steve Sloan (Alabama '65)
Tommy Tolleson (Alabama '66)

ALABAMA 1969
Ken Donahue
Mal Moore
Jack Rutledge
Sam Bailey
Pat Dye
Tom Rogers
Carney Laslie
Hayden Riley
Clem Gryska
Dude Hennessey
Jimmy Sharpe
Steve Sloan
John David Crow (Texas A&M
    '58)
Tommy Tolleson

ALABAMA 1970
Ken Donahue
Mal Moore
Jack Rutledge
Sam Bailey

Pat Dye
Clem Gryska
Dude Hennessey
Hayden Riley
Jimmy Sharpe
Tom Rogers
Steve Sloan
John David Crow
Ken Martin (Alabama '68)
Jim Tanara (UT Chattanooga
'65)

ALABAMA 1971
Ken Donahue
Mal Moore
Jack Rutledge
Sam Bailey
Pat Dye
Hayden Riley
Clem Gryska
Dude Hennessey
Jimmy Sharpe
John David Crow
Ken Martin
Richard Williamson
Bill Oliver (Alabama '62)
Bob Tyler (Mississippi '58)
Jim Tanara
Bobby Field (Arkansas '71)

ALABAMA 1972
Ken Donahue
Mal Moore
Jack Rutledge
Sam Bailey
Clem Gryska
Dude Hennessey
Jimmy Sharpe
Bill Oliver
Hayden Riley
Ken Martin
Pat Dye
Bobby Marks (Texas A&M '58)
Bud Moore (Alabama '61)
Danny Ford (Alabama '70)
Jim Tanara
Bobby Field

ALABAMA 1973
Ken Donahue
Mal Moore
Jack Rutledge
Bobby Marks
Clem Gryska
Sam Bailey

*Former Tide assistant Danny Ford is
now Arkansas head coach.*

Jimmy Sharpe
Hayden Riley
Dude Hennessey
Bill Oliver
Bud Moore
Pat Dye
Danny Ford
Ken Martin
Jim Tanara
John Mitchell (Alabama '73)

ALABAMA 1974
Ken Donahue
Mal Moore
Jack Rutledge
Bobby Marks
Clem Gryska
Dee Powell
Sam Bailey
Hayden Riley
Dude Hennessey
Ken Martin
Bud Moore
Bill Oliver
John Mitchell
Al Kincaid (Virginia Tech)
Paul Crane (Alabama '66)
Curley Hallman (Texas A&M
'68)
Jim Tanara

ALABAMA 1975
Ken Donahue
Mal Moore
Jack Rutledge

Bobby Marks
Clem Gryska
Dee Powell
Sam Bailey
Hayden Riley
Paul Crane
Curley Hallman
Dude Hennessey
John Mitchell
Bill Oliver
Al Kincaid
Shorty White (Jacksonville
State)
Louis Campbell (Arkansas '72)
Jim Tanara

ALABAMA 1976
Ken Donahue
Mal Moore
Jack Rutledge
Bobby Marks
Bill Oliver
Shorty White
Dee Powell
Louis Campbell
Paul Crane
Curley Hallman
Dude Hennessey
John Mitchell
Sylvester Croom (Alabama '75)
Jim Tanara

ALABAMA 1977
Ken Donahue
Mal Moore
Bobby Marks
Dee Powell
Jack Rutledge
Paul Crane
Bill Oliver
Shorty White
Sylvester Croom
Bryant Pool (East Texas State
'73)
Jeff Rouzie (Alabama '74)
Jim Tanara

ALABAMA 1978
Ken Donahue
Mal Moore
Bobby Marks
Dee Powell
Sylvester Croom
Bryant Pool
Jeff Rouzie

The 1979 Alabama coaching staff included (front, L-R), Bill Oliver, Bobby Marks, Jack Rutledge, K.J. Lazenby, Perry Willis, Shorty White and Mal Moore; (back, L-R), Mike Marks, Sylvester Croom, Ken Donahue, Andy Gothard, Jeff Rouzie, Dee Powell, Bryant Pool and Coach Bryant.

Jack Rutledge
Bill Oliver
Shorty White
Perry Willis (Alabama '70)

ALABAMA 1979
Ken Donahue
Sylvester Croom
Bobby Marks
Mal Moore
Bryant Pool
Dee Powell
Jeff Rouzie
Jack Rutledge
Bill Oliver
Shorty White
Perry Willis
K. J. Lazenby (Alabama '77)
Andy Gothard (Alabama '77)

ALABAMA 1980
Ken Donahue
Sylvester Croom
Bobby Marks
Mal Moore
Bryant Pool
Dee Powell
Jeff Rouzie
Jack Rutledge
K. J. Lazenby
Shorty White
Perry Willis
Louis Campbell

ALABAMA 1981
Ken Donahue
Sylvester Croom
Paul Davis (Mississippi '47)
Bobby Marks
Mal Moore

Bryant Pool
Dee Powell
Jeff Rouzie
Jack Rutledge
Bruce Arians (Virginia Tech '74)
Louis Campbell

ALABAMA 1982
Ken Donahue
Sylvester Croom
Bobby Marks
Mal Moore
Bryant Pool
Dee Powell
Jack Rutledge
Louis Campbell
Paul Davis
Bruce Arians
Steve Hale (East Carolina '78)
Murray Legg (Alabama '79)

Former Bryant assistant Curley Hallman later became head coach at Southern Miss and LSU.

Bryant Assistant Coaches, 1945-1982

(Alphabetical listing, with alma mater and year in parentheses)

Allen, Ermal (Kentucky '42), Kentucky, 1948-53

Arians, Bruce (Virginia Tech '74), Alabama, 1981-82

Atkinson, Joe (Vanderbilt '42), Kentucky, 1946-49

Balitsaris, Mike (Tennessee '42), Kentucky, 1946-47

Ball, Herman (Davis Elkins), Maryland, 1945

Bailey, Sam (Ouachita '49), Texas A&M, 1956-57, Alabama, 1958-69, 1972-75

Blevins, Jim (Alabama '60), Alabama, 1962-63

Bradford, Vic (Alabama '39), Kentucky, 1951

Bradshaw, Charley (Kentucky '50), Alabama, 1959-61

Brooks, Jim (Kentucky '49), Kentucky, 1949

Browning, Charles (Kentucky '48), Kentucky, 1948

Campbell, Louis (Arkansas '72), Alabama, 1975-76, 1980-82

Chapman, George (Georgia '35), Kentucky, 1950

Claiborne, Jerry (Kentucky '50), Kentucky, 1952-53, Texas A&M, 1954-55, Alabama, 1958-60

Cochran, Don (Alabama '59), Alabama, 1961

Crane, Paul (Alabama '66), Alabama, 1974-77

Croom, Sylvester (Alabama '75), Alabama, 1976-82

Crow, John David (Texas A&M '58), Alabama, 1969-71

Cutchin, Phil (Kentucky '43), Kentucky, 1952-53, Texas A&M, 1954-57, Alabama, 1958-62

Davis, Paul (Mississippi '47), Alabama, 1981-82

Dietzel, Paul (Miami, Ohio, '47), Kentucky, 1951-52

Donahue, Ken (Tennessee '51), Alabama, 1964-82

Dye, Pat (Georgia '62), Alabama, 1965-73

Field, Bobby (Arkansas '71), Alabama, 1971-72

Ford, Bob (Memphis State '55), Alabama, 1959-60

Ford, Danny (Alabama '70), Alabama, 1972-73

Genito, Ralph (Kentucky '50), Alabama, 1965-68

Goostree, Jim (Tennessee '51), Alabama, 1957-1983 (Trainer)

Gothard, Andy (Alabama '77), Alabama, 1979

Gryska, Clem (Alabama '49), Alabama, 1960-75

Hale, Steve (East Carolina '78), Alabama, 1982

Hallman, Curley (Texas A&M '68), Alabama, 1974-76

Heagy, Al (Maryland '30), Maryland, 1945 (Part-time)

Hennessey, Larry "Dude" (Kentucky '55), Alabama, 1960-76

James, Pat (Kentucky '51), Kentucky, 1953, Texas A&M, 1954-57, Alabama, 1958-63

Keith, Bobby D. (Texas A&M '57), Alabama, 1958-59

Kettler, Elwood (Texas A&M '55), Alabama, 1961-62

Kincaid, Al (Virginia Tech), Alabama, 1974-75

King, J. T. (Texas '38), Texas A&M, 1957

Lacewell, Larry (Arkansas A&M '59), Alabama, 1959

Langley, J. D. (Chattanooga '43), Kentucky, 1951

Laslie, Carney (Alabama '33), Maryland, 1945, Kentucky, 1946-50, Texas A&M, 1957, Alabama, 1958-69

Lazenby, K. J. (Alabama '77), Alabama, 1979-80

Legg, Murray (Alabama '79), Alabama, 1982

Lindsey, Don (Arkansas A&M '65) Alabama, 1965-66

Luna, Bobby (Alabama '54), Alabama, 1958

Marks, Bobby (Texas A&M '58), Alabama, 1972-82

Marks, Mike (Oklahoma State '74), Alabama, 1977-81 (Strength Coach)

Martin, Ken (Alabama ('68), Alabama, 1970-74

McClendon, Charles (Kentucky '51), Kentucky, 1951

McCubbin, Bill (Kentucky '40), Kentucky, 1946-51 (Part-time)

McGaughy, Frank (Memphis State), Alabama, 1967

Meyer, Ken (Denison '50), Alabama, 1963-67

Bryant and staff intently watch the play of the Alabama team.

Miller, Al (Northeast Louisiana '70), Alabama, 1982 (Strength Coach)

Mitchell, John (Alabama '73), Alabama, 1973-76

Moore, Bud (Alabama '61), Alabama, 1972-74

Moore, Mal (Alabama '62), Alabama, 1965-82

Moseley, Bill (Kentucky '48), Kentucky, 1948 (Part-time)

Moseley, Frank (Alabama '34), Maryland, 1945, Kentucky, 1946-50)

Oliver, Bill (Alabama '62), Alabama, 1971-79

Osborn, Ted (Ohio Wesleyan '31), Kentucky, 1948-49

Owens, Jim (Oklahoma '50), Kentucky, 1951-53, Texas A&M, 1954-55

Pell, Charley (Alabama '63), Alabama, 1963

Phillips, O. A. "Bum" (Stephen F. Austin '50), Texas A&M, 1956-57

Pool, Bryant (East Texas State '73), Alabama, 1977-82

Powell, Dee (Texas A&M '57), Alabama, 1963-64, 1974-82

Powers, Clayton (Kentucky), Alabama, 1967-68

Richards, Charley (Livingston '50), Alabama, 1966-68

Riley, Hayden (Alabama '48), Alabama, 1958-60, 1968-75

Rogers, Tom (Delta State '56), Alabama, 1967-70

Rouzie, Jeff (Alabama '74), Alabama, 1977-81

Rutledge, Jack (Alabama '62), Alabama, 1966-82

Saylor, Unis (Kentucky '49), Kentucky, 1950

Sengel, George (Kentucky '49), Kentucky, 1949

Schnellenberger, Howard (Kentucky '56), Alabama, 1961-65

Sharpe, Jimmy (Alabama '63), Alabama, 1963-73

Sloan, Steve (Alabama '65), Alabama, 1968-70

Smith, Elmer (Hendrix '31), Texas A&M, 1954-57

Stallings, Eugene (Texas A&M '57), Alabama, 1958-64

Tanara, Jim (UT-Chattanooga '65), Alabama, 1970-77

Tipps, Tom (Sul Ross '38), Texas A&M, 1954-55

Tolleson, Tommy (Alabama '66), Alabama, 1968-69

Tyler, Bob (Mississippi '58), Alabama, 1971

Underwood, Clarence (Marshall '38), Kentucky, 1948-53

White, George "Shorty" (Jacksonville State), Alabama, 1975-80

Whitlow, Ken (Rice '41), Maryland, 1945

Williamson, Richard (Alabama '64), Alabama, 1964-67

Willis, Perry (Alabama '70), Alabama, 1978-80

Yarutis, Leo (Kentucky '48), Kentucky, 1948 (Part-time)

Zapalac, Willie (Texas A&M '47), Texas A&M, 1954-57

8

He Was Both

Feared and Revered

"I have tried to teach them to show class, to have pride and to display character. I think football—winning games—takes care of itself if you do that."
—Paul "Bear" Bryant

BRYANT COACHED OVER 5,000 PLAYERS

Coach Bryant always gave his players credit for winning the games. "I've never won a game, but I've lost some," he said. "The players win the games." He genuinely cared about the players. Some of them knew it, but most didn't because of the tough image he presented and protected so well.

Over his 38-year career as head coach at Maryland, Kentucky, Texas A&M and Alabama, Bryant coached nearly 4,000 players, producing over 100 all-conference players, more than 60 All-Americas and a Heisman Trophy winner in John David Crow at Texas A&M in 1957.

Bryant was both feared and revered by his players. Fear often dominated, however, especially during the players' early days on his teams. Allen "Bunk" Harpole, a defensive lineman at Alabama, 1965-67, recalled his first opportunity to speak with Coach Bryant as a sophomore making his first road trip.

"Coach Bryant stopped as he walked by our table at breakfast and asked me my father's name," Harpole said. " I stuttered and choked and tried to speak, but I was so scared I couldn't say a word. Jackie Sherrill finally spoke up and answered for me."

Bryant had a special relationship with his quarterbacks, and with a purpose. He wanted them, as the on-field team leaders, to have the respect and confidence of the other players. To accomplish that, he spent extra time with them and often shared meals with them, transferring his own stature to them as he gave them extra lessons on the game of football. Pat Trammell, a quarterback from Scottsboro, Ala., who made the All-America team while playing for Bryant from 1959 to 1961, of all Bryant's players came closest to epitomizing Bryant's ideal. In his driving desire to win, he was in many ways a model of the coach. "Pat Trammell was," Bryant said of him, "the favorite person of my entire life. As a quarterback he had no ability. He

Page 176: Quarterback Pat Trammell led Alabama to a national championship in 1961, giving Coach Bryant the first of six in his career.

couldn't do anything but win. He was not a great runner, but he scored touchdowns. He didn't pass with great style, but he completed them. As a leader, I've never seen another one like him."

The relationship that Bryant had with his quarterbacks was partly responsible for his having five of them make All-America, nine all-conference and nine of them to play professional football.

Bryant coached a few second-generation players—sons of some of those who had played for him early in his career. Those included John David Crow Sr. and John David Crow Jr., and Bobby and Keith Marks.

Bryant Lettermen 1945-82

The following players are listed in programs, media guides, etc., as having lettered for Coach Bryant during his coaching career:

MARYLAND (1945)

Barkalow, Gerald
Barnes, George
Bissell, John
Bonk, Harry
Chisari, Thomas
Crosland, Robert
Daly, Leslie
Drach, Joseph
Evans, Francis
Fehr, Walter
Fritz, Emile
Gleasner, Donald
Greer, William
Johnston, Richard
Kinney, Eugene
McCarthy, Joseph
Morter, LaRoy
Pietrowski, Joseph
Piker, Robert
Poling, William

KENTUCKY (1946-53)

A
Adkins, Tommy, 1951-52-53

B
Babb, Jim, 1946-47
Bailey, John, 1952
Baldwin, John, 1950-51-52
Bassitt, Bob, 1952
Bentley, Charles, 1946-47-48-49

Bryant demonstrates blocking techniques during a practice session. He always gave credit where credit was due, saying, "I've never won a game, but I've lost some. The players win the games."

Bezuk, Bob, 1949
Bibin, Arvon, 1953
Blanda, George, 1946-47-48
Boller, Bill, 1946-47-48-49
Bradshaw, Charles, 1946-47-48-49
Brooks, Bobby, 1948-49
Browning, Charles, 1946-47
Bruno, Al, 1948-49-50

C
Callahan, Ray, 1953
Chambers, Bill, 1946
Claiborne, George, 1951
Claiborne, Jerry, 1946-48-49
Clark, Emery, 1949-50-51
Conde, Bill, 1949-50-51
Correll, Ray, 1951-52-53

Curnette, Delmas, 1953
Cutchin, Phil, 1946

D
Dawson, Bill, 1946
Donaldson, Gene, 1950-51
Dyer, Don, 1952

F
Farley, Bill, 1950-51
Ferrell, Doc, 1946-47-48
Fillion, Tom, 1951-52-53
Ford, Ray, 1948
Frampton, Don, 1948-49
Frye, Bob, 1950-51-52
Fucci, Dom, 1948-49-50
Fuller, Frank, 1950-51-52

G
Gain, Bob, 1947-48
Genito, Ralph, 1947-48-49
Griffin, Bill, 1946-47
Griggs, John, 1950-51-52
Gruner, Bucky,1951

H
Haas, Gene, 1946
Hamilton, Allen, 1946
Hamilton, Ed, 1949-50-51
Hanley, Jack, 1952-53
Hardy, Bob, 1953
Harper, Tom, 1952-53
Heinzinger, Ben, 1946
Hennessey, Larry "Dude", 1951-52-53
Hensley, Dick, 1946-47
Holt, Bobby, 1953 (Manager)
Holway, Dick, 1947-48-49
Hooper, Hayden, 1952
Howe, Jim, 1948-49
Hughes, Delmar, 1953
Hunt, Herbie, 1951-52-53

I
Ignarski, John, 1949-50-51

J
Jamerson, Wilbur, 1947-48
James, Pat, 1948-49-50
Jirschele, Don, 1951
Jones, Harry, 1950-51-52
Jones, Larry, 1950-51-52
Jones, Paul, 1949-51
Jones, Roscoe, 1946-47
Jones, Wallace, 1946-47-48

K
Karlbo, Lou, 1952-53
Kennard, Jim, 1946
Kirk, Harry, 1951-52-53
Klein, Norman, 1946-47-48
Koch, Joe, 1952-53
Kuhn, Dave, 1953

L
Lair, Matt, 1946-47
Lawson, Cliff, 1949-50-51
Leskovar, Bill, 1949-50-51
Lowry, Neil, 1952-53
Lukawski, Chet, 1950-51

M
Martin, Dick, 1947-48-49-50
Mason, Max, 1951

Mayo, Jim, 1952
McClendon, Charles, 1949-50
McDermott, Lloyd, 1947-48-49
Meeks, Gene, 1946
McKenzie, Jim, 1949
Mehaus, Johnny, 1948
Meilinger, Steve, 1951-52-53
Mills, Bradley, 1952-53
Mingus, Jerry, 1952
Mitchell, Dick, 1952-53
Moseley, Bill, 1946-47
Moseley, Doug, 1949-50-51

N
Netoskie, Don, 1953
Netoskie, John, 1949-50-51

O
Odivak, Nick, 1947-48-49

P
Paolone, Ralph, 1952-53
Parilli, Vito "Babe," 1949-50-51
Phelps, Don, 1946-47-49
Platt, Joe, 1952-53
Pope, Bob, 1948-49-50
Porter, Ray, 1947-48-49
Preston, Leonard, 1946-47
Proffitt, Jim, 1951-52-53

R
Rhodemyre, Jay, 1946-47
Rice, Dennis, 1946
Ridge, Don, 1946-47
Rogers, Harry, 1949-50
Rudd, O. T., 1951
Rushing, Dick, 1952-53

S
Sadler, Frank, 1946-47 (Manager)
Saylor, Unis, 1948-49 (Manager)
Schaffinit, Bill, 1948-49-50
Schenk, Jim, 1952-53
Schnellenberger, Howard, 1952-53
Serini, Walsh, 1946-47
Shatto, Dick, 1953
Smith, Calvin, 1951
Smotherman, Frank, 1947
Strange, Leo, 1953

T
Tunstill, Jesse, 1946

U
Ulinski, Harry, 1946-47-48-49

Coach Bryant instilled both fear and reverence in his players. It was an image he worked hard to achieve and protect.

V
Vance, Wendell, 1949-50

W
Walker, Charlie Bill, 1946
Wannamaker, Bill, 1948-49-50
Webb, Clayton, 1948-49-50
Weinman, Al, 1950-51 (Manager)
Willard, Miles, 1951-53
Wodke, Bob, 1948
Wooddell, Harold, 1949-50
Yarutis, Leo, 1946-47
Yowarsky, Walt, 1948-49-50

Z
Zampino, Al, 1951-53
Zaranka, Ben, 1947-48-49-50

TEXAS A&M (1954-57)

B
Barnett, Ray R., 1954

Beck, Kenneth, 1956-57
Brown, Darrell W., 1954-55-57
Bruton, Alfred L., 1954 (Manager)

C
Clark, Henry F., 1955
Clendennan, Robert J., 1955-56
Conrad, Bobby Joe, 1955-56-57
Crow, John David, 1955-56-57

D
Darwin, William B., 1957
Dendy, Billy G., 1955
Doucet, Raymond L., 1957
Dudley, Edward R., 1955

E
Easley, Robert A. Jr., 1954
Esquivel, Carlos, 1956-57

G
Gay, Richard C., 1956-57
Gilbert, John R., 1955-56-57
Gillar, George E., 1955-56
Godwin, Willis H. Jr., 1957
Goehring, Allen G., 1957
Goehring, Dennis H., 1954-55-56
Grant, Donald G., 1955
Greene, Taylor H., 1954
   (Manager)

H
Hale, Lloyd R., 1954-55-56
Hall, Charles L., 1954
Howard, Thomas V. Jr., 1956-57
Huddleston, Billy P., 1954-55

J
Johnson, George R, 1955

K
Kachtik, Edward D., 1954
Keith, Robert D., 1954-55-56
Kettler, Elwood N., 1954
Krueger, Charles A., 1955-56-57

L
Langston, James E., 1956
LeBoeuf, Gordon E., 1957
Lockett, Bobby J., 1956
Luna, Otie C., 1957

M
Marks, Robert E., 1955-56-57
McClelland, Don A., 1957

McGowan, Billy Joe, 1954
Milstead, Charles F., 1957
Munson, Joe U. Jr., 1957

O
Oliver, Gale G., 1957
Osborne, Carl R., 1955-56-57

P
Pardee, John P. "Jack," 1954-55-56
Payne, Howard, 1957
Pearson, Henry A., 1957
Powell, Jack E., 1955
Powell, William D., 1954-55-56
Price, Harold L., 1956

R
Robbins, Donald, 1955
Rollins, Gerald D., 1956 (Manager)

S
Sanders, Robert W., 1957
Schero, Joe E., 1954
Schmid, Joe H., 1957 (Manager)
Schroeder, William H., 1954
Simmons, A. L., 1956-57
Sinclair, Bennie C., 1954
Smith, Don G., 1956-57
Stallings, Eugene C., 1954-55-56
Stanley, James L., 1955-56-57

T
Tate, Marvin P., 1954
Taylor, Loyd F., 1955-56-57
Theriot, Sidney J., 1954
Tracey, John, 1956-57
Trimble, Murry H., 1955-56

V
Vaden, Frank S., 1955 (Manager)
Vick, Richard P., 1954

W
Watson, Donald A., 1954-55-56
Winkler, Lawrence E., 1954
Wolf, Herbert J., 1954-55
Wright, James, 1955-56-57

ALABAMA (1958-82)

A
Abruzzese, Raymond (HB), Philadelphia, Pa., 1960-61
Adcock, Mike (OT), Huntsville, Ala., 1981-82
Adkinson, Wayne (HB), Dothan, Ala., 1970-71-72
Allen, Charles (T), Athens, Ala., 1958-59

Coach Bryant is carried off the field atop his players' shoulders.

Allen, Steve (G), Athens, Ala., 1961-62-63
Allison, Scott (OT), Titusville, Fla., 1978-79-80
Allman, Phil (OB), Birmingham, Ala., 1976-77-78
Andrews, Mickey (HB), Ozark, Ala., 1963-64
Aydelette, William L. "Buddy" (TE), Mobile, Ala., 1977-78-79

B
Bailey, David (SE), All-SEC, Bailey, Miss., 1969-70-71
Barnes, Ronnie Joe (DE), Abbeville, Ala., 1973-74
Barnes, Wiley (C), Marianna, Fla., 1978-79
Barron, Marvin (G-T), Troy, Ala., 1970-71-73
Barron, Randy (DT), Dadeville, Ala., 1966-67-68
Bates, Tim (LB), Tarrant, Ala., 1964-65
Batey, Joseph D. "Bo" (OG), Jacksonville, Ala., 1976

Battle, William "Bill" (E), Birmingham, Ala., 1960-61-62

Baumhower, Robert G. "Bob" (DT), All-SEC, Tuscaloosa, Ala., 1974-75-76

Bean, Dickie (HB), Childersburg, Ala., 1966

Beard, Jeff (DT), Bessemer, Ala., 1969-70-71

Beard, Ken (T), Bessemer, Ala., 1963

Beazley, Joe (DT), Woodbridge, Va., 1979-80-81-82

Beck, Ellis (HB), Ozark, Ala., 1971-72-73

Beddingfield, David (QB), Gadsden, Ala., 1969

Bedwell, David (DB), Cedar Bluff, Ala., 1965-66-67

Bell, Stanley (E), West Anniston, Ala., 1959

Bendross, Jesse (SE), Hollywood, Fla., 1980-81-82

Bentley, Edward K. Jr. (DB), Sylacauga, Ala., 1970

Billingsley, Randy (HB), Sylacauga, Ala., 1972-73-74

Bird, Ron (T), Covington, Ky., 1963

Bisceglia, Steve (FB), Fresno, Calif., 1971-72

Blair, Bill (DB), Nashville, Tenn., 1968-69-70

Blevins, James Allen (T), Moulton, Ala., 1958-59

Blitz, Jeff (DB), Montgomery, Ala., 1972

Blue, Al (DB), Maitland, Fla., 1981-82

Bolden, Ray (DB), Tarrant, Ala., 1974-75

Boler, Clark (T), Northport, Ala., 1962-63

Boler, Thomas (OT), Northport, Ala., 1980

Boles, John "Duffy" (HB), Huntsville, Ala., 1973-75

Bolton, Bruce (SE), Memphis, Tenn., 1976-77-78

Booker, David (SE), Huntsville, Ala., 1979

Booker, Steve (LB), Huntsville, Ala., 1981-82

Booth, Baxter (E), Athens, Ala., 1958

Boothe, Vince (OG), Fairhope, Ala., 1977-78-79

Boschung, Paul (DT), Tuscaloosa, Ala., 1967-68-69

Bowman, Steve (FB), All-SEC, Pascagoula, Miss., 1963-64-65

Box, Jimmy (E), Sheffield, Ala., 1960

Boyd, Thomas (LB), All-America, All-SEC, Huntsville, Ala., 1978-79-80-81

Boylston, Robert W. "Bobby" (T), Atlanta, Ga., 1959-60

Bradford, James J. "Jim" (OG), Montgomery, Ala., 1977

Bragan, Dale (LB), Birmingham, Ala., 1976

Braggs, Byron (DT), All-SEC, Montgomery, Ala., 1977-78-79-80

Bramblett, Gary (OG), Dalton, Ga., 1979-80-81-82

Brannen, Jere Lamar (E), Anniston, Ala., 1958

Brewer, Richard (SE), Sylacauga, Ala., 1965-66-67

Britt, Gary (LB), Mobile, Ala., 1977

Brock, Jim (OG), Montgomery, Ala., 1981

Brock, Mike (OG), All-SEC, Montgomery, Ala., 1977-78-79

Brooker, Johnny (PK), Demopolis, Ala., 1982

Brooker, William T. "Tommy" (E), Demopolis, Ala., 1959-60-61

Brown, Bill (DB), Dekalb, Miss., 1982

Brown, Halver "Buddy" (G), All-America, All-SEC, Tallahassee, Fla., 1971-72-73

Brown, Jerry (TE), Fairfax, Ala., 1974-75

Brown, Larry (TE), Pembroke Pines, Fla., 1979-80-81-82

Brown, Randy (T), Scottsville, N.Y., 1968

Brungard, David A. (FB), Youngstown, Ohio, 1970

Bryan, Richard (DT), Vernoa, N.J., 1972-74

Buchanan, Richard W. "Woody" (FB), Montgomery, Ala., 1976

Buck, Oran (K), Oak Ridge, Tenn., 1969

Bunch, Jim (OG), All-America, All-SEC, Mechanicsville, Va., 1976-77-78-79

Busbee, Kent (DB), Meridian, Miss., 1967

Busby, Max (OG), Leeds, Ala., 1977

Butler, Clyde (OT), Scottsboro, Ala., 1970

C

Callaway, Neil (LB-DE), Macon, Ga., 1975-77

Callico, Kelly (DT), Fairhope, Ala., 1977

Calvert, John (G), All-SEC, Cullman, Ala., 1965-66

Canterbury, Frank (HB), Birmingham, Ala., 1964-65-66

Carroll, Jimmy (C), Enterprise, Ala., 1965-66

Carruth, Paul Ott (RB), Summit, Miss., 1981-82

Carter, Joe (RB), Starkville, Miss., 1980-81-82

Cary, Robert H. Jr. "Robin" (DB), Greenwood, S.C., 1972-73

Cash, Jeraull Wayne "Jerry" (E), Bogart, Ga., 1970-71

Cash, Steve (DL), Huntsville, Ala., 1980

Castille, Jeremiah (DB), All-America, All-SEC, Phenix City, Ala., 1979-80-81-82

Cavan, Peter Alexander (HB), Thomaston, Ga., 1975-76-77

Cayavec, Bob (OT), All-SEC, Largo, Fla., 1980-81-82

Chaffin, Phil (FB), Huntsville, Ala., 1968-69-70

Chambers, Jimmy (C), Fort Payne, Ala., 1967

Chapman, Roger (K), Hartselle, Ala., 1977-78

Chatwood, David (FB), Fairhope, Ala., 1965-66-67

Childers, Morris (B), Birmingham, Ala., 1960

Childs, Bob (LB), Montgomery, Ala., 1966-67-68

Ciemny, Richard (K), Anthony, Kan., 1969-70

Clark, Cotton (HB), Kansas, Ala., 1961-62

Clark, Tim (SE), Newnan, Ga., 1978-79-80-81

Clay, Hugh Stephen (G), Gadsden, Ala., 1969

Clements, Mike (DB), Center Point, Ala., 1978-79-80

Cline, Jackie (DT), McCalla, Ala., 1980-81-82

Cochran, Donald G. (G), Birmingham, Ala., 1958-59

Cokely, Donald (T), Chickasha, Okla., 1970-71

Colburn, Rocky (DB), Cantonment, Fla., 1982

Cole, Richard (DT), Crossville, Ala., All-America, 1965-66

Coleman, Michael (SE), Anaheim, Calif., 1978

Coley, Ken (DB), Birmingham, Ala., 1979-80-81-82

Collins, Danny (DE), Birmingham, Ala., 1976-77

Collins, Earl (FB), Mobile, Ala., 1980-81

Cook, Elbert (LB), Jacksonville, Fla., 1960-61-62

Cook, Leroy (DE), Abbeville, Ala., All-America, All-SEC, 1972-73-74-75

Cook, Wayne (TE), Montgomery, Ala., 1964-65-66

Cowell, Vince (OG), Snellville, Ga., All-SEC, 1978-79-80

Cox, Allen (OT), Satsuma, Ala., 1972

Crane, Paul (C-LB), All-America, All-SEC, Prichard, Ala., 1963-64-65

Crenshaw, Curtis (T), Mobile, Ala., 1961

Croom, Sylvester (C), All-America, All-SEC, Tuscaloosa, Ala., 1972-73-74

Crow, John David Jr. (HB), El Cahon, Calif., 1975-76-77

Crowson, Roger (FB), Jackson, Miss., 1968

Cross, Andy (LB), Birmingham, Ala., 1972

Croyle, John (DE), Gadsden, Ala., 1971-72-73

Crumbley, Allen (DB), Birmingham, Ala., 1976-78

Cryder, Robert J. (OG), O'Fallon Township, Ill., 1975-76-77

Culliver, Calvin (FB), East Brewton, Ala., 1973-74-75-76

Culwell, Ingram (HB), Tuscaloosa, Ala., 1961-62

D

Dasher, Bob (OG), Plymouth, Miss., 1981

Davis, Bill (K), Columbus, Ga., 1971-72-73

Davis, Fred Jr. (T), Louisville, Ky., 1964

Davis, Johnny Lee (FB), Montgomery, Ala., 1975-76-77

Davis, Mike (K), Columbus, Ga., 1975

Davis, Ricky (S), All-SEC, Bessemer, Ala., 1973-74

Davis, Steve (K), Columbus, Ga., 1965-66-67

Davis, Terry Ashley (QB), All-SEC, Bogalusa, La., 1970-71-72

Davis, Terry Lane (E), Birmingham, Ala., 1970

Davis, Tim (K), Columbus, Ga., 1961-62-63

Davis, William (DT), Fort Deposit, Ala., 1978

Davis, William "Junior" (T), Birmingham, Ala., 1967-68

Dawson, Jimmy Dale (LB), Excel, Ala., 1973

Dean, Mike (DB), Decatur, Ga., 1967-68-69

Dean, Steve (HB), Orlando, Fla., 1972-73

DeNiro, Gary (DE), Youngstown, Ohio, 1978-79-80

Dichiara, Ron (K), Bessemer, Ala., 1974

Dill, Jimmy (E), Mobile, Ala., 1962-63

Dismuke, Joe (OT), Gadsden, Ala., 1982

Dixon, Dennis (TE), Orange, Calif., 1967-68

Doran, Stephen Curtis (TE), Murray, Ky., 1969-70

Dowdy, Cecil (OT), All-America, All-SEC, Cherokee, Ala., 1964-65-66

Danny Ford was All-SEC while at Alabama from 1967-69.

Drinkard, Reid (OG), Linden, Ala., 1968-69-70

Dubose, Mike (DE), Opp, Ala., 1972-73-74

Duncan, Conley (LB), All-SEC, Hartselle, Ala., 1973-74-75

Duncan, Jerry (OT), Sparta, N.C., 1965-66

Duke, Jim (DT), Columbus, Ga., 1967-68-69

Durby, Ron (T), Memphis, Tenn., 1963-64

Dyar, Warren E. (T-E), Florence, Ala., 1972-73

Dyess, Johnny (RB), Elba, Ala., 1981

Dyess, Marlin (HB), Elba, Ala., 1958-59

E

Eckenrod, Michael Lee (C), Chattanooga, Tenn., 1973

Edwards, Randy (DT), Marietta, Ga., 1980-81-82

Elder, Venson (LB), Decatur, Ga., 1982

Elias, Johnny (MG), Columbus, Ga., 1981-82

Ellard, Butch (Mgr), Tuscaloosa, Ala., 1982

Elmore, Grady (K-HB), Ozark, Ala., 1962-63-64

Emerson, Ken (DB), Columbus, Ga., 1969-70

Quarterback Alan Gray (1979-81) receives instructions on the sidelines from Coach Bryant.

F

Fagan, Jeff (RB), Hollywood, Fla., 1979-80-81-82

Faust, Donald W. (FB), Fairhope, Ala., 1975-76-77

Faust, Douglas (DT), Fairhope, Ala., 1972

Ferguson, Charles M. (OG), Cuthbert, Ga., 1968-69

Ferguson, Richard (OG), Fort Payne, Ala., 1969

Fields, Paul (QB), Gardendale, Ala., 1982

Flanagan, Thad (SE), Leighton, Ala., 1974-75-76

Florence, Craige (DB), Enterprise, Ala., 1981-82

Ford, Danny (OT), All-SEC, Gadsden, Ala., 1967-68-69

Ford, Mike (DE), All-SEC, Tuscaloosa, Ala., 1966-67-68

Ford, Steven (DB), Tuscaloosa, Ala., 1973-74

Fowler, Conrad (SE), Columbiana, Ala., 1966-67-68

Fowler, Les (DB), Hartselle, Ala., 1976

Fracchia, Mike (FB), All-SEC, Memphis, Tenn., 1960-61-63

Fraley, Robert (QB), Winchester, Tenn., 1974-75

Frank, Milton (G), Huntsville, Ala., 1958-59

Frank, Morris (C), Huntsville, Ala., 1962

Freeman, Wayne (OG), All-America, All-SEC, Fort

Alabama's 1961 national championship team

Payne, Ala., 1962-63-64
French, Buddy (K), Decatur, Ala., 1963-64
Fuller, Jimmy (T), Fairfield, Ala., 1964-65-66
Fuller, Leon (HB), Nederland, Tex., 1959-60

G
Gantt, Greg (K), All-SEC, Birmingham, Ala., 1971-72-73
Gay, Stan (DB), Tuskegee, Ala., 1981-82
Gellerstedt, Sam (NG), All-America, All-SEC, Montgomery, Ala., 1968
Gerasimchuk, Davis (OG), All-SEC, Lomita, Calif., 1975-76
Gilbert, Danny (DB), Geraldine, Ala., 1968-69-70
Gilliland, Rickey (LB), Birmingham, Ala., 1976-77-78
Gilmer, Creed (DE), All-SEC, Birmingham, Ala., 1964-65
Gossett, Don Lee (MG), Knoxville, Tenn., 1969
Gothard, Andrew "Andy" (DB), Alexander City, Ala., 1975-76
Grammer, James W. (C), All-SEC, Hartselle, Ala., 1969-71
Grammer, Richard (C), Hartselle, Ala., 1967-68-69
Gray, Alan (QB), Tampa, Fla., 1979-80-81
Green, Louis E. (OG), Birmingham, Ala., 1974-76-77
Grogan, Jay (TE), Cropwell, Ala., 1981-82
Guinyard, Mickey (TB), Atlanta, Ga., 1981-82

H
Hall, Mike (LB), All-America, All-SEC, Tarrant, Ala., 1966-67-68
Hall, Randy Lee (DT), Huntsville, Ala., 1972-73-74
Hall, Wayne (LB), Huntsville, Ala., 1971-72-73
Hamer, Norris (DE), Tarrant, Ala., 1967-68
Hamilton, Wayne (DE), Okahumpka, Fla., 1977-78-79

Hand, Jon (DT), Sylacauga, Ala., 1982
Hand, Mike (LB, OG), Tuscumbia, Ala., 1968-69-70
Haney, James (RB), Rogersville, Ala., 1979
Hannah, Charles (DT), All-SEC, Albertville, Ala., 1974-75-76
Hannah, David (OG), All-SEC, Albertville, Ala., 1975-77-78-79
Hannah, John (OG), All-America, All-SEC, Albertville, Ala., 1970-71-72
Hannah, William C. (T), Indianapolis, Ind., 1958-59
Hanrahan, Gary (OG), Pompano Beach, Fla., 1973
Harkness, Fred (MG), Winfield, Ala., 1980
Harpole, Allen "Bunk" (DG), Columbus, Miss., 1965-66-67
Harrison, Bill (DT), Ft. Walton Beach, Fla., 1976
Harris, Charles (DE), Mobile, Ala., 1965-66-67
Harris, Don (DT), Vincent, Ala., 1968-69-70
Harris, Hudson (HB), Tarrant, Ala., 1962-63-64
Harris, Jim Bob (DB), All-SEC, Athens, Ga., 1978-79-80-81
Harris, Joe Dale (SE), Uriah, Ala., 1975
Harris, Paul (DE), Mobile, Ala., 1974-75-76
Hayden, Neb (QB), Charlotte, N.C., 1969-70
Heath, Donnie (C), Anniston, Ala., 1960
Henderson, Josh (DB), Panama City, Fla., 1982
Henderson, William T. "Bill" (TE), Tuscaloosa, Ala., 1975-77
Henry, Butch (E), Selma, Ala., 1961-62-63
Higginbotham, Steve (DB), All-SEC, Hueytown, Ala., 1969-70-71
Higginbotham, Robert (DB), Hueytown, Ala., 1967-68
Hill, John (RB), Centre, Ala., 1979-80
Hill, Roosevelt (LB), Newnan, Ga., 1982
Hines, Edward T. (DE), LaFayette, Ala., 1970-72
Hodges, Bruce (DE-T), Sarasota, Fla., 1977
Holcombe, Danny (OG), Marietta, Ga., 1980-81-82
Holsomback, Roy (G), West Blocton, Ala., 1959-60

Alabama's 1964 national championship team

Holt, Darwin (LB), Gainesville, Tex., 1960-61

Holt, James J. "Buddy" (P), Demopolis, Ala., 1977-79

Homan, Dennis (SE), All-America, All-SEC, Muscle Shoals, Ala., 1965-66-67

Homan, Scott (DT), Elkhart, Ind., 1979-80-81-82

Hood, Sammy (DB), Ider, Ala., 1982

Hopper, Mike (E), Huntsville, Ala., 1961-62-64

Horstead, Don (HB), Elba, Ala., 1982

Horton, Jimmy (DE), Tarrant, Ala., 1971

Hubbard, Colenzo (LB), Mulga, Ala., 1974-75-76

Hufstetler, Thomas R. Jr. (C), Rossville, Ga., 1977-78

Hunt, Morris Parker (OT), Orlando, Fla., 1972-73

Hunter, Scott (QB), Prichard, Ala., 1968-69-70

Hurlbut, Jack (QB), Houston, Tex., 1962-63

Hurst, Tim (OT), DeArmandville, Ala., 1975-76-77

Husband, Hunter (TE), Nashville, Tenn., 1967-68-69

Husband, Woodward A. "Woodie" (LB), Nashville,

Tenn., 1969-70

I

Israel, Jimmy Kent (QB), Haleyville, Ala., 1966

Israel, Thomas Murray (G), Haleyville, Ala., 1969

J

Jackson, Billy (RB), All-SEC, Phenix City, Ala., 1978-79-80

Jackson, Bobby (QB), Mobile, Ala., 1958

Jackson, Mark (C), Houston, Tex., 1981-82

Jackson, Wilbur (HB), All-SEC, Ozark, Ala., 1971-72-73

Jacobs, Donald (QB), Scottsboro, Ala., 1979-80

James, Kenneth Morris (T), Columbus, Ga., 1969-70

Jilleba, Pete (FB), Madison, N.J., 1967-68-69

Johns, Bobby (DB), All-America, All-SEC, Birmingham, Ala., 1965-66-67

Johnson, Billy (C), Selma, Ala., 1965-66-67

Bryant with Joe Namath, one of Alabama's most successful and recognizable players

Johnson, Cornell (HB), High Point, N.C., 1959-60
Johnston, Donny (HB), Birmingham, Ala., 1966-69
Jones, Amos (RB), Aliceville, Ala., 1980
Jones, Joe (RB), Thomaston, Ga., 1978-79-80
Jones, Joey (SE), Mobile, Ala., 1980-81-82
Jones, Kevin (QB), Louisville, Ky., 1977-78
Jones, Robbie (LB), Demopolis, Ala., 1979-80-81-82
Jones, Terry Wayne (C), Sandersville, Ga., 1975-76-77
Jordan, Lee Roy (LB), All-America, All-SEC, Excel, Ala., 1960-61-62
Junior, E. J. III (DE), All-America, All-SEC, Nashville, Tenn., 1977-78-79-80

K

Kearly, Dan (DT), All-America, All-SEC, Talladega, Ala., 1962-63-64
Kelley, Joe (QB), Ozark, Ala., 1966-67-68
Kelley, Leslie (FB), Cullman, Ala., 1964-65-66
Kerr, Dudley (K), Reform, Ala., 1966-67
Killgore, Terry (C), Annandale, Va., 1965-66-67
Kim, Peter (KS), Honolulu, Hawaii, 1980-81-82
King, Emanuel (DE), Leroy, Ala., 1982
King, Tyrone (DB), All-SEC, Docena, Ala., 1970-71-72
Kramer, Michael T. (DB), Mobile, Ala., 1975-76-77
Krapf, James Paul (C), All-America, All-SEC,

Newark, Del., 1970-71-72
Krauss, Barry (LB), Pompano Beach, Fla., 1976-77-78
Krout, Bart (TE), All-SEC, Birmingham, Ala., 1978-79-80-81
Kubelius, Skip (DT), Morrow, Ga., 1972-73
Kulback, Steve Joseph (DT), Clarksville, Tenn., 1973-74

L

LaBue, John (RB), Memphis, Tenn., 1976
LaBue, Joseph II (HB), Memphis, Tenn., 1970-71-72
Lambert, Buford (OT), Warner Robins, Ga., 1976
Lambert, Randolph (C), Athens, Ga., 1973-74
Lancaster, John (DE), Tuscaloosa, Ala., 1979
Langston, Griff (SE), Birmingham, Ala., 1968-69-70
Law, Phil (OT), Montgomery, Ala., 1971
Lawley, Lane (SE), Citronelle, Ala., 1970
Layton, Dale (E), Sylacauga, Ala., 1962
Lazenby, K. J. (OT), Monroeville, Ala., 1974-75-76
Lee, Mickey (FB), Enterprise, Ala., 1976-77-78
Legg, Murray (DB), Homewood, Ala., 1976-77-78
Lewis, AL (G), Covington, Ky., 1961-62-63
Lewis, Walter (QB), Brewton, Ala., 1980-81-82
Lowe, Eddie (LB), Phenix City, Ala., 1980-81-82
Lowe, Woodrow (LB), All-America, All-SEC, Phenix

Alabama's 1965 national championship team

City, Ala., 1972-73-74-75

Lusk, Thomas Joseph III (DE), Clarksville, Tenn., 1970-72

Lyles, Warren (NG), All-SEC, Birmingham, Ala., 1978-79-80-81

Lyons, Martin A. "Marty" (DT), St. Petersburg, Fla., 1977-78

M

Maddox, Sam H. (TE), Orlando, Fla., 1976-77

Mallard, James (SE), Tampa, Fla., 1980

Mann, Frank (K), Birmingham, Ala., 1968-69-70

Marcello, Jerry (DB), McKeesport, Pa., 1973

Mardini, Georges (PK), Damascus, Syria, 1980

Marks, Keith (SE), Tuscaloosa, Ala., 1979-82

Marshall, Fred H. (C), Montgomery, Ala., 1970-71

Martin, Gary (HB), Dothan, Ala., 1961-62-63

Mauro, John (DE), South Bend, Ind., 1978-79-80

Maxwell, Raymond Edward (OT), Flat Rock, Ala., 1973-74-75

Mikel, Bobby (DE), Fort Walton Beach, Fla., 1976

Miller, Noah Dean (LB), Oneonta, Ala., 1973

Mitchell, David Dewey (LB), Tampa, Fla., 1975-76-77

Mitchell, John (DE), All-America, All-SEC, Mobile, Ala., 1971-72

Mitchell, Ken "Tank" (G), Florence, Ala., 1964

Montgomery, Greg (LB), Macon, Ga., 1972-73-74-75

Montgomery, Robert M. (DE), Shelbyville, Ky., 1970

Mooneyham, Marlin (FB), Montgomery, Ala., 1962

Moore, Harold (FB), Chattanooga, Tenn., 1965-66

Moore, John (HB), Montgomery, Ala., 1962

Moore, Mal (QB), Dozier, Ala., 1962

Moore, Pete (FB), Hopkinsville, Ky., 1968-69

Moore, Randy (TE), Montgomery, Ala., 1970-73

Moore, Ricky (FB), Huntsville, Ala., 1981-82

Moore, Robert "Bud" (E), Birmingham, Ala., 1958-59-60

Morgan, Ed (FB), Hattiesburg, Miss., 1966-67-68

Morrison, Duff (HB), Memphis, Tenn., 1958-59-61

Morton, Farris (E), Sardis, Ala., 1962

Moseley, Elliott (C), Selma, Ala., 1960

Mosley, John (HB), Thomaston, Ala., 1964-65-66

Moss, Stan (LB), Birmingham, Ala., 1965-66-67

Mott, Steve (C), New Orleans, La., 1980-81-82

Murphy, Philip (HB), Anniston, Ala., 1973

Musso, Johnny (HB), All-America, All-SEC, Birmingham, Ala., 1969-70-71

Mc

McClendon, Frankie (T), Guntersville, Ala., 1962-63-64

McCullough, Gaylon (C), Enterprise, Ala., 1962-63-64

McCombs, Eddie (OT), Birmingham, Ala., 1978-79-80

McCrary, Tom (DT), Scottsboro, Ala., 1982

McElroy, Alan (PK), Tuscaloosa, Ala., 1978-79

McGee, Barry (OB), Birmingham, Ala., 1975

McGill, Larry (HB), Panama City, Fla., 1962-63

McGriff, Curtis (MG), Cottonwood, Ala., 1977-78-79

McIntyre, David (OT), Columbus, Miss., 1975-76

McKewen, Jack II (T), Birmingham, Ala., 1968

McKinney, Robert B. Jr. (DB), All-SEC, Mobile, Ala., 1970-71-72

McLain, Rick (TE), Walnut Hill, Fla., 1974-75

McLeod, Ben (DE), Pensacola, Fla., 1965

McMakin, David (DB), All-SEC, Tucker, Ga., 1971-72-73

McNeal, Don (DB), All-America, All-SEC, McCollough, Ala., 1977-78-79

McQueen, Mike (OT), Enterprise, Ala., 1981-82

McRae, Scott (LB), Huntsville, Ala., 1982

N

Namath, Joe Willie (QB), All-America, All-SEC, Beaver Falls, Pa., 1962-63-64

Nathan, Tony (HB), Birmingham, Ala., 1975-76-77-78

Bryant and All-SEC quarterback Steadman Shealy discuss their options during a crucial 1979 game.

Neal, Rick (TE), Birmingham, Ala., 1976-77-78

Neighbors, Billy (T), All-America, All-SEC, Northport, Ala., 1959-60-61

Nelson, Benny (HB), All-SEC, Huntsville, Ala., 1961-62-63

Nelson, Rod (K), Birmingham, Ala., 1974-75-76

Newsome, Ozzie (SE), All-America, All-SEC, Leighton, Ala., 1974-75-76-77

Nix, Mark (RB), Altoona, Ala., 1979-80-81

Norman, Haywood Eugene "Butch" (DE), Luverne, Ala., 1973

Norris, Lanny S. (DB), Russellville, Ala., 1970-71-72

O

O'Dell, Richard (E), Lincoln, Ala., 1959-60-62

Odom, Earnest Lavant (E), Birmingham, Ala., 1973

Ogden, Ray (HB), Jesup, Ga., 1962-63-64

Ogilvie, Morgan Oslin "Major" (RB), All-SEC, Birmingham, Ala., 1977-78-79-80

O'Linger, John (C), Scottsboro, Ala., 1959-60-61

Oliver, William "Brother" (DB), Livingston, Ala., 1960-61

Orcutt, Ben (RB), Arlington Heights, Ill., 1981

O'Rear, Jack (QB), Tarrant, Ala., 1974-76-77

Oser, Gary (C), New Orleans, La., 1976

Osteen, Robert "Gary" (FB), Anniston, Ala., 1958-59

O'Toole, Mike (DB), Palmerdale, Ala., 1982

Owen, Wayne (LB), Gadsden, Ala., 1966-67-68

P

Palmer, Dale (LB), Calera, Ala., 1978

Pappas, Peter George (SE), Birmingham, Ala., 1973

Parker, Calvin (DE), Eastoboga, Ala., 1976-78

Parkhouse, Robin (DE), All-America, All-SEC, Orlando, Fla., 1969-70-71

Parsons, Don (G), Houston, Tex., 1958

Patrick, Linnie (RB), Jasper, Ala., 1980-81-82

Patterson, Jim (OG), Annandale, Va., 1971

Patterson, Steve (OG), Omaha, Neb., 1972-73-74

Patton, James "Jap" (E), Tuscumbia, Ala., 1959-60

Pell, Charles B. (T), Albertville, Ala., 1960-61-62

Perkins, Ray (E), All-America, All-SEC, Petal, Miss., 1964-65-66

Perrin, Benny (DB), Decatur, Ala., 1980-81

Perry, Anthony "Lefty" (DB), Hazel Green, Ala., 1973

Pettee, Robert A. "Bob" (G), Bradenton, Fla., 1960-61-62

Phillips, Gary (G), Dothan, Ala., 1958-59-60

Piper, Billy (HB), Poplar Bluff, Mo., 1960-62-63

Pitts, Mike (DE), All-America, All-SEC, Baltimore, Md., 1979-80-81-82

Pittman, Alec Noel (LB), New Orleans, La., 1970

Pizzitola, Alan (DB), All-SEC, Birmingham, Ala., 1973-74-75

Poole, John Paul (E), Florence, Ala., 1958

Pope, Herman "Buddy" (OT), Bradenton, Fla., 1973-74-75

Prestwood, Thomas A. (DE), Chattanooga, Tenn., 1975

Propst, Eddie (DB), Birmingham, Ala., 1966-67

Prudhomme, John Mark (DB), Memphis, Tenn., 1973-74-75

Pugh, George (TE), Montgomery, Ala., 1972-73-74-75

Pugh, Keith Harrison (SE), Evergreen, Ala., 1977-78-79

R

Raburn, Gene (FB), Jasper, Ala., 1965-66

Raines, James Patrick (C), Montgomery, Ala., 1970-71-72

Raines, Vaughn Michael (DT), All-SEC, Montgomery, Ala., 1972-73

Ranager, George (SE), Meridian, Miss., 1968-69-70

Rankin, Carlton (QB), Piedmont, Ala., 1962

Ray, David (SE-K), All-America, All-SEC, Phenix City, Ala., 1964-65

Reaves, Pete (G), Bessemer, Ala., 1958

Reed, Wayne, Tuscaloosa, Ala., 1978 (Mgr.)

Reilly, Mike (DG), Mobile, Ala., 1966-67-68

Reitz, John David (DE-OT), Morristown, Tenn., 1965-66-67

Rhoads, Wayne R. (DE), Jackson, Miss., 1969-70

Rhoden, Steve (K), Red Bay, Ala., 1981

Rhodes, D. Wayne Jr. (DB), All-SEC, Decatur, Ga., 1973-74-75

Rice, William J. "Bill" (E), Troy, Ala., 1959-60-61

Rich, Jerry (HB), Attalla, Ala., 1959

Richardson, Ron (DB), Columbus, Ga., 1971

Richardson, W. E. "Billy" (HB), Jasper, Ala., 1959-60-61

Ridgeway, Danny Howard (K), Fyffe, Ala., 1973-74-75

Riley, Mike (DB), Corvallis, Ore., 1974

Rippetoe, Benny (QB), Greenville, Tenn., 1971

Robbins, Joe (C), Opp, Ala., 1978-79-80

Roberts, Kenneth (C), Anniston, Ala., 1958

Roberts, Larry (DT), Dothan, Ala., 1982

Robertson, Ronald Dale (LB), Signal Mountain, Tenn., 1973-74

Roddam, Ronnie (C), Birmingham, Ala., 1968-69

Rodriguez, Mike (MG), Melbourne, Fla., 1981-82

Rogers, Eddie Bo (LB), Bessemer, Ala., 1966-67

Rogers, John David (OG), All-SEC, Montgomery, Ala., 1972-73-74

Rogers, Richard (OG), Boise, Id., 1973

Ronsonet, Norbie (E), Biloxi, Miss., 1958-59-60

Root, Steve (LB), Indio, Calif., 1971

Rosser, Jimmy Lynn (OT), Birmingham, Ala., 1969-70-71

Rouzie, Jefferson Carr (LB), Jacksonville, Fla., 1970-71-73

Rowan, Robert "Robby" (DB), Huntsville, Ala., 1972

Rowell, Terry (DT), Heidelberg, Miss., 1969-70-71

Ruffin, Larry Joe (OG), Fayette, Ala., 1973-74-75

Rumbley, Roy (OG), Moss Point, Miss., 1981-82

Rustin, Nathan (DT), Phenix City, Ala., 1966-67

Rutledge, Gary (QB), Birmingham, Ala., 1972-73-74

Rutledge, Jack (G), Birmingham, Ala., 1959-60-61

Rutledge, Jeffrey R. (QB), Birmingham, Ala., 1975-76-77-78

S

Sadler, David A. (OG), Cadiz, Ky., 1975-76-77.

Samples, Alvin (OG), All-America, All-SEC, Tarrant, Ala., 1967-68-69

Sanders, Terry (K), Birmingham, Ala., 1981-82

Sansing, Walter (FB), West Blocton, Ala., 1958

Sasser, Mike (DB), Brewton, Ala., 1966-69

Sawyer, Bubba (SE), Fairhope, Ala., 1969-71

Schamun, Russ (SE), Napa, Calif., 1974-76

Schmissrauter, Kurt (OT), Chattanooga, Tenn., 1981-82

Schumann, Eric (DB), Blue Island, Ill., 1977

Scissum, Willard (OG), Huntsville, Ala., 1981-82

Scott, Randy (LB), All-SEC, Decatur, Ga., 1978-79-80

Scroggins, Billy (SE), Jacksonville, Fla., 1967-68

Searcy, Bill (OG), Savannah, Ga., 1978-80

Seay, Buddy (HB), Dadeville, Ala., 1969-70

Sebastian, Mike (DT), Columbus, Ga., 1978

Sewell, Ray (QB), Breman, Ga., 1976

Shankles, Don (E), Fort Payne, Ala., 1967

Sharpe, Jimmy (OG), Montgomery, Ala., 1960-61-62

Sharpless, John Waylon Jr. (SE), Elba, Ala., 1972-73

Shealy, Steadman (QB), All-SEC, Dothan, Ala., 1977-78-79

Shelby, Willie (HB), All-SEC, Purvis, Miss., 1973-74-75

Sherrill, Jackie (FB-LB), Biloxi, Miss., 1963-64-65

Shinn, Richard (DT), Columbiana, Ala., 1980-82

Sides, John "Brownie" (DT), Tuskegee, Ala., 1966-67

Simon, Kenny (RB), Montgomery, Ala., 1979-81

Simmons, Jim (T), Piedmont, Ala., 1962-63-64

Simmons, Jim (TE), Yazoo City, Miss., 1969-70-71

Simmons, Malcolm (P), Montgomery, Ala., 1981-82

Sims, Wayne (G), Columbiana, Ala., 1958-59

Sington, Dave (T), Birmingham, Ala., 1958-59

Sington, Fred Jr. (T), Birmingham, Ala., 1958-59

Sisa, Joe (T), Clark, N.J., 1960

Skelton, Robert "Bobby" (QB), Pell City, Ala., 1959-60

Sloan, Steve (QB), All-America, All-SEC, Cleveland, Tenn., 1963-64-65

Smalley, Jack Jr. (LB), Douglasville, Ga., 1976-77

Smiley, Anthony (DE), Birmingham, Ala., 1981-82

Smith, Barry S. (C), Anniston, Ala., 1977-78-79

Smith, Bobby (DB), Fairhope, Ala., 1978-79

Smith, Bobby (QB), Brewton, Ala., 1958

Smith, James Sidney (C), Warner Robins, Ga., 1974-75-76

Somerville, Tom (OG), White Station, Tenn., 1965-66-67

Spencer, Tom (DB), Fairfax, Va., 1979

Spivey, Paul Randall (FB), Montgomery, 1972-73

Sprayberry, Steve (OT), All-SEC, Sylacauga, Ala., 1972-72

Sprinkle, Jerrill (DB), Chamblee, Ga., 1980-81-82

Spruiell, Jerry (E), Pell City, Ala., 1960

Stabler, Ken "Snake" (QB), All-America, All-SEC, Foley, Ala., 1965-66-67

Stanford, Robert "Bobby" (OT), Albany, Ga., 1969-72

Stapp, Laurien "Goobie" (QB-K), Birmingham, Ala., 1958-59-60

Steakley, Rod (SE), Huntsville, Ala., 1971

Stephens, Bruce (G), All-SEC, Thomasville, Ala., 1965-66-67

Stephens, Charles (E), Thomasville, Ala., 1962-63-64

Stephens, Gerald (C), Thomasville, Ala., 1962

Stephenson, Dwight (C), All-America, All-SEC, Hampton, Va., 1977-78-79

Stevens, Wayne (E), Gadsden, Ala., 1966

Stickney, Ravis "Red" (FB), Key West, Fla., 1959

Stock, Mike (HB), Elkhart, Ind., 1973-74-75

Stokes, Ralph Anthony (HB), Montgomery, Ala., 1972-74

Stone, Rocky (G), Birmingham, Ala., 1969

Strickland, Charles "Chuck" (LB), All-SEC, East Ridge, Tenn., 1971-72-73

Strickland, Lynwood (DE), Alexander City, Ala., 1965

Strickland, William Ross (T), Birmingham, Ala., 1970

Sullivan, Johnny (DT), Nashville, Tenn., 1964-65-66

Surlas, Tom (LB), All-America, All-SEC, Mt. Pleasant, Pa., 1970-71

Sutton, Donnie (SE), Blountsville, Ala., 1966-67-68

Wide receiver Ozzie Newsome (82) makes a spectacular catch over a defender. Newsome was first team All-America in 1977.

Sutton, Mike (DB), Brewton, Ala., 1978

Swafford, Bobby "Hawk" (SE), Heflin, Ala., 1967-68

Swann, Gerald (DB), Ashville, Ala., 1982

T

Taylor, James E. (HB), Citronelle, Ala., 1973-74-75

Thomas, Daniel Martin (C), Clinton, Tenn., 1970

Thompson, Louis (DT), Lebanon, Tenn., 1965-66

Thomas, Richard "Dickey" (DB), All-SEC, Thomasville, Ga., 1965-66-67

Tillmann, Homer Newton "Chip" (OT), Panama City, Fla., 1976-77

Todd, Richard (QB), All-SEC, Mobile, Ala., 1973-74-75

Tolleson, Tommy (SE), All-SEC, Talladega, Ala., 1963-64-65

Trammell, Pat (QB), All-America, All-SEC, Scottsboro, Ala., 1959-60-61

Travis, Timothy Lee "Tim" (TE), Bessemer, Ala., 1976-77-78-79

Trimble, Wayne (QB), Cullman, Ala., 1964-65-66

Trodd, Paul (PK), Eufaula, Ala., 1981

Tucker, Michael V. (DB), Alexandria, Ala., 1975-76-77

Tucker, Richard Glenn "Ricky" (DB), All-SEC, Florence, Ala., 1977-78-79-80

Turner, Craig (FB), Gaithersburg, MD, 1982

Turpin, John R. (FB), Birmingham, Ala., 1977-78

Turpin, Richard "Dick" (DE), Birmingham, Ala., 1973-74-75

U

Umphrey, Woody (P), Bourbonnais, Ill., 1978-79-80

V

Vagotis, Chris (OG), Canton, Ohio, 1966

Valetto, Carl (E), Oakmont, Pa., 1958

Varnado, Carey Reid (C), Hattiesburg, Miss., 1970

Versprille, Eddie (FB), Norfolk, Va., 1961-62-63

Vickers, Doug (OG), Enterprise, Ala., 1981-82

Vines, Jay (OG), Birmingham, Ala., 1978

W

Wade, Steve (DB), Dothan, Ala., 1971-72

Wade, Tommy (DB), Dothan, Ala., 1968-69-70

Walker, Hardy (OT), Huntsville, Ala., 1981

Wall, Larry "Dink" (FB), Fairfax, Ala., 1961-62-64

Washco, Gerard George (DT), West Orange, N.J., 1973-74-75

Washington, Mike (DB), All-America, All-SEC, Montgomery, Ala., 1972-73-74

Watkins, David (DE), Rome, Ga., 1971-72-73

Watts, Jimmy (DE), Gulf Breeze, Fla., 1981-82

Watson, Rick (FB), Birmingham, Ala., 1974-75-76

Weigand, Tommy (HB), Enterprise, Ala., 1968

Wesley, William Earl "Buddy" (FB), Talladega, Ala., 1958-59-60

Whaley, Frank (DE), Lineville, Ala., 1965-66

Wheeler, Wayne (SE), All-America, All-SEC, Orlando, Fla., 1971-72-73

White, Darryl (SE), Tuscaloosa, Ala., 1981-82

White, Gus (MG), Dothan, Ala., 1974-75-76

White, Jack (OG), Louisville, Miss., 1971

White, Tommy (FB), West Blocton, Ala., 1958-59-60

Whitman, Steven K. (FB), Huffman, Ala., 1977-78-79

Wiesman, Bill (G), Louisville, Ky., 1962-63

Wilcox, Tommy (DB), All-America, All-SEC, Harahan, La., 1979-80-81-82

Wilder, Ken (OT), Columbiana, Ala., 1968-69

Wilkins, Red (E), Bay Minette, Ala., 1961

Williams, Charlie (FB), Bessemer, Ala., 1980

Williams, John Byrd (G), Decatur, Ala., 1965-66

Williams, Steven Edward (DB), Moline, Ill., 1969-70-71

Williamson, Richard (SE), Fort Deposit, Ala., 1961-62

Willis, Perry (SE), Dadeville, Ala., 1967

Wilson, George "Butch" (HB), Hueytown, Ala., 1960-61-62

Wilson, Jimmy (OG), Haleyville, Ala., 1961-62

Wingo, Richard Allen "Rich" (LB), Elkhart, Ind., 1976-77-78

Wood, Russ (DE), Elba, Ala., 1980-81-82

Wood, William Dexter (SE), Ozark, Ala., 1970-71-72

Woodruff, Glen (TE), Aliceville, Ala., 1971

Wright, Steve (T), Louisville, Ky., 1962-63

Y

Yelvington, Gary (DB), Daytona Beach, Fla., 1973-74

Bryant All-America Players
(Includes First and Second Team Selections)

Kentucky

1949   Bob Gain (Tackle; First Team)

1950   Bob Gain (Tackle; First Team)
Vito "Babe" Parilli (Quarterback; First Team)

1951   Doug Moseley (Center; First Team)
Vito "Babe" Parilli (Quarterback; First Team)

1952   Steve Meilinger (End; First Team)

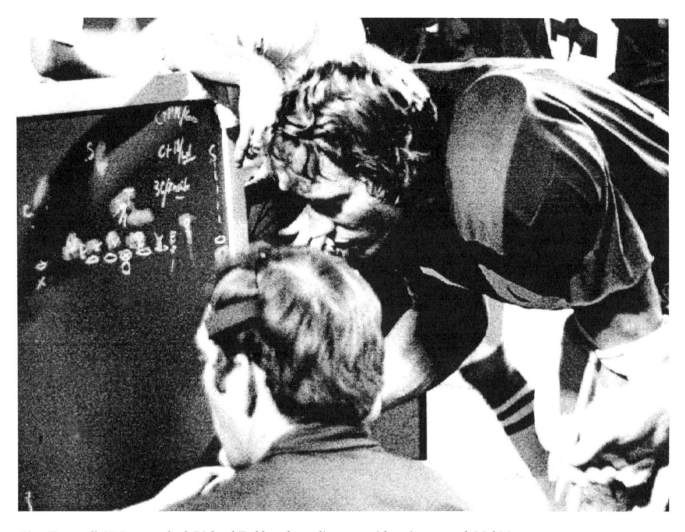

First Team All-SEC quarterback Richard Todd analyzes diagrams with assistant coach Mal Moore.

1953 Ray Correll (Guard; First Team)
Steve Meilinger (End; First Team)

Texas A&M

1956 Dennis Goehring (Guard; First Team)
Charles Krueger (Tackle; First Team)
Jack Pardee (Fullback; First Team)

1957 John David Crow (Halfback; First Team)
Charles Krueger (Tackle; First Team)

Alabama

1961 Lee Roy Jordan (Center)
Billy Neighbors (Defensive Tackle; First Team)
Pat Trammell (Quarterback)

1962 Lee Roy Jordan (Center; First Team)
1963 Benny Nelson (Halfback)

1964 Wayne Freeman (Offensive Guard; First Team)
Dan Kearley (Offensive Tackle; First Team)
Joe Namath (Quarterback; First Team)
David Ray (Halfback; First Team)
Mickey Andrews (Halfback)

1965 Paul Crane (Center; First Team)
Steve Sloan (Quarterback; First Team)
Steve Bowman (Fullback)

1966 Richard Cole (Defensive Tackle; First Team)
Cecil Dowdy (Offensive Tackle; First Team)
Bobby Johns (Defensive Back; First Team)
Ray Perkins (Split End; First Team)

1967 Dennis Homan (Split End; First Team)
Bobby Johns (Defensive Back; First Team)
Kenny Stabler (Quarterback; First Team)

1968 Sam Gellerstedt (Defensive Guard; First

Johnny Musso (22) and Steve Sloan were two of Bryant's favorite players.

Team)
Mike Hall (Linebacker; First Team)

1969   Alvin Samples (Defensive Guard; First Team)

1970   Johnny Musso (Halfback; First Team)

1971   John Hannah (Offensive Guard; First Team)
        Johnny Musso (Halfback; First Team)
        Robin Parkhouse (Defensive End)
        Tom Surlas (Linebacker)
        Jim Krapf (Center)

1972   John Hannah (Offensive Guard; First Team)
        Jim Krapf (Center; First Team)
        John Mitchell (Defensive End; First Team)

1973   Buddy Brown (Offensive Tackle; First Team)
        Woodrow Lowe (Linebacker; First Team)
        Wayne Wheeler (Split End; First Team)
        Mike Washington (Defensive Back)

1974   Leroy Cook (Defensive End; First Team)
        Sylvester Croom (Center; First Team)
        Woodrow Lowe (Linebacker; First Team)
        Mike Washington (Defensive Back; First Team)

1975   Leroy Cook (Defensive End; First Team)
        Woodrow Lowe (Linebacker; First Team)
        Bob Baumhower (Defensive Tackle)

1976   Bob Baumhower (Defensive Tackle)
        Ozzie Newsome (Wide Receiver)

1977   Bob Cryder (Offensive Guard)
        Johnny Davis (Fullback)
        Wayne Hamilton (Defensive End)
        Ozzie Newsome (Wide Receiver; First Team)

1978   Barry Krauss (Linebacker; First Team)
        Marty Lyons (Defensive Tackle; First Team)
        Dwight Stephenson (Center)

1979   Jim Bunch (Offensive Tackle; First Team)
        Don McNeal (Defensive Back; First Team)
        Dwight Stephenson (Center; First Team)
        E. J. Junior (Defensive End; First Team)
        Byron Braggs (Defensive Tackle)

1980   Thomas Boyd (Linebacker; First Team)
        E. J. Junior (Defensive End; First Team)
        Byron Braggs (Defensive Tackle)

1981   Thomas Boyd (Linebacker; First Team)

Alabama's 1973 national championship team

Tommy Wilcox (Defensive Back; First Team)
Warren Lyles (Nose Guard)

1982   Jeremiah Castille (Defensive Back; First Team)
Mike Pitts (Defensive End; First Team)
Tommy Wilcox (Defensive Back; First Team)
Steve Mott (Center)

Bryant All-Conference Players
First Team Selections Only

Kentucky (Southeastern Conference, 1946-53)

1946   Wallace Jones (End)

1947   Jay Rhodemyre (Center)

1949   Bob Gain (Tackle)
Harry Ulinski (Center)

1950   Bob Gain (Tackle)
Vito Parilli (Quarterback)

1951   Gene Donaldson (Guard)
Steve Meilinger (End)
Doug Moseley (Center)
Vito Parilli (Quarterback)

1952   Steve Meilinger (Quarterback)
1953   Ray Correll (Guard)
Steve Meilinger (halfback)

Texas A&M (Southwest Conference, 1954-57)

1954   Elwood Kettler (Quarterback)
Bennie Sinclair (End)

1955   Gene Stallings (End)
Dennis Goehring (Guard)

1956   Jack Pardee (Fullback)
Lloyd Hale (Center)
Dennis Goehring (Guard)
John David Crow (halfback)
John Tracey (End)
Charles Krueger (Tackle)
Roddy Osborne (Quarterback)

1957   John David Crow (Halfback) (Heisman Trophy Winner)
Charles Krueger (Tackle)
Bobby Marks (End)

Alabama (Southeastern Conference, 1958-82)

1961   Pat Trammell (Quarterback)
Billy Neighbors (Guard)
Lee Roy Jordan (Center)
Mike Fracchia (Back)

1962   Lee Roy Jordan (Center)

1963   Benny Nelson (Back)

1964   Steve Bowman (Back)
Joe Namath (Quarterback)
David Ray (Back)
Wayne Freeman (Guard)
Dan Kearley (Tackle)

1965   Tommy Tolleson (End)
Paul Crane (Center)
Steve Bowman (Fullback)
Creed Gilmer (End)
Bobby Johns (Defensive Back)

1966   Cecil Dowdy (Tackle)
Bobby Johns (Defensive Back)
Ray Perkins (End)
John Calvert (Guard)
Dicky Thompson (Back)

Alabama's 1978 national championship team

1967   Mike Ford (End)
        Ken Stabler (Quarterback)
        Dennis Homan (End)
        Mike Hall (Linebacker)
        Bruce Stephens (Guard)
        Bobby Johns (Defensive Back)

1968   Mike Hall (Linebacker)
        Sam Gellerstedt (Guard)
        Mike Ford (End)
        Alvin Samples (Guard)

1969   Alvin Samples (Guard)
        Danny Ford (Tackle)

1970   Johnny Musso (Tailback)

1971   Johnny Musso (Halfback)
        John Hannah (Guard)
        Tom Surlas (Linebacker)
        Jimmy Grammer (Center)
        Steve Higginbotham (Defensive Back)
        Robin Parkhouse (Defensive End)
        Jim Krapf (Tackle)
        David Bailey (End)

1972   John Hannah (Guard)
        Greg Gantt (Punter)
        Jim Krapf (Center)
        Terry Davis (Quarterback)
        Wayne Wheeler (End)
        Chuck Strickland (Linebacker)
        Bobby McKinney (Defensive Back)
        John Mitchell (Defensive End)
        Buddy Brown (Tackle)

1973   Wilbur Jackson (Halfback)
        Wayne Wheeler (End)
        Buddy Brown (Offensive Tackle)
        Mike Raines (Defensive Tackle)

        Woodrow Lowe (Linebacker)
        Mike Washington (Defensive Back)
        Greg Gantt (Punter)
        Steve Sprayberry (Offensive Tackle)
        David McMakin (Defensive Back)
1974   Willie Shelby (Halfback)
        Sylvester Croom (Center)
        John Rogers (Guard)
        Leroy Cook (Defensive End)
        Woodrow Lowe (Linebacker)
        Mike Washington (Defensive Back)
        Ricky Davis (Safety)

1975   Leroy Cook (Defensive End)
        Bob Baumhower (Defensive Tackle)
        Conley Duncan (Linebacker)
        Wayne Rhodes (Defensive Back)
        Tyrone King (Defensive Back)
        Alan Pizzitola (Safety)
        Woodrow Lowe (Linebacker)
        Richard Todd (Quarterback)
        David Gerasimchuk (Guard)

1976   Davis Gerasimchuk (Guard)
        Ozzie Newsome (End)
        Bob Baumhower (Defensive Tackle)
        Charley Hannah (Defensive Tackle)

1977   Jim Bunch (Offensive Tackle)
        Dwight Stephenson (Center)
        Ozzie Newsome (End)
        Johnny Davis (Fullback)
        Mike Kramer (Defensive Back)
        Marty Lyons (Defensive Tackle)
        Mike Tucker (Defensive Back)
        Wayne Hamilton (Defensive End)
        Bob Cryder (Offensive Guard)

1978   Mike Brock (Offensive Tackle)
        Dwight Stephenson (Center)

Alabama's 1979 national championship team

Jim Bunch (Offensive Tackle)
E. J. Junior (Defensive End)
Marty Lyons (Defensive Tackle)
Barry Krauss (Linebacker)
Murray Legg (Safety)
Wayne Hamilton (Defensive End)

1979   E. J. Junior (Defensive End)
David Hannah (Defensive Tackle)
Byron Braggs (Defensive Tackle)
Thomas Boyd (Linebacker)
Jim Bob Harris (Defensive Back)
Don McNeal (Defensive Back)
Tommy Wilcox (Defensive Back)
Jim Bunch (Offensive Tackle)
Mike Brock (Offensive Guard)
Dwight Stephenson (Center)
Steadman Shealy (Quarterback)
Major Ogilvie (Back)

1980   E. J. Junior (Defensive End)
Byron Braggs (Defensive Tackle)
Thomas Boyd (Linebacker)
Jim Bob Harris (Defensive Back)
Vince Cowell (Guard)
Tommy Wilcox (Defensive Back)

1981   Tommy Wilcox (Defensive Back)
Jeremiah Castille (Defensive Back)
Jim Bob Harris (Defensive Back)
Warren Lyles (Defensive Lineman)
Mike Pitts (Defensive End)
Thomas Boyd (Linebacker)
Bart Krout (Tight End)
Bob Cayavec (Offensive Tackle)

1982   Jeremiah Castille (Defensive Back)
Mike Pitts (Defensive End)
Joe Beazley (Offensive Tackle)
Steve Mott (Center)

Epilogue

He Won Because
He Never Quit

"Many of our teams had only three, four or five great players. I had some with only one or two. But we usually had a dozen or so guys in the fourth quarter who got to thinking they were great."
—Paul "Bear" Bryant

BRYANT TEAMS STOOD TALLEST IN THE FOURTH QUARTER

The legacy of Paul W. "Bear" Bryant's life was—and is—perseverance. He stressed never quitting above size, talent and all else, and that more than anything else, made him and those who played for him winners.

"If you believe in yourself and have dedication and pride and never quit, you'll be a winner," he said in one of his most reproduced and reflective comments. Perseverance was his signifying lesson, and he lived and taught it well.

In the final analysis, winning football games was almost a mere by-product of Coach Bryant's primary mission, that of shaping lives by teaching his players to become winners. And wasn't that what football once was all about?

Coach Bryant knew first-hand of the temptation to quit, to let up in the fourth quarter when the strain and pain were greatest, but he didn't, and his teams didn't. Because of that, his teams—and especially his Alabama teams over a quarter of a century—came to claim the fourth quarter as their own. His teams played for that final period and welcomed it, even cheered its arrival, confident they would rise to the challenge of those final, deciding and often glorious moments. Opponents tried but could not ignore the inspired determination which Bryant-coached teams displayed in those final 15 minutes.

The fourth quarter was that defining hour when Bryant and his teams stood tallest, most confident, most poised, most dedicated to scratching and clawing and fighting and laying it on the line on every play, determined to win if possible but even more determined not to quit until the final whistle. And they did it game after game, season after season, rarely allowing opponents to come from behind for a victory.

Lee Roy Jordan, an All-America linebacker at Alabama (1960-62) and a member of Bryant's first national championship team in 1961 (and later

Page 200: Winning football games was a by-product of Coach Bryant's primary mission: shaping lives by teaching his players to become winners.

Dallas Cowboys star), has recalled Bryant's fourth-quarter plan often throughout the years.

"Coach Bryant always wanted to win the fourth quarter," Jordan said. "It was a big thing with him because it showed the outstanding mental and physical conditioning of his players.

"He wanted us to always get stronger as the game went on, to wear down the other teams in the fourth quarter. And he convinced us that we could do it against Georgia Tech in 1960 (Alabama won 16-15 on the final play of the game after trailing 15-0 at halftime) and in a lot of other games after that," Jordan said.

Coach Bryant prepared his players for that fourth-quarter challenge by testing them individually in carefully planned practice sessions which placed them in difficult, game-like situations designed to build confidence by taking them to an inspired level of personal achievement even beyond their own dreams and expectations.

Jim Goostree, University of Alabama athletic trainer during each day of Bryant's 25 years at the school, remembered those special tests also. "Coach Bryant always exposed every player to a 'gut check' as he called it at some time during the season. It was done with the purpose of taking the player to the brink of failure and leading him through that to show him that he could succeed."

That lesson is often remembered by his former players and followers in difficult times as the years turn life into a series of fourth quarters. Those who played for him or knew him well can often still see and hear him on the sideline even today, clapping and talking about "big play time," "gut-check time" or "reaching down inside for that something extra" when the doctor walks in with heart-breaking news or the job suddenly disappears. One can remember him, poised and confident because he knew his teams wouldn't quit, as 80,000 fans scream and gasp and clutch each other in a game-deciding moment against Tennessee or Georgia Tech or Penn State and try to imitate him and his teams in some small way by refusing to give up, by vowing to stand and fight, to give it all and make a difference, even when you're hurt or sick or scared and frustrated with the hand life has dealt you.

"Football teaches a boy to win, to work for maybe the first time in his life and sacrifice and suck up his guts when he's behind. It's the only place left where you can learn that," Bryant once said. "I believe a player who comes here and stays four years is going to be better prepared to take his place in society and better prepared for life because I think he'll learn some lessons that are very difficult to teach in the home, in the church or in the

Bryant players learned the value of perseverance. One of Bryant's favorite slogans hung in the Alabama dressing room to spur players on to victory. It read, "A winner never quits and a quitter never wins." To him, it was not simply a slogan; it was the gospel. Never quitting was the trait that was most responsible for making him a winner.

classroom." He believed that because he knew what football had taught him, and he proved it with thousands of players.

That lesson of never quitting is what Coach Bryant most symbolized. The signs in the dressing room proclaiming, "A winner never quits and a quitter never wins" and "When the going gets tough, the tough get going" were not simply slogans to Coach Bryant. To him, they were the gospel. His never quitting was the trait that most made him a winner. And he lived for and took pride in the moments when his players faced and made the big plays in practice and in games to prove—not to him but to themselves—that they were winners.

Steve Sloan, an All-America quarterback at Alabama who helped win two national championships (1964 and 1965), was reminded of that fourth-quarter tradition once as an assistant coach under Bryant at Alabama.

Late in a game against Tennessee in 1970,

Coach Bryant approached Sloan, the quarterback coach, on the sideline and asked him if a certain formation had been set up to call automatic plays at the line of scrimmage.

"Yes, sir," Sloan replied, "in a desperate situation."

Coach Bryant looked at the scoreboard and Sloan's eyes followed. It was 24-0, Tennessee.

"I don't know about you," Coach Bryant said, "but the situation is desperate enough to suit me right now!"

Bryant did not take kindly to losing any game, or any other challenge, any way, any time, any how. In the late sixties, Alabama lost an in-state football prospect Bryant wanted badly when Richmond Flowers Jr. signed with Tennessee, partly because of the Volunteers' superior track facilities and program. Flowers, a Dothan native and high school standout in both track and football in Montgomery, went on to become a star performer in

Bryant's tenacity and perception made him a coach to be reckoned with. He was acutely perceptive of the people and circumstances surrounding him. He went jaw to jaw with every tough situation he faced—and always came out a winner.

both sports at Tennessee.

Bryant didn't accept the recruiting loss happily, and shortly thereafter announced plans for new track facilities and the hiring of a new track coach at Alabama. His comment at the time was that he didn't plan to lose another football prospect because of poor facilities or programs in any sport. As athletic director, Bryant saw that University of Alabama athletic programs and facilities were equal to or better than any in the conference from that time on.

A story circulated a few years later that illustrated the premium Bryant placed on winning. Seems the coach of a so-called minor sport was called on the carpet by Bryant to explain the morning headlines proclaiming an Auburn win over his Alabama team. The coach is said to have gone into rather lengthy detail to explain the loss, including mentioning his strategy of not wanting his team to peak prior to conference and NCAA competition coming up soon.

"So, what you're saying is that Auburn was trying to whip us, and we weren't trying to whip them," Bryant both asked and concluded at the same time. He then explained to the coach, in his own special way, his position as athletic director and his preference for winning, or at least trying very hard to win, every time out, no matter what, where or when, and especially when the opponent was Auburn.

He Inspired More Reverence Than Respect

Coach Bryant will likely fade into distant memory a generation or two from now. Those who recall the many stories about him or knowing him or playing for him will be viewed then only as old-

timers reliving the glory days of some near-mythical legend.

New fans will learn about Coach Bryant in bits and pieces by visiting the Paul W. Bryant Museum on Paul W. Bryant Drive, or at a game in Bryant-Denny Stadium, or on a visit to Paul Bryant Hall or by seeing his statue in a mall or his picture somewhere.

Unfortunately, they may learn only that he coached football for 38 seasons, the last 25 at the University of Alabama, and that he won more games than any other major college coach (323); carried his teams to more bowl games than any other coach (29); was honored as college football's coach of the year more times (three), and won more national championships than any other coach (six). They will learn much about his many records, but perhaps little about the man himself.

A coach from Nebraska or Notre Dame or Penn State or Alabama or Auburn, or some less likely

To Alabama fans—even the youngest ones—Bryant was a legend in his own time. Fans elsewhere in the country admired and respected him as a great leader and winner. What he symbolized will remain a part of many lives.

place, may one day break his record for career wins. Another may eclipse his consecutive bowl record, or maybe even win more national championships.

But what Coach Bryant most symbolized—and continues to symbolize today—will remain a part of many lives because of him, with or without the records. His lessons of discipline, teamwork, pride, sportsmanship, perseverance, sacrifice, blood and sweat and class have proven true. His principles offer not simply hope, but expectations—if not an outright guarantee—for success, not only on the football field, but in life.

Youngsters who fight and scrap and sweat and bleed to achieve excellence and refuse to quit until they do will become winners on football fields from east to west and north to south. In doing so, they will learn the lessons he taught, directly or indirectly, and will grow from boys into men in the process, perhaps never knowing that much of what they learn was taught by Coach Bryant.

The American Football Coaches Association has named its coach of the year award the Paul W. Bryant award in his honor, symbolizing the respect his peers held for him. He had a way of earning a higher degree of respect—more reverence than respect—than those who did not know him can imagine, even among his fellow coaches.

A personal experience illustrates that reverence so many had for him. Coach Bryant was driving from Tuscaloosa to Marion one late spring evening in the early seventies to speak at the Marion Institute Sports Banquet, and I was riding along.

He told story after story as he drove slowly along, and was in the middle of one of the stories as we approached a turn we needed to make. I saw the sign, but swallowed hard, looked dead ahead and kept listening. I didn't even consider interrupting. Coach Bryant kept on with his story and his dri-

Bryant chats with Vanderbilt coach George MacIntyre following Alabama's 1982 win over the Commodores. Former Ohio State coach Woody Hayes said that Bryant "was honorable, and he won with good, clean ball clubs."

ving, and we drove several miles beyond the turn before he finished the story.

Then and only then did I mention that I thought we "might" have missed the turn a few miles back. Coach Bryant didn't raise an eyebrow. Instead, he kept on driving even farther, as if by plan, to a small roadside cafe. We went in and he had a cup of coffee and smoked a cigarette in his usual casual style, just relaxing and chatting with the owners and customers as I had a glass of tea. By my watch, it was already past banquet time, and I was a bit on the nervous side.

Reluctantly, I reminded him of the time and mentioned that maybe we'd better get moving.

"They probably won't start without me, since I'm the speaker," he said with a broad smile as we got up to leave. He didn't hurry as we drove back, and the banquet had not started without him when we arrived, just as he predicted.

That special personal respect did not diminish over the years, either, and was demonstrated again in a "Bear Bryant Classic" golf tournament a decade later. The annual tournament, hosted by Coach Bryant, brought together the Alabama coaching staff, media and others associated with Alabama athletics each summer before the start of

fall practice. The outing allowed all parties to become acquainted, provided the media with preseason stories, and resulted in surprisingly few serious injuries to the participants.

Coach Bryant played in most of the tournaments and was better than average at the game (and quite excellent at drawing partners), as I recall.

In one of his last tournaments in the early eighties, Coach Bryant was seated in a golf cart behind the 18th green, watching the last groups finish, when my foursome approached. The other three players in my group hit onto or toward the green, going ahead of me at my insistence. I was hoping Coach Bryant would leave in the meantime. I was reluctant to hit toward the green because I feared I might actually hit him with the ball. I was lousy at golf, and the last man on earth I wanted to hit with a golf shot was Coach Bryant.

I delayed as long as I could, and the other players were having a good laugh about it because they had seen me in action, and they knew my "respect" for Coach Bryant. Finally, in desperation, I decided to aim the ball off to the left of the green into some woods, as far away from Coach Bryant as possible. That choice seemed far better than taking a chance at going for the green with him no more than 30 feet away.

I took a deep breath and swung, but to my immediate horror the ball didn't head for the woods as planned. It was instead a high, beautiful shot, and it sailed straight for the flag. I gasped and held my breath until it plopped down on the green no more than 10 feet from the hole. I breathed a long sigh of relief and whispered a prayer of thanks.

Coach Bryant applauded and said, "Nice shot," never knowing or imagining that it was all luck, and very bad luck at that.

He Seized—and Squeezed Tightly—Every Moment

Coach Bryant was a rare man who seized every opportunity and moment in life, and he held tightly onto them for a long, long time, choking every ounce of glory from them, just as he had done when he wrestled that bear. Throughout his life, he looked every man in the eye, and because he did you had to believe what he said was true. He went jaw to jaw with every tough situation he faced, fighting hardest when the situation seemed darkest, never once backing down.

He was a man of principle, a man of action and a man of his word. He was acutely perceptive—almost psychic—in his awareness and knowledge of the people and circumstances surrounding him. He was tough and he had guts. No one crushed his hat, no one dumped a tub of ice water on his head and no one called his hand.

But even Coach Bryant cannot be credited with being a completely self-made man, and he was always quick to say as much. He came out of Moro Bottom, Arkansas, with many character traits already instilled by his parents—especially his mother—and his older siblings. He learned much about life from the hard times of his youth and he learned about football from his high school coach, Bob Cowan, and from coaches Frank Thomas, Red Drew and Hank Crisp as a player and four-year assistant coach at Alabama.

A great deal of credit for his success must also go to the loyal and dedicated assistant coaches and players who believed in his word and his way and paid the price time and time again through 38 seasons to prove him true. Sam Bailey (28 years); Jim Goostree (25 years); Clem Gryska (23 years); Hayden Riley and Gary White (21 years each); Carney Laslie and Ken Donahue (19 years each); Mal Moore (18 years); Dude Hennessey, Jack Rutledge and Willie Meadows (17 years each);

Coach Bryant was almost universally respected. Here even the Auburn mascot honored him with an imitation.

Henry "Sang" Lyda and Rebecca Christian (15 years each); Jimmy Sharpe, Bobby Marks, Pat James and Dee Powell (11 years each) and Phil Cutchin (10 years) were among Bryant's longest associates as assistant coaches and administrators, but there were countless others, and he would not leave out the secretaries, groundskeepers, managers, etc., when passing out the praise himself.

And much credit goes to his number one fan, Mary Harmon Black Bryant, a true and gentle lady who stood by him and shared him with the game of football as his wife for almost 50 years. Perhaps because the game took so much of him from her, she liked basketball more than football.

Mrs. Bryant died August 26, 1984, and Coach and Mrs. Bryant's only daughter, Mae Martin Tyson, died shortly thereafter. Bryant is survived by a son, Paul W. Bryant Jr., a Tuscaloosa businessman with national interests, and five grand-

Coach Bryant's funeral procession passes Bryant-Denny stadium at the University of Alabama as his fans line the streets.

children.

Bryant's contributions to college football are immeasurable, and he will continue to have unprecedented and lasting impact on the game and its participants through the thousands of players and coaches he influenced on the field, at coaching clinics and in other ways. His impact on the University of Alabama is even greater, of course, and goes far beyond his won-lost record; his innovative ideas and achievements as athletic director; the numerous scholarships he established, and the standards of excellence he set.

Gene Stallings, Alabama's head football coach since 1990, is proof of that lingering influence. Stallings had been Coach Bryant's personal choice to succeed him as the head coach at Alabama when Bryant retired after the 1982 season, but certain circumstances prevented that from happening at the time.

"I knew Coach Bryant wanted me to follow him at Alabama because he told me," Stallings said. "Only a few people knew that. When Ray Perkins was hired, I thought my chances of coaching at Alabama were gone."

Seven years later, however, Bryant's wishes were honored when Stallings was chosen to replace Bill Curry, who had followed Perkins as head coach after the 1986 season.

Stallings was hired only after an upheaval by the Bryant "family" of former players and other influential supporters and alumni triggered the departure of Curry, a former Georgia Tech player and coach, after only three seasons at Alabama. The Bryant "family" had been disappointed in the hiring of Curry over a coach with Alabama and/or Bryant ties from the start, and he was never fully accepted by many Alabama fans.

The upheaval became so tumultuous that it also resulted in the departure of athletic director Steve Sloan, a former Bryant quarterback and assistant and a favorite of Alabama fans who apparently was caught in the crossfire.

In the end, however, Bryant got the man he wanted as Alabama's head coach, even though it came seven years late. His influence remained great in the hiring of Stallings in 1990, and that influence continues today. Stallings proved Coach Bryant's choice a sound one by winning a national championship in 1992; therefore, it is not unlikely that those selecting Stallings' successor, when that

Bryant set the standard for excellence and provided a foundation for winning by future Alabama teams. Gene Stallings, Bryant's choice as his successor as Alabama head coach, coached the Crimson Tide to the 1992 national championship, which he celebrated with a victory ride on the shoulders of players.

time comes, will attempt to guess who Bryant might have preferred in the job, just to be on the safe side.

He Not Only Expected, But Demanded Excellence

Whatever the ingredient that causes a man to rise up again when he falls, to fight back against often insurmountable odds and to maintain poise in the face of adversity—to refuse to quit short of that final whistle—Coach Bryant had, and he had plenty of it.

Perhaps it was pride, perhaps character or class; but it was the quality he sought most to find or to inspire in others, and it was the quality others found most evident in him. It was the quality which drew Darwin Holt from Texas to Alabama to play

for him. It was the quality which drew All-America quarterbacks Joe Namath and Ken Stabler back to the team after he had suspended them. It was the quality which turned the smaller, so-called average players on so many Bryant teams into winners. It was the quality which brought his teams back so many times in the fourth quarter to claim or to preserve victory.

It was the quality which most made him a winner, and he spent his life demonstrating and teaching that quality to others the only way he knew how—through the game of football.

Along the way, just the way he planned and promised they would, his teams won 323 games and six national championships.

His teams won because he not only demanded discipline, class and excellence but personally demonstrated it and expected it from each player. And they won because they never quit.

And they never quit because he never quit.